The Anime Boom in the United States

HARVARD EAST ASIAN MONOGRAPHS 406

The Anime Boom in the United States

Lessons for Global Creative Industries

Michal Daliot-Bul and Nissim Otmazgin

Published by the Harvard University Asia Center
Distributed by Harvard University Press
Cambridge, Massachusetts, and London 2017

The Harvard University Asia Center publishes a monograph series and, in coordination with the Fairbank Center for Chinese Studies, the Korea Institute, the Reischauer Institute of Japanese Studies, and other facilities and institutes, administers research projects designed to further scholarly understanding of China, Japan, Vietnam, Korea, and other Asian countries. The Center also sponsors projects addressing multidisciplinary and regional issues in Asia.

HEROMAN © B,P,W/HEROMAN Production Committee

Library of Congress Cataloging-in-Publication Data

Names: Daliot-Bul, Michal, author. | Otmazgin, Nissim, author.
Title: The anime boom in the United States : lessons for global creative industries / Michal Daliot-Bul and Nissim Otmazgin.
Other titles: Harvard East Asian monographs ; 406.
Description: Cambridge, Massachusetts : Published by the Harvard University Asia Center, 2017. | Series: Harvard East Asian monographs ; 406 | Includes bibliographical references and index.
Identifiers: LCCN 2016053022 | ISBN 9780674976993 (hardcover : alk. paper)
Subjects: LCSH: Animated television programs—United States—Japanese influences. | Animated television programs—Japan—History and criticism. | Television broadcasting—Japan—Influence.
Classification: LCC PN1992.8.A59 D35 2017 | DDC 791.45/3—dc23 LC record available at https://lccn.loc.gov/2016053022

Index by Alexander Trotter

⊖ Printed on acid-free paper

Last figure below indicates year of this printing
26 25 24 23 22 21 20 19 18 17

Dedicated with much love to my parents,
Mitzi and Shaike Daliot
Michal Daliot-Bul

To my beloved family, for their many years of
encouragement and support
Nissim Otmazgin

Contents

List of Tables, Plates, and Figures

Tables

Plates:

1. *Tetsuwan atomu* (*Astro Boy*)
2. *Hakuja den* (*The White Snake Enchantress*, also titled *Panda and the Magic Serpent*)
3. *Shōnen sarutobi sasuke* (*The Magic Boy*)
4. *Saiyu-ki* (*Enchanted Monkey*)
5. In *Voltron*, the footage from two of Tōei's *mecha* anime series was combined to create a new story.
6. American-style Cheetara, *Thunder Cats*
7. *Dragon Ball Z* protagonists
8. Anime-inspired American cartoon: *Teen Titans*

Figures

Acknowledgments

This book is the product of five years of research conducted mostly in Japan and the United States. Throughout the research for this book, we have been assisted by many people who shared our enthusiasm and dedicated their time and energy in helping us get into the field, answered our questions, or read parts of the manuscript, in some cases more than once. We must begin by thanking Shichijō Naohiro, whose broad knowledge of the industry and effective assistance in directing us to relevant materials and in introducing us to key personnel in Japan's anime industry were crucial for this book; we cherish the friendship he extended to us. We would also like to thank Satō Chiyoko, who generously stepped in to help us contact people we never thought we could meet, always doing this with the kindest smile, as if it were nothing at all. We also thank Marco Pellitteri, whose detailed reading was very helpful in fleshing out the content to improve and strengthen the manuscript, and Sharalyn Orbaugh for her insightful comments on parts of the manuscript.

While working on this book, we met scholars and media specialists who openly shared with us their ideas and thoughts. We wish to thank in particular Ishikawa Shinichiro, George Wada, Makihara Ryōtarō, Mihara Ryōtarō, and Ian Condry. We would also like to thank wholeheartedly our interviewees, too numerous to mention here, who shared their knowledge and experience with us patiently. As anyone doing fieldwork will attest, there is nothing as rewarding and as exciting while doing research as a good interview! It is always a pleasure to work with promising students, and we were privileged to work with wonderful research assistants: Nadav Rotdchild, Muneera Abu Roken, and Nave Barlev. Last but not least, we thank Robert Graham for encouraging us and guiding us through the process of publishing this manuscript, and the two anonymous readers for their invaluable advice and critical comments.

The research for this book was generously funded by the Israel Science Foundation (ISF), grant number 1056/10. We acknowledge the following sources, where earlier versions of some parts of chapters 1 and 3 appeared as "Reframing and Reconsidering the Cultural Innovations of the Anime Boom on US Television," *International Journal of Cultural Studies* 17, no. 1 (2014): 75–91, and "Anime in the US: The Entrepreneurial Dimensions of Globalized Culture," *Pacific Affairs* 84, no. 1 (2014): 53–69.

Michal Daliot-Bul, Haifa, and Nissim Otmazgin, Jerusalem

Preface

For a certain period in the 1990s and 2000s, anime was defying the U.S. domination of the global animation market. The broadcasting rights of Japanese anime series and movies were being sold on an unprecedented scale around the world, with the United States being one of the biggest buyers. Overseas sales of anime soared, and reached a peak between 2003 and 2005; in the United States alone, in 2003, anime and anime-related business sales amounted to almost US$5 billion. Somewhat alarmingly, however, overseas sales of Japanese anime have declined in recent years. In 2012, sales were less than they had been ten years earlier and less than the overseas sales in 2009, the year after the global financial crisis. Notwithstanding anime's commercial decline, Japan's animation industry has remained a strong player in the global animation market, but to quote Japan's Anime Industry Association survey from 2015, "reality is challenging."

This book addresses a neglected dimension of contemporary studies of anime. Although in the past few years anime, and more generally, Japanese popular culture, have become an academic growth industry, we both felt that the literature on anime presents only part of the entire picture. While much that is written today on the globalization of anime explores the bottom-up mechanisms of globalization, emphasizing the artistic sensibilities of anime and the role of fans in consuming, interpreting, and adopting anime, we want to contribute a complementary top-down perspective. Specifically, we want to offer a scholarly perspective

on the companies and promoters responsible for the production, circulation, regulation, and hybridization of anime, their global expansion strategies, marketing and global distribution infrastructures, and the increasing involvement of the Japanese state as it attempts to capitalize on the
anime boom and attain "soft power."

In this book, we set out to provide a comprehensive and empirically
grounded study of the various stages of anime's commercial expansion
in the United States and its organizational and cultural impact on the
American market. What caused the rise of the commercial anime market in the United States and what triggered its recent decline? What can
be learned about anime as a cultural commodity and about the legacy of
the anime boom years in the United States? Beyond the case of anime's
expansion into the United States, what are the social processes and organizational mechanisms that enable the globalization of anime? Does the
state play a significant role in shaping contemporary transnational cultural flows? And lastly, what does the future hold for the globalization of
media products in an age of media digitalization and media convergence?

We address the above questions by combining textual analysis and
cultural history with insights from political economy and organizational
theories, in ways that merge our different academic backgrounds and disciplines. We thus explore the networks of production and circulation
that made anime popular outside of Japan, and particularly in the United
States, as well as analyze the artistic quality of anime, its cultural and
emotional appeal, and the historical and social context of its globalization. We also discuss the business opportunities offered to Japanese anime promoters in the American market, the dialogue between the Japanese and American animation industries, and the rise of the "cool Japan"
phenomenon in the United States.

To examine the role of the industry in the cultural globalization of
anime, there can hardly be a better perspective than the United States–
Japan case. The United States is not only the world's biggest producer and
consumer of animation and television content, but it is also home to some
of the globe's biggest animation studios and media conglomerates. Looking at the expansion of anime in the United States illuminates the mechanisms and processes involved in the interaction between media industries that have evolved in different contexts, and shows how cultural
globalization actually works. In other words, the expansion and success

of anime in the United States provides an excellent opportunity to examine how the commercial globalization of cultural and media industries takes place in highly competitive, cutting-edge markets.

Although this book emphasizes an economic-industrial perspective of the globalization of anime, after spending so much of our time engulfed in the world of anime and surrounded by the talented people who create it, one of our most important personal conclusions is that anime is much more than a valorized creative product. Anime's artistic quality has greatly enriched the work of animators and media specialists across the globe, providing them with a new tool kit to produce new images. For many fans in North America (and elsewhere), anime remains an important part of their lives. It sometimes influences dramatically the way they grow up and how they perceive themselves. Indeed, it determines who their friends are and their place in the world. The global success of anime has also influenced policymakers in Japan and in other Asian countries, who, in recent years, have highlighted the importance of anime and other "creative industries" in boosting their economies. The case of anime thus suggests that a reversal of priorities should be considered, namely, that it is time to deliberate on how to harness the economy for boosting creativity and culture rather than the other way around.

A Note to the Reader

Romanization follows the Hepburn style; macrons indicate long vowels: ā, ī, ū, ē, ō, except in those cases of well-known place-names or terms (e.g., Tokyo). Japanese names follow the practice of surname first except for those authors who regularly publish in English. Japanese words are translated according to the Kenkyūsha dictionary system. Anime titles are given first in English unless they are referred to in the context of their appearance in Japan, in which case the titles are given first in Japanese. Yen-to-dollar exchange rates are calculated according to the Research and Statistics Department of the Bank of Japan (www.stat.go.jp).

List of Abbreviations

ACA	Agency for Cultural Affairs (under the Ministry of Education, Culture, Sports, Science, and Technology)
AFA	Anime Festival Asia (held since 2008 in Southeast Asia)
CGI	computer-generated imagery
IP	intellectual property
JASIAS	Japan Society of Image Arts and Sciences
JETRO	Japan External Trade Organization
JSAS	Japan Society for Animation Studies
METI	Ministry of Economy, Trade, and Industry (Japan)
MEXT	Ministry of Education, Culture, Sports, Science, and Technology (Japan)
MG	minimum guaranty
MIPTV	Marché International des Programmes de Télévision (France)
MOFA	Ministry of Foreign Affairs (Japan)
NATPE	National Association of Television Program Executives (United States)
ODA program	Official Development Assistance (Japan)
OVA	original video animation
RIETI	Research Institute of Economy, Trade and Industry (Japan)
SAS	Society of Animation Studies (an international organization)
SF	science fiction

INTRODUCTION

The first Japanese animation series (hereafter "anime series") to debut in the United States was *Astro Boy* (*Tetsuwan atomu* [see color insert, plate 1], created and directed by Tezuka Osamu) in 1963. Organized anime fandom in the United States started as early as 1977 with the formation of the first fan club created expressly to promote Japanese animation to American fans (Patten 2004: 22–43, 53–56). Since then, anime has gradually made inroads in the United States, reaching mainstream audiences in 1998 with the introduction of the popular *Pokémon* series and continuing with a range of other popular series such as *Yugioh!* (*Yūgiō dyueru monsutāzu*, 2000), and movies such as *Spirited Away* (*Sen to Chihiru no kamikakushi*, written and directed by Miyazaki Hayao, 2001). In the following few years, child-oriented anime and related merchandise were marketed and consumed in the United States on an unprecedented scale. At the same time, the Web 2.0 revolution turned the Internet into a prominent platform for anime fans, who could now easily interact and collaborate with each other in a social media dialogue, sharing and discussing their favorite Japanese anime titles. Encouraged by these developments, entrepreneurs expanded the range of anime genres imported to the United States, distributing them on television or as DVDs.

Beyond export/import and the long-standing outsourcing relations between the American and Japanese animation industries, the impact of anime on American animation styles since then has become noticeable in so-called anime-inspired cartoons and in American animated and live-action remakes of Japanese intellectual properties (IPs). Experimental collaborations between Japanese and American production companies and talents have also taken place, with *Animatrix, Demashita! PowerPuff Girls Z,* and *Afro Samurai* (see fig. 1) being some well-known examples. Hundreds of anime fan gatherings, the most famous being the Los Angeles Anime Expo and Baltimore's Otakon, have grown every year, drawing hundreds of thousands of American fans.

Commercially, the golden age of anime in the United States lasted for about a decade, which we roughly frame from 1998 to 2008, and generated considerable economic revenues, peaking in 2003 with more than US$4.84 billion in sales, which included movies (US$2 million), videos (US$72 million), DVDs (US$316 million), and character-related merchandise (US$4.45 billion) (JETRO [Japan External Trade Organization] 2003). This is 3.2 times greater than the value of Japanese steel exports to the United States in the same year.[1] In the following years, however, the numbers dropped due to the saturation of the American market with low-quality anime series and the death of the DVD market in the United States, combined with illegal online downloading and a reduction in consumer spending in the aftermath of the 2008 economic crisis. According to JETRO, anime sales in the United States generated US$2.93 billion in 2007. In 2009, the numbers dropped again, reaching US$2.74 billion, which included movies (US$15 million), DVDs (US$306 million), and character-related merchandise (US$2.42 billion) (JETRO 2011: 39).

The anime boom in the United States has widely influenced American animation and, more broadly, American popular culture. According to media critic Roland Kelts, it was the biggest cultural invasion into the United States since the Beatles in the 1960s.[2] While "invasion" may not be the accurate term to describe the penetration of anime into mainstream American animation, since, as we show in this book, it was anything but the result of a coordinated strategy of Japanese media companies, Kelts's strong words encapsulate the dramatic change brought by anime. Anime introduced to American consumers a new set of sophisticated visual images, imaginative narratives, and artistic qualities that were dramatically different from those they knew before. Anime held great appeal for consumers, but it also influenced American animation creators, who gradually came to appreciate and adopt anime qualities and creative vision, and integrated these in their own work. If Walt Disney, the Fleischer Brothers,

FIGURE I. *Afro Samurai* (created by Okazaki Takashi, 2007).
© 2006 Takashi Okazaki, Gonzo.

and other great American cartoonists had a big impact on Japanese modern manga and anime during their emerging stage (Schodt 2007: 44), Japanese animation reciprocated in kind during the 1990s and 2000s.

This book analyzes the anime boom in the United States, the biggest market in the world for animation and home to the world's largest animation production houses and other media-related companies. Using historical and contemporaneous perspectives, the book details the various stages of anime production, marketing, and global distribution, and the supporting organizational and cultural processes, thereby describing a transnational embedded system for globalizing and localizing commodified culture. It investigates the ways in which anime—primarily television anime series but also significant theatrical releases—has been exported to the United States since the 1960s and explores the transnational networks of production and marketing of anime while investigating the cultural and artistic processes it inspired.

This book's analysis of the anime boom in the United States is the starting point for a wider investigation of the multidirectional globalization[3] of contemporary culture and the ways in which global creative industries operate.[4] Methodologically, the underlying premise of this study is that to understand such a cultural phenomenon in global markets, one should look not only into the cultural content of media commodities but also at the networks of distribution and dissemination, and at the specific industrial, historical, and cultural contexts that have shaped them. This book is thus the integrated product of two research approaches combining the specialty and experience of two scholars from political economy (Nissim Otmazgin) and cultural and media studies (Michal Daliot-Bul).

Analytically, we suggest that the media digitalization and convergence that have enabled the anime boom since the 1990s have dramatically changed the ecosystem for global media products, including animation. Our research suggests that creative international coproductions are emerging today as the most promising strategy for capitalizing on global opportunities. But while the pool of talent and knowledge in the anime industry in Japan continues to be outstanding in the global sphere, the organizational culture of the anime industry is, with some exceptions, quite antagonistic to the pursuit of daring international adventures. At present, the Japanese anime industry is still weak in distribution channels, especially when compared with Hollywood. Unless this changes, the anime industry may find itself yielding its prominent place in the global market of animation to emerging rival national animation industries.

* * *

The expansion and success of anime in the United States provides an excellent opportunity to examine how the globalization of cultural and media industries actually works in highly competitive, cutting-edge markets. This book's investigation is thus relevant not only to the case of anime in the United States but also to address wider questions related to how best to understand, nurture, and capitalize value in the creative industries. Specifically, identifying the actors as well as the mechanisms and processes that have affected and are still affecting media globalization is, in general, beneficial in suggesting a framework for assessing other instances of transnational marketing and dissemination of media. In other words, by following the three classic questions of cultural research—how is culture produced, how is it being transferred, and how is it being received?—our study uses historical reflection and contemporary empirical research to lead the reader all the way from the early stages of the globalization of animation to the complexities and dilemmas of current media globalization.

To begin with, an examination of the mass movement of cultural commodities from Japan to the United States tells us not only about the artistic qualities of anime or about the American market, but more basically about the way globalization works in the cultural and media industries. It illuminates overlooked mechanisms and processes that connect artistic innovation with corporate mechanisms and maps out the way individuals, large and small studios and firms, and state regulations influence the transnational transfer of cultural commodities in free market economies. It also allows us to recognize the social and cultural mechanisms that support or hinder cultural transformation—for example, to delineate the fragile balance between cultural and marketing factors that together determine the success or failure of imported media/cultural products. We can thus explore the dialectical relation between the celebration of and demand for otherness in postmodern culture and the expressed understanding that foreign media/cultural products must be domesticated to make them less foreign and to thus ensure their reception in foreign markets. In other words, it enables theory formulation related to the movements of culture.

Second, as mentioned earlier, besides opening up a new market in the United States for imported media from Japan, anime has had a substantial normative impact on the American animation industry and youth culture. Anime visual styles and storytelling techniques have been adapted and incorporated into the making of television cartoons and other animated genres in the United States over the past twenty years, thus becoming part of the tool kit available to contemporary animation artists. The result is that television cartoons that American children, young adults, and adults watch often carry traces of cultural hybridization. The warm reception of anime has also helped to push U.S. animation from being child-oriented to being young adult– and adult-oriented (Patten 2001: 66).

Anime-related merchandising has influenced the toy industry in the United States, and anime-related fan practices (such as compiling fan-subs,[5] drawing derivative works, costume playing, or participating in conventions) have a significant impact on the way many young Americans grow up. In the past decade or so, anime has provided occasional inspiration for the design and packaging of other American media–related industries, such as music, and of course, street fashion. The normative impact of anime on American animation, American youth culture, and other American media teaches us about mechanisms of cultural transformation and about the ways in which popular culture works in the global sphere.

Third, the exploration of the heyday of the anime boom in the United States provides us with another perspective on a large sector of Japan's economy that the Japanese government increasingly regards both as a means to enhance the country's "content industries" (an important segment of the cultural/creative industries) and as a diplomatic tool to boost the country's image abroad and to attain "soft power." The latter is no minor issue. Political scientist Joseph Nye coined the term "soft power" to describe the way a country can use its cultural influence as part of international politics (1990: 167; 2004: 68–69). According to Nye, the proof of power in world politics today lies in the ability of leading nations to affect what other countries want and to shape other societies' preferences while transcending the protective shield of the state. In a great shift from the more traditional power structures, soft power derives mostly from intangible resources such as culture and ideology rather than from military action or economic incentives (see Daliot-Bul 2009). In the 1990s, when the Cold War was over and the geopolitical structure of Asia was shifting, the Japanese government found this very tempting. Shortly after the turn of this century, Japanese popular culture became widely referred to in the media, academic circles, and government agencies as a national resource of soft power. Nowadays, soft power is used as a rhetorically invigorating term by Japanese officials to encourage investment in the country's creative and media industries, which are deemed harbingers of Japan's "cool" image in the world (Otmazgin 2017).

For the Japanese government, anime is increasingly regarded as an economically emerging sector. In 2003, the Japanese Ministry of Economy, Trade and Industry (METI) estimated that approximately 65 percent of the world's production of animated cartoon series was taking place in Japan, with annual sales of licensed goods and events worth US$17 billion (METI 2003: 8–9). By March 2017, Pokémon sales alone had generated JPY 6 trillion worldwide (approximately U.S. $5.4 billion) coming from movies, anime TV series, video games, trading cards, and other licensed products.[6] Anime is also important for two other economic sectors— Japan's electronic and game industries—since it provides the necessary visual images and sounds. The phenomenal success of the mobile game *Pokémon Go,* released in July 2016, is an example of the close synergy between anime and hardware industries. Making use of GPS and the camera of compatible devices such as smartphones, the game allows players to capture virtual creatures drawn from the popular anime series *Pokémon,* who appear on device screens as though in the real world. Following the success of *Pokémon Go,* on the day of its Japan launch, Nintendo's shares on the Tokyo market almost doubled, from ¥14,490 to ¥28,220. As succinctly summarized by Howard Stringer, Sony's former chief executive, "without content, most gadgets are just junk."[7] The Japanese government, for its part, has been cognizant of the overseas success of anime and is, accordingly, initiating policies to support it. At the same time, many of these initiatives have not had great success, and the inherent tension between organized and bureaucratic action and cultural creativity continues. To put it another way, our case study is also an investigation of the challenges cultural policymakers face today as we question the relevance of the modernistic approach to the state as a regulatory cultural planning apparatus in a world of media convergence and intensive cultural globalization powered by individuals.

* * *

This book hopes to contribute to the burgeoning scholarly field created by crossing two major fields of study, namely, cultural globalization and anime. The majority of academic literature on anime and its globalization since the 1990s has detailed the artistic qualities of the genre, the images projected, and its acceptance by groups of fans in Japan and abroad. (Notable recent examples include Brophy et al. 2010; Brown 2008; Oshita 2014; Pellitteri 2011; Salkowitz 2012; and Shiraishi 2013). In the available literature, the globalization of anime has been attributed to the role of fans as cultural agents (Kelts 2007; Lee 2001; Napier 2001), the deterritorializing effects of globalization in which culture flows rapidly between markets (Iwabuchi 2002a; Shita 2005), the domestication and heavy editing of anime to suit American taste (Allison 2006; Brienza 2016; McKevitt 2010), the ability of the Japanese anime industry to constantly produce new creative images and genres (Condry 2013; LaMarre 2009; Steinberg 2012; Ueno 2002), and the wider global flow of Japanese pop culture and "soft power" (Daliot-Bul 2009; Sakurai 2009; Takada 2011; Yano 2013). A few studies, especially those from Japan, have provided convincing testimony for the presence of anime in the United States over the past few decades and have offered detailed accounts of the history of anime in the United States, and specific successful anime series and movies (Kusanagai 2003; Ladd and Deneroff 2010; Mascias 2006; Ōtsuka and Ōsawa 2005; Yamaguchi 2009). They tend to be encyclopedic in nature, however, and overlook the organizational mechanism responsible for the transfer and marketing of anime, and in particular, the role of entrepreneurship connecting the Japanese and American markets.

Our book, in contrast, joins with other research projects to adopt an integrative approach to the study of the globalization of anime. Shiraishi Saya's (2013) comprehensive study, for example, showed how the emergence of overseas markets for Japanese manga and anime are the result of both globalizing and localizing forces, which worked dialectically and complemented each other. Similarly, in his book *The Dragon and the Dazzle* (2011), Marco Pellitteri dealt with both the language anime uses and its success in terms of popular culture and consumption, as well as with the economic/productive/strategic dimensions of the arrival and success of anime in Western Europe (namely, in Italy and France, with some references to Germany and Spain). Pellitteri described anime's arrival in Italy and France, which was enabled by the flexible models of the import/export of small distribution companies working with big public networks, and the function of European fairs of international television content. Our book aims to expand and empirically enrich these integrative approaches to the study of anime by combining historical reflection, textual analysis, and an organizational study. We investigate the historical-cultural context of the globalization of anime and its acceptance and domestication in the United States as directly relating to and depending on networks and mechanisms of production and dissemination.

Goldstein-Gidoni 2010: 181). This marketing strategy resulted in a rather interesting construction of pleasure, which, drawing on Freud, Anne Allison (2006: 9–10) has called "polymorphous perverse play" in reference to the way in which producers cut across new borders, media, and technologies to make and market fun and child-oriented fantasy.

HOW TO STUDY ANIME?

Many years before animation and anime became legitimate academic topics, they were addressed and discussed passionately by fans and cultural critics in popular fan-oriented journals, popular books, and conventions. They constructed a canon as well as detailed expertise, tracing cultural history, and mapping aesthetic norms. These publications have later become useful for a more scholarly investigation that seeks to explore broader theoretical issues relating to animation and anime.

An academic approach to the study of animation began taking shape in the Euro-American academic sphere in the late 1970s and became more institutionalized with the establishment of the Society of Animation Studies (SAS) in 1988. As with every medium that becomes the subject of growing academic scholarship (such as film studies), the question of whether animation represented a medium so different from others and of enough interest to warrant its own discipline was addressed seriously and critically by supporters and opponents. For some scholars, animation was different from other media, even from its closest relative, the live films medium (Pilling 1997: xii).

Nicole Lipitz (2010) has nicely summarized some of the unique underlying characteristics of animation:

> Animation has an emblematic stylization that arose from its work-intensive frame-by-frame nature. Using drawings as diagrams, animation sectionalizes movement (Halas 1976: 10–11). Each motion is divided into parts; in each part an element changes position. To facilitate this division of movement, images are simplified through symbols. Rarely does animation refer to life through accurate representation. Elements are exaggerated and reduced to better emphasize the nature of the motion depicted (Ibid: 12). The image transforms through the frames. Heather Crow, describing the animated gesture, writes, "Animated film is characterized by shape-shifting

bodies: bodies squashed and stretched, organs that jump out of the skin, human figures that transform into animals or objects" (Crow 2007: 51). Motion manifests through the frame-by-frame duplication and transformation of an image (Ibid). . . . Like comics and graphic novels, animation ties images together. Animation is specific in that the images are not arranged on a page, but in time, projected on a screen. Norman McLaren of the National Film Board of Canada defined the nature of animation: "Animation is not the art of drawings that move, but the art of movements that are drawn. What happens between each frame is more important than what exists on each frame. Animation is therefore the art of manipulating the invisible interstices that lie between frames." (Hoffer 1981: 5)

Different platforms such as conferences organized by the Society of Animation Studies (SAS) and its *Animation Studies Journal* (established in 1991) have enabled scholars to discuss and develop animation theories in a global intellectual milieu whose lingua franca is English. In Europe, parallel interests have been pursued in local languages, remaining, unfortunately, unknown to those who cannot speak those languages.[8] Many studies that are available to the global English-speaking milieu of animation studies focus on what makes animation different from films, such as the creation of movement across frames in animation and its semiotic consequences. Other studies use contemporary animation as a point of entry into analyses of postmodern media conditions (e.g., simulation, media mix, information theory, intermediality; see LaMarre 2009: xxii).

In Japan, efforts to establish an academic animation studies forum began in 1975 with the establishment of the Animation Research Group by Tōei Animation Studio (Tōei Dōga), anime directors Yabushita Taiji and Ikeda Hiroshi, and Tokyo University of the Arts professor Uchiyama Shotaro. The initiative was soon abandoned for reasons unexplained and was picked up again many years later, in 1992, by members of the Japan Society of Image Arts and Sciences (JASIAS), who kept the same title for their research project: (the second) Animation Research Group. In 1998, the Japan Society for Animation Studies (JSAS) was established by members of the JASIAS, and in 1999 they launched its *Japanese Journal of Animation Studies*. According to Koide Masashi—a core member of both entities—the Animation Research Group of JASIAS remained active even after the establishment of the Japan Society for Animation

Studies due to their different agendas. Whereas the Animation Research Group of JASIAS sees animation studies as based on film or image studies, the Japan Society for Animation Studies promotes animation studies as cross-disciplinary or independent. This subbranching repeats, to some extent, what happened in animation studies in the Euro-American academic sphere. In 2003, the first academic (as opposed to applied) programs of animation studies opened at Tokyo Polytechnic University and Tokyo Zōkei University (Koide 2013: 51–52).

In 2009, Thomas LaMarre (2009) attempted to change the face of animation studies within Western academia by looking at the specificity of animation and (interestingly for us) by using Japanese anime as a case study. LaMarre stressed one of the unique technological features of animation making that has a determining (though not deterministic) semiotic impact on the meanings of the result. Key to LaMarre's theory is the space that occurs between the panels layered in the animation stand during the compositing of the frame, that is, the "animetic interval." The animetic interval creates a unique spatiality in the animation text and separates animation from other forms of the moving image such as traditional cinematic film. In his work, LaMarre demonstrated how an analysis of animation must first explore the movement within images before attempting to understand the movement across them.

While the search for new theoretical and methodological approaches that are exclusive to the study of animation (and anime) remains fresh and exciting, in recent years interdisciplinarity has become the accepted norm in animation studies in both Euro-American and Japanese academia. Different methodologies shaped within a wide range of existing disciplines—such as art history, literature, media and cultural studies, gender studies, sociology, anthropology, film studies, and even economics and political sciences—are mobilized for the study of animation. Exhibiting this approach is *Animation: An Interdisciplinary Journal*, which was launched in 2006. Quite distinct from the previously mentioned *Animation Studies Online Journal*, this newer journal, *Animation: An Interdisciplinary Journal*, promises on its website not only to be interdisciplinary but also to "re-mediate and inter-mediate a range of moving image platforms and to re-think the premises that have thus far found it proper to separate the 'mashed potatoes' of film theory from the 'peas' of animation theory and the 'carrots' of digital media theory."[9]

Multidisciplinarity has also become a major feature of animation studies today. The study of animation and of anime is being increasingly intertwined with a growing number of media studies interests, ranging from comics, manga, video games, and new media. It has grown into a field of knowledge that is shaped by fans, media journalists, and media critics as much as by scholars, even after they have been institutionalized in academia. This fusion brings forth a new set of questions relating to the production of knowledge today. This fusion also positions the study of animation and animation-related practices as a very inclusive endeavor, out of the hands of professional academic scholars, with an expanding focus of research for wider groups of investigators.

Against this backdrop, we agree that there is a benefit to studying animation and anime in relation to their own shared and separate traditions, and to speaking about them using their own shared and separate vocabularies. Nonetheless, this should be part of a multidisciplinary and inclusive approach to the study of animation and anime that relates to and considers the research questions being tackled in order to be productive and true to the nature of the object of study. More specifically, for the purpose of this book, we believe that such a dialogue is crucial for understanding the rise and fall of the anime boom in the United States and the different processes and trajectories that the anime industry is currently undergoing. Admittedly, this approach reflects our own education as scholars of political economy and of media and cultural studies, disciplines that reject the notion of predetermined and inflexible methodologies.

As part of our interdisciplinary move, in this book we introduce a "big picture" approach to the study of anime and analyze anime both as the products of a creative industry and as texts. We examine the production, circulation, and consumption of anime in the United States as well as its wider cultural and industrial impact on the American market; we also look closely at some of the anime genres broadcast in the United States and their dialogue with American animation productions.

Similar to other creative industries, the anime industry is based on the merging of individual creativity and talent with industrial infrastructures, thereby generating an economic exchange of material products and intellectual property. By contextualizing historically our field of investigation, we use quantitative and qualitative research methods from the social sciences to study and analyze the contexts of industrial factors as well as the organizational procedures that have shaped the anime industry in Japan, the globalization of anime, and its reception and domestication in the United States. At the same time, we use textual analysis to try to understand more deeply how the world is viewed in anime and how meanings are reproduced, domesticated, and transformed when cultural contexts are changed.

ANIME AS A MAINSTREAM PHENOMENON

The origins of anime can be traced as far back as the nineteenth century, to the time when Japan was rapidly opening to the West. Back then, manga, and later on anime, were products of the artistic interaction between Japanese, European, and American cultures, combined with new printing and media technologies (Poitras 2008: 48–49). The first Japanese animated work known to have been shown in a movie theater in Japan was *Imokawa Mukuzo genkanban no maki* (Mukuzo Imokawa the Doorman, created and directed by Shimokawa Ōten), which was released in 1917, and the first animated (almost) feature-length film was *Momotaro no umiwashi* (Momotaro's Divine Sea Warriors, Mitsuyo Seo), released in Japan in 1943.

During the American occupation (1945–52), anime remained a relatively small and undeveloped medium that was rather restricted by the authorities' attempts to supervise its content. From the mid-1950s, however, freed from much of the censorship in the newly established democratic Japan, an anime industry started taking shape. It was television that increased the demand for animation and gave animators a new platform and the financial resources for producing and delivering animation. The first Japanese anime to air on Japanese television was the three-part *Mitsu no hanashi* (Three Tales, created and directed by Osonoe Keiko) in 1960. This was followed in 1961 by the daily historical series *Insutanto hisutorī* (Instant History, created and directed by Yokoyama Ryuichi), renamed *Otogi manga karendā* (Otogi Manga Calendar) in the second season, which featured animation mixed with photographs and film footage. In 1961, Tezuka Osamu established his own animation production studio, Mushi Productions, and created Japan's first television cartoon, the highly popular *Tetsuwan atomu* (*Astro Boy*). Other series that became popular among children in the following years included *Tetsujin 28–gō* (Gigantor, created by Yokoyama Mitsuteru, directed by Watanabe Yonehiko, 1963) and *Mahōtsukai sarii* (*Sally, The Witch*, created by Yokoyama Mitsuteru, directed by Katsuta Toshio and Ikeda Hiroshi, 1966). Mushi Productions, Tōei Animation, Tele-Cartoon Japan, and other newly established animation studios provided content for Japan's growing television industry. As television became a popular home appliance, animation grew into a massive industry (Hu 2010: 83–103).

The 1960s brought a greater degree of collaboration between the anime industry, toy companies, music studios, and manga publishers (Steinberg 2012). Companies in Japan paid particular attention to the marketing of merchandise and toys based on popular anime series. The 1970s saw the rise of genres such as *mecha* anime (anime featuring fighting robots) and space opera anime (featuring futuristic, character- and plot-driven stories that take place in space). Some anime directors, such as Matsumoto Reiji, Tomino Yoshiyuki, Miyazaki Hayao, Takahata Isao, and Osamu Dezaki, began acquiring recognition and fame. The 1970s also saw the birth of the first generation of committed fans of Japan's "media mix" ecosystem in which manga and anime are key features, together with other media and commodity goods. More manga and anime clubs were established at universities, and the first Comiket (Comic Market) convention, during which old anime were screened along with other activities, took place in 1975.[10] These committed fans, the first generation of Japanese "media geeks," were later nicknamed *otaku* and became infamous for their obsessive engagement in fandom practices that celebrate and fetishize fictional worlds and characters of manga, anime, science fiction, video games, computer games, and all related information.[11]

By the 1980s, anime had become a mainstream phenomenon that had diversified into various genres and subgenres, and was shown on television, in movie theaters, and on video game consoles, loved by both the young and old. These developments peaked in the 1990s with a huge variety of products being promoted on television and in movie theaters, and later via the Internet, cellular phones, and advertising billboards (Poitras 2008: 49–58). By the turn of the century, there were at least three generations of children born in postwar Japan who had been raised with anime as a major component of their cultural heritage.

Due to the aging of Japanese society and the lingering economic stagnation, one of the key characteristics of the anime industry over the past decade has been that many products are more attuned to the tastes and aesthetic sensibilities of the *otaku,* its most avid financial supporters. This trend is heavily criticized for producing formulaic results that are often characterized by more sexually suggestive characters and content, by being more character-driven than plot-driven, and by the overuse of iconic symbols that are meaningful only for the *otaku* community (Azuma 2009). One of the evolving features of anime nowadays has been the strong incorporation of the so-called *moe* (infatuating) element, defined by cultural critic Patrick Galbraith (2014: 17) as "an affectionate response to fictional characters." Others, such as cultural critic Ōtsuka Eiji (2015), argue that while anime in Japan was initially based on Disney-oriented universal aesthetics, nowadays the anime industry is basically a sort of mechanical reproduction system within the context of "Galapagosizing" Japanese society.

Anime Goes to America

When did commercial animation start going abroad on a massive scale? Ōtsuka and Ōsawa (2005: 256–58) argued that we need to view the transnational flow of anime as part of a growing trend in which cultural products came to be seen as an integral component of international politics, beginning with U.S. support of the export of American movies in the aftermath of World War I.

Although the anime industry did not enjoy such government support for local or international distribution, it can be argued that in 1956, when Tōei Animation was established as Disney's Far East rival, a global market for media content already existed. Tōei Animation is one of the few animation production houses in Japan that was established with the specific purpose of becoming a global player. In the early 1960s, it distributed three theatrical features in the United States: *The White Snake Enchantress* (*Hakuja den,* directed by Yabushita Taiji, 1958; released in the United States, 1961), *The Magic Boy* (*Shōnen sarutobi sasuke,* directed by Yabushita Taiji, 1959; released in the United

States, 1961), and *Enchanted Monkey* (*Saiyu-ki*, directed by Yabushita Taiji and Tezuka Osamu, 1960; released in the United States, 1961). (See plates 2, 3, and 4 in the color insert.) They did not do well in American box offices for several reasons, which will be elaborated later in this book. Television anime, however, was a different story, due to the growing need for television content around the world, including in the United States, and because television animation can be easily and cheaply domesticated to local audiences. Thus, as soon as the television anime industry was established in Japan, a small group of American and Japanese visionary entrepreneurs began the export/import of its products. The imported anime series were heavily edited and dubbed. Meanwhile, on a different trade trajectory, outsourcing from American animation production houses to Japanese production houses began in 1966 when *The King Kong Show* became the first American cartoon produced in Japan (outsourced to Tōei Animation by the U.S. company Videocraft, later renamed Rankin/Bass Productions). As will be explained in chapter 1, American animation companies, American television producers, and Japanese anime producers created complex and sophisticated transnational production and trade trajectories throughout the years.

According to Shiraishi Saya's (2013: 287–303) ethnographic study of a few top universities in the United States, although anime conventions started in the United States in the late 1970s, it was only in the early 1990s that anime started to forge its way onto American campuses. This new interest coincided—not incidentally as we shall discuss in chapter 1—with the release of the theatrical feature *Akira* (Otomo Katsuhiro, 1988) in the United States. Impressed by the high graphic qualities of anime and manga, and the possibility of imitating some of the images, university students were a significant factor in raising awareness and interest in anime. Design and animation students were proactively looking to Japan for inspiration. Later on, computer science students used the Internet to import and distribute anime content. Soon enough, student clubs were formed where members could meet to watch and discuss their favorite anime series, and even think about ways to translate some of the scenes into English. Some of the members started to take Japanese classes or study the language on their own. These gatherings created modicum markets for importing these products from Japan. According to Shiraishi's description (2013: 40–41):

> Initially, it [the globalization of manga and anime] had been set out almost disorderly at the grass-root level by various "fans" in different places. After coming across anime during their trip to Japan on summer vacations or getting in the habit of reading manga while they studied in Japan, they would start asking their siblings, classmates or roommates from high schools or universities, and later their friends and relatives, to send them these products, while detecting the distribution networks of the pirated products translated into various languages and exchanging information through internet networks. Out of such chaos of antecedent demands, the market has been formed all around the world, followed by publication funds, intermediary agents, advertising businesses, TV and so forth that made their entrance into this emerging market. The result was stirring secondary and thirdly demands [for anime and manga].

Anime conventions and anime fandom have played a profound role in the spread of anime in the United States (Tsutsui 2010a: 45). Anime and manga clubs foster networks of fans in schools and universities, and act as a sort of volunteer-based PR machine. In the smaller gatherings, avid fans tend to spread the word about anime and encourage family members and friends to start watching anime series with an almost religious zeal. These days, many of the fan activities rely on the Internet to distribute (often illegally) anime content, share ideas and opinions, create a buzz, and generally cultivate attention to anime. There are, at present, over 260 fan gatherings every year in the United States in which anime plays a central role. The largest of these gatherings—Otakon on the East Coast and Anime Expo on the West Coast—are meticulously organized events, drawing hundreds of thousands of visitors who often attend the event wearing the costume of their favorite anime character. Beyond anime, these gatherings are a huge celebration of Japanese-inspired pop culture, including everything from trinkets to concerts, DVDs to movie premiers, autograph sessions to scholarly roundtables, and, in the bigger conventions, sometimes special panels explaining to parents what it is that so fascinates their children.

The commercial anime boom in the United States began with the introduction of the famous *Pokémon* series to American audiences in what Anne Allison called "the 'Pokémonization' of America" (Allison 2006: 234). The export and localization of anime in the United States during its successful decade brought it to the attention of wider audiences there rather than merely small groups of dedicated fans. According to our survey,[12] between 1993 and 2010, no less than 533 anime series and short anime films were broadcast on American television or offered on DVD, several of them creating lucrative markets for anime-related merchandise and toys.

THE CULTURAL IMPACT OF ANIME
IN THE UNITED STATES

Some television anime series had become very successful in the United States already in the 1960s. Anime-related toys hit the American market in the 1970s, even before their media properties, inspiring the local toy industry. Moreover, the influence of anime storytelling techniques and visual design on American animation can be traced back to long before the anime boom years. In the 1990s, however, something important happened. This was when a meteoric rise of animation in global media occurred, and Japanese animation emerged as one of the key global players in the field. As put by LaMarre (2009: xxii):

> Given that Japan is the world's largest producer of animation, one might well argue that anime did not simply ride the wave of animation's new visibility and popularity but played a central role in it. Japanese animations were central to the tectonic shift in modes of image production and reception that generated the wave of interest in animation and animated media.

With the beginning of the marketing of anime in the United States as "made in Japan" in the late 1990s, and with the diversification of Japanese anime on television and in DVD rental shops (including titles that would previously have been considered too foreign for the American palate), the cultural impact of anime in the United States grew substantially. It should be noted that during these years, there was also hype in the United States surrounding Japanese popular culture in general, including niche and mainstream cultural products, such as video games, street fashion, food, design, television shows, manga, and character goods (such as Hello Kitty). It is, therefore, quite impossible to extricate and evaluate the impact of anime as a separate medium with its own distinct spheres of influence. This is particularly acute because, to begin with, many if not all genres and products of Japanese popular culture are closely interwoven either thematically or on the production level (as a result of the previously mentioned media mix strategy). Different popular culture forms fuse into each other. Furthermore, beyond themes and production strategies, the aesthetics of Japanese media-centered popular culture (i.e., anime, manga, video games, related derivative fan practices) have had a formative influence on the aesthetics of Japanese popular music, street fashion, design, and the public sphere in general.

With this in mind, we can outline some of the more obvious examples of the influences of Japanese anime on American animation and popular culture. Many American animators have acknowledged that anime has been a major source of inspiration for them since the 1980s. This was artistically expressed in anime-inspired cartoons such as *Avatar: The Last Airbender* (created by Michael Dante DiMartino and Bryan Konietzko, 2005–08) and *The Boondocks* (created by Aaron McGruder, 2005–14). This has also been expressed in the conscious effort of some producers to collaborate with Japanese talents to give a Japanese feel to locally produced animated series, such as *Thunder Cats* (a remake of Rankin/Bass Productions series from 1985 by the same name. Warner Bros. Animation, together with Japanese animation Studio 4°C, 2011). Japanese IPs, such as *Transformers* (based on the toy line of the Japanese toy company Takara), *Mahha GōGōGō* (*Speed Racer*), and *Tetsuwan atomu* (*Astro Boy*) were remade in American animated or live-action productions. The broadcasting of young adult anime series on American television, such as *Cowboy Bebop* (created and directed by Watanabe Shinichirō, 1998), helped to expand the domain of animation in the United States from one that was child-oriented to a sophisticated medium appropriate for adults as well. In a 2010 interview, Disney and Pixar animator and animation director Glen Keane argued that Japanese animation is part of Disney's animation heritage.[13]

Anime's influence on U.S. media has stretched beyond American animation series. Since the late 1990s, some of the biggest American blockbuster live-action films have been heavily inspired by Japanese anime, such as *Kill Bill: Volume 1* (Quentin Tarantino, 2003), *The Matrix Trilogy* (the Wachowski Brothers, 1999–2003), *Avatar* (James Cameron, 2009), and *Pacific Rim* (Guillermo del Toro, 2013). In the video game industry, with the advent of Japanese video games in the United States in the 1980s, anime design became part of the gamers' world, and of game designers' inspiration. While Western game design has come to dominate the industry over the last decade, the influence of anime can still be seen in video games produced outside of Japan. The distinctly Japanese design of robots and *mecha* is a common sight in games created by non-Japanese studios, from the exotic war machines in the American game series *Command and Conquer* to the svelte ships of the Canadian game *Mass Effect* (Lambie 2011). Proving yet further the close affinity between video games and anime, an anime feature film set in the *Mass Effect* universe was coproduced in 2012 by Canadian BioWare, American Funimation, and Japanese T.O. Entertainment, and animated by the Japanese anime production house Production I.G.

In the music industry, Japanese pop artist Murakami Takashi designed an anime- and manga-inspired colorful cover for American rapper Kanye West's album *Graduation*. Multidisciplinary artist, producer, and hip-hop singer RZA composed the music for the American–Japanese anime *Afro Samurai*. In 2013, Canadian singer-songwriter Avril Lavigne came out with a single entitled "Hello Kitty," inspired by the aesthetics of Japanese media–centered popular culture. Singer-songwriter Gwen Stefani draws much inspiration from Japanese culture and fashion in her performances, including backup dancers known as the Harajuku Girls, who appear in costumes influenced by the Japanese Gothic Lolita fashion, itself inspired by video games and anime. Gwen Stefani also has her own fashion label, L.A.M.B., which is inspired by Japanese street fashion.

But perhaps the most significant impact of anime in the United States is that which cannot be quantified or easily demonstrated and is expressed in how anime and anime-related merchandise have become part of children's mainstream culture and, for some kids and young adults, some of their warmest childhood memories. For the smaller niche of committed anime fans, it is even arguable that anime and anime-related fan practices are influencing the way they grow up, the way they spend their free time, and the friends (virtual and real) with whom they hang out.

THREE OVERLAPPING STAGES
IN THE LOCALIZATION OF ANIME
IN THE UNITED STATES

It is possible to divide the expansion and localization of anime in the American market into three main overlapping stages (Otmazgin 2014: 60–62). (See table 1.) The first stage, beginning in the early 1960s, was the localization of anime for American television by a small number of American companies, such as NBC Enterprise and Delphi Associates, which understood the financial potential of importing Japanese anime into the United States. Localizing anime series not only entails translating the texts into English but also rewriting some of the stories to suit American tastes and broadcasting regulations, reproducing the theme music with new lyrics in English, rewriting the dialogue so that it sounds better in American English, and adjusting the length of the episode to meet broadcasters' demands. This trend grew in scale in the 1970s and early 1980s, as will be seen in chapter 1.

In the late 1980s, a new demand from small groups of enthusiastic fans and college students who saw anime as an alternative to Hollywood-made

Table 1
Stages of Anime Localization in the United States

Stage 1	Broadcast of imported anime from Japan, heavily edited and dubbed into English.	Since the early 1960s
Stage 2	Active localization of anime to suit American taste continues.	Since the late 1980s
	A growing interest in anime among aficionados.	
	Growing influence of anime storytelling techniques and visual styles on American animators and producers.	
	Growth in the number of anime series on American television.	
	New companies are established for importing anime to the United States.	
	Anime is marketed as "Japanese."	
Stage 3	A new era of experimental American–Japanese collaborations.	Since the late 1990s

animation ushered in a new era for anime in the United States. The popularity of anime gradually took off, reflected and enhanced by the increasing involvement of a few American and Japanese companies and promoters who began marketing anime as "Japanese" to mainstream consumers. Funimation is a notable example of this process; the company was established in 1994 for the expressed purpose of importing and localizing anime for the American market, beginning with the *Dragon Ball* franchise. Other companies established for the same purpose (some even earlier), include Streamline Pictures (1988–2002), VIZ Media (1986–), U.S. Renditions (1987–mid-1990s), AnimEigo (1988–), Central Park Media (1990–2009), ADV Films (1992–2009), Urban Vision Entertainment Inc. (1996–), Bandai Entertainment (1998–2012), Synch-Point (2001–2008), and Geneon Entertainment USA (originally Pioneer Entertainment, 2003–2007).

This second stage, which began in the late 1980s, saw some of the first American productions that closely adopted storytelling techniques and visual styles of anime. These productions include early birds such as Rankin/Bass Productions' *Thunder Cats* (1985) and *Tiger Sharks* (1987), as well as Universal Cartoon Studios' 1993 *Exosquad*, which was marketed as the first attempt by an American studio at a series with anime-like complexity. Since the late 1990s and the turn of the century, there have been at least twenty major productions of American anime-inspired cartoons, including *Teen Titans, Samurai Jack, My Life as a Teenage Robot,* and *Kappa Mikey.* Moreover, our survey documented thirty-six Japanese–American and Japanese–European collaborations between 1982 and 2011 producing anime that was aired on American and European television, including such series as *The Mysterious Cities of Gold* (French–Japanese), *Bionic Six* (American–Japanese), *Around the World with Willy Fog* (Spanish–Japanese), *Mega Man* (American–Japanese), and *Ōban Star Racers* (French–Japanese).

While this was going on, a third stage began in the late 1990s with Hollywood live-action remakes of Japanese anime IPs, such as those mentioned previously. More experimental collaborations between American and Japanese animation production houses included, for example, *Animatrix* (Village Roadshow Pictures and Silver Pictures, together with Square Enix, Studio4°C, Madhouse, DNA, 2003), *Demashita! PowerPuff Girls Z* (Cartoon Network, Tōei Animation, and Aniplex, 2006), and *Afro*

Samurai (Studio Gonzo, with the creative collaboration of Samuel L. Jackson and a music score by RZA, 2007). Although these and other collaborations are not necessarily experimental from an artistic point of view as they target a mainstream audience, such collaborations that go beyond outsourcing relations can still be considered as experimental due to their high cost of production and the new production paradigms they create.

The result is a multifaceted presence of different anime productions at different levels of localization, from a basic attempt to introduce anime to American consumers, to actively intervening in the story line and visual techniques of anime series, and finally, to experimenting in producing a new hybrid form of animation. These three overlapping stages have had commercial as well as cultural impact on the anime market in the United States. They created a market that was saturated with different productions, and in this sense, richer in content. From a cultural point of view, their increasing presence inspired dialogue between the Japanese and American animation industries, which for most of the postwar period had developed separately, with the former being domestic in essence and the latter oriented globally from the very beginning.

Empirical Research and a Road Map for the Book

The history of anime in the United States spans a period of more than half a century, and any attempt to narrate such a long period within a single book is bound to be selective. In this book, we chose to emphasize two dimensions related to the spread of anime in the United States during its boom years: the historical roots of the 1990s boom and the industrial and cultural factors that determined the success and then the commercial downfall of anime in the United States. While some chapters in the book adopt a broader perspective on anime products in the United States by referring also to anime theatrical releases and anime-related merchandise, in chapters 1, 2, and 4 we chose to focus on television anime series to avoid too broad a generalization and to emphasize our view that television series were the most important medium for the exposure of anime in the United States and the commercial expansion of the anime industry into the United States.

This book is the product of five years of research (2011–16). Empirically, it is based on wide-scale surveys of the anime series that were commercialized in the United States (see note 12 of the Introduction). We have categorized and analyzed hundreds of anime series that were aired in the United States and conducted a focused textual analysis of American-Japanese anime and anime-inspired productions during these years. We have also gathered additional information from primary sources in Japanese and English, and conducted a comprehensive review of works in English and Japanese on the commodification, marketing, and consumption of anime.

The book also draws insights from in-depth interviews with key personnel in the Japanese and American animation industries. The people interviewed for this research include media specialists, producers, executives of anime/animation companies, and government officials. The interviews were conducted in Tokyo, Los Angeles, Baltimore, Tel Aviv, Seoul, and Singapore. The semistructured interviews included five types of questions: (1) general questions regarding anime in Japan and the United States; (2) questions regarding industrial infrastructure for the production, collaboration, and dissemination of animation in Japan, Europe, and the United States; (3) more specific questions regarding the popularity, appreciation, marketing, and capacity of the anime market in the United States; (4) questions regarding existing collaborations between Japanese, American, and European companies in promoting and producing anime; and (5) questions concerning the interviewees' views on various aspects of anime, including its economic impact, relations between the anime sector and the state, and difficulties and prospects for the global anime industry. The aim of the interviews was to learn about the different organizational and cultural processes involved in the globalization of anime, and specifically in the United States, as well as to bring out the interviewees' voices and opinions about the direction in which the anime industry is headed.

In this introduction, we have framed the topic of this book, namely, the rise and fall of the anime market in the United States and the insights that can be drawn from this cultural episode, for wider research on the cultural and industrial mechanisms of media globalization. We have also introduced the main questions that the book addresses: What caused the rise and fall of the anime market in the United States? What can we learn about anime as a commodity of great cultural and financial significance?

What is the cultural legacy of the anime boom years in the United States? What are the industrial mechanisms that enable the globalization of media products from historical and contemporaneous perspectives? How can we theorize the transnational flow of popular culture? Does the state have a role in shaping transnational cultural flows? And lastly, what is the future of the globalization of media products in an age of media digitalization and media convergence? The following chapters will examine these questions in depth.

In chapter 1, we explore the history of anime on American television since *Astro Boy* (*Tetsuwan atomu*) in 1963 until today. We propose a reconsideration of the anime boom as another chapter in the ongoing business and artistic relationship between the American and Japanese animation industries since the 1960s. By focusing on the adaptation, distribution, and reproduction of Japanese animated television series in the United States since the 1960s, we suggest examining the anime boom within what we see as its primary context: postwar animation as a global creative industry. Within the global animation industry, the American and Japanese animation industries have a determining role. We also show how in the creation of new animation products for local and global markets, commercial and artistic considerations are at least equally important.

Chapter 2 emphasizes the importance of global distribution infrastructures for the success of media products overseas. We offer a comparative analysis of the organizational structures of the television animation industry in the United States and the television anime industry in Japan, and their impact on the organizational culture of both industries as well as on the production and globalization of media content. We argue that it is the differences in the long-standing organizational structures and business models of the animation industries in the United States and Japan, particularly their export infrastructures and strategies, that have determined, and are still determining, their global reach and profitability.

Chapter 3 focuses on the actors who have driven the marketing and localization of anime in the United States from the 1990s, when anime started to occupy a sizable market share. We examine the business models developed by Japanese and American entrepreneurs for producing, marketing, and profiting from anime in the American market. Analytically, this chapter investigates the role of human agency in the media and cultural industries, and describes the construction of new markets with a transnational embedded mechanism. More specifically, this chapter emphasizes the role of entrepreneurship as a central feature in the process of transnational penetration, distribution, reproduction, and consumption of anime in the U.S. market.

Chapter 4 uses a textual analysis approach to explore one of the most colorful legacies of the anime heydays in the United States, namely, American anime-inspired cartoons. This chapter offers a study of cross-cultural flows and adaptations. There are several patterns of cross-cultural interactions that are exhibited repeatedly in anime-inspired cartoons. Each of these interactions reveals something about the potential and possibilities in cross-cultural hybridism, as well as about cross-cultural politics of identity. This chapter analyzes three prominent patterns: the emulation of visual styles, storytelling techniques, and narration themes; the reproduction of a certain Japaneseness by way of expressing in animated stories a fetish for Japan; and the transformation of the symbolic meaning of established forms when they cross cultural borders. We argue that anime-inspired cartoons were a transitional stage, and hence the genre is almost obsolete today. Anime is now an established part of a sophisticated and diverse tool kit available to the contemporary American animator and producer, which includes varied sources of inspiration. In that sense, anime has become a transcultural animation style.

Chapter 5 analyzes the response of the Japanese state to the warm reception of anime overseas, which has gradually come to be viewed as both economically profitable and diplomatically beneficial for boosting Japan's image abroad. We point out the inherent tension in state–anime industry relations and the difficulty of cultivating creativity within a highly formalized and bureaucratized organization such as the state. Based on interviews with both government officials and industry personnel, the chapter discusses the different actions taken by the Japanese government to enhance global animation.

The conclusion of this book argues that the rise and fall of the anime boom in the United States should be viewed as a reflection of the upheaval of the media convergence revolution, thus explaining why this case study has broader implications for media globalization in general. The global media landscape today is a stage of fierce competition that provides opportunities for emerging animation centers and for those willing to take risks. The Japanese anime industry, however, is struggling to find business models that might fit the rapidly changing global media ecosystem and thus help it maintain its position as a leader in the global animation industry. While this has caused many Japanese critics to lament the general decline of the anime industry, we contend that the pool of talent and knowledge in the anime industry is, and will continue being, outstanding in the global sphere.

CHAPTER I

Reframing the Anime Boom
in the United States

The anime-related market in the United States peaked in 2003. American producers and buyers of television content were feverishly looking for the next *Pokémon,* and Japanese producers raced to produce an incredible number of series. According to Sam Register, the president of Warner Bros. Animation and Warner Digital Series,[1] everyone got greedy. Between 2002 and 2006, the huge demand from American producers and distributors for new Japanese anime series found Japanese animation studios overwhelmed and unprepared (Kelts 2007: 69–85). The number of anime series produced in Japan rose from 64 in 2000 to 180 in 2006 (*Anime Sangyō Repōto* 2012). It is perhaps not surprising that many of these series did not deliver quality; they were overly formulaic, and American producers who got burnt once or twice did not try again. For Register, who sees himself as an expert on entertaining American kids and who is personally responsible for some of the most interesting anime-inspired cartoons of the early twenty-first century,[2] "Cool Japan has become boring." In 2005, some Japanese scholars were already talking about the "defeat of Japanimation" (Ōtsuka and Ōsawa 2005).

Some important perspectives have been prominent in the academic analysis of the anime boom in the United States: the role of fans in introducing anime to the United States (e.g., Patten 2004: 45); the crucial importance of global distribution channels to the globalization of anime (e.g., Iwabuchi 2002a: 38); the significance of marketing in the reception of anime in the United States (e.g., Allison 2000); and the real and potential sociocultural and political implications of the rise of Japan as a global cultural center (e.g., Kondo 2008). These perspectives share the underlying assumption that the anime boom in the United States was a groundbreaking cultural phenomenon with no previous history and that anime broke out of its cultural isolation at some point in the 1990s due to several related factors. This assumption is also sustained by a strong cultural narrative among Japanese artists that anime is specific to Japan and pertains to some Japaneseness; its global popularity is, therefore, all the more puzzling (see LaMarre 2002: 336). This premise ignores, however, the substantial market share of anime in the United States and its cultural influence even before the anime boom years.

In this chapter, we reconsider the anime boom as another phase (albeit an important one) in the ongoing business and artistic relationship between the American and Japanese animation industries since the 1960s, which includes imports and exports, outsourcing, and transnational productions, as well as cross-cultural experimentations with themes and styles—an ongoing cross-cultural pollination much like that of the film industry (see Trifonova 2006). By focusing on the adaptation, distribution, and reproduction of Japanese animated television series in the United States since the 1960s, we propose examining the anime boom in the United States within what we see as its primary context: postwar animation as a global creative industry comprising many local industries, among which the American and Japanese industries are key and in which artistry and commercial considerations merge (see Caves 2000). Whereas other mediums were also responsible for the surging popularity of Japanese animation in the early 2000s (e.g., the video games industry and the Internet), it was television that had the potential to turn anime into mainstream content. It is for this reason that this chapter focuses on the role of U.S. television content buyers, producers, and animators in introducing anime to American audiences, while referring also to a few theatrical releases of anime and anime-inspired animation and live action movies, which became watershed moments in the wider exposure of Japanese animation in the United States.

By thus positioning the anime boom on a longer time line of transnational/transcultural exchange, we expand the discourses on the agencies and marketing strategies that brought wider American recognition to Japanese animation. In doing so, we flesh out older and newer paradigms of cultural appropriation of anime, of cultural production of anime-inspired cartoons, and of transnational collaborations.

A Global Industry Avant la Lettre

Animation is a labor-intensive industry. Attracted by stable and inexpensive labor supplies, North American and West European animation studios have, since the 1960s, established overseas production facilities while also cooperating with existing overseas facilities, first in Japan, then in South Korea and Taiwan, and later also in the Philippines, Malaysia, Singapore, Vietnam, Thailand, India, Indonesia, China, and even North Korea. Today, the economics of the industry makes it feasible for Asia to feed the cartoon world to the extent that it is estimated that about 90 percent of all "American" television animation is produced in Asia (Yoon and Malecki 2010: 246).

In 2D animation, the usual procedure is for preproduction (preparing the script, storyboard, and exposure sheets) to be done in the headquarter country, after which the package is sent to an outsourcing location for production (drawing cells, coloring by hand, inking, painting, and camera work). The work is then sent back to the headquarter country for postproduction (film editing, color grading, and sound) (*Asian Animation Industry: Strategies, Trends & Opportunities* 2010). In 3D animation, however, until just a few years ago it was difficult, if not impossible, to separate the creative tasks from the technical or mechanical tasks. This has since changed, and today, while preproduction and postproduction in 3D animation are handled by the headquarter studios, the technical aspects are outsourced to specialized studios, many of which are located in Asia (Yoon and Malecki 2010: 257). Nevertheless, the huge cost of 3D animation keeps the entry barrier into 3D productions very high and only major studios can afford to produce them.

In a few outsourcing locations, such as China, India, and North Korea, the local animation industry had some professional experience and history before engaging in production for other animation centers around the world (Lent 2001: 239). In these locations, as well as in most of the others, a recurrent cultural process has been noted: after years of transferring skills through outsourcing and training by the foreign head-quarter studio, a domestic animation industry can develop into a serious global player (Lent 2001: 245). Japan was a different case, however. In 1966, when *The King Kong Show* became the first American cartoon produced in Japan (outsourced to Tōei Animation by the U.S. company Videocraft, later renamed Rankin/Bass Productions), Japan already had an animation industry that produced animation shorts and features, and had already entered the era of television animation productions. Moreover, some entre-preneurs in Japan's animation industry had already started targeting the global market.

Early in the 1960s, three Japanese animation theatrical features by Tōei Animation were distributed in the United States: *The White Snake Enchantress* (*Hakuja den,* directed by Yabushita Taiji, 1958; released in the United States, 1961), *The Magic Boy* (*Shōnen sarutobi sasuke,* di-rected by Yabushita Taiji, 1959; released in the United States, 1961), and *Enchanted Monkey* (*Saiyu-ki,* directed by Yabushita Taiji and Tezuka Osamu, 1960; released in the United States, 1961). (See plates 2, 3, and 4 in the color insert.) The first two were selected for international distribu-tion after winning awards at the Venice Children's Film Festival. Al-though these features were produced according to the Disney formula for feature animations (i.e., adventures based on folktales, cute human-ized animals for protagonists, and catchy music) and references to their foreign origins were blurred before distribution, they nonetheless did not do well in American box offices. One interpretation attributes their fail-ure at the box office to the use of Asian tales (Patten 2001: 56). It is also possible that they suffered from a lack of branding, in contrast to the popular and quality-guaranteed Disney productions, and were not dis-tributed or publicized as efficiently as Hollywood productions.

Japanese television animation, however, was a completely different story. Due to its cost effectiveness, the potential in finished animation products that can be used after editing was recognized and exploited by American production companies in extremely creative ways from very early on. Often considered Japan's first television animated series, *Astro Boy* (*Tetsuwan atomu,* created and directed by Tezuka Osamu, 1963) was licensed by NBC Enterprise (plate 1). It underwent reediting and dubbing, and was aired with great success on American syndicated television as early as 1963 (Schodt 2007: 87–88).[3] It was swiftly followed by other titles that were similarly adapted to suit the American audience: *Gigantor,* the 1964 adaptation of *Tetsujin 28-gō* (fig. 2) (created by Yokoyama Mitsuteru, directed by Watanabe Yonehiko Television Corporation of Japan (TCJ), 1963) by Delphi Associates Inc.; *Prince Planet,* the 1966 adaptation of *Yūsei shōnen papī* (created by Inoue Hideaki and Yoshikura Shoichiro, directed by Ōkura Sato, Television Corporation of Japan (TCJ), 1965) by American International Television Production; *Kimba the White Lion,* the 1966 adaptation of the first Japanese colored television animated series *Janguru taitei* (created and directed by Tezuka Osamu, Mushi Productions, 1965) by NBC Enterprises; and *Speed Racer,* the 1967 adaptation of *Mahha GōGōGō* (created by Yoshida Tatsuo, directed by Sasagawa Hiroshi, Tatsunoko Production, 1967) by Trans-Lux.

From a production point of view, perhaps the most interesting 1960s American adaptation of a Japanese animated series involved the reproduction of *Ganbare marin kiddo* (Terebi Doga [Japan Tele-Cartoons], 1966). The American company Seven Arts Productions (which later merged with Warner Bros.) expressed an interest in using footage from this series, which was cancelled in Japan due to low ratings. The series was extended from thirteen to seventy-eight episodes and repackaged for English-speaking audiences. The script and storyboard were prepared in both English and Japanese, and were produced in Japan. The English version, entitled *Marine Boy,* was first broadcast in the United States and other countries in 1967, whereas the Japanese version, *Kaitei shōnen marin* (Marine, the Bottom of the Sea Boy), was aired in Japan only from 1969. It is therefore fair to conclude that American studios selected Japan as their first outsourcing location because it could provide cheap and skilled labor, and because of its good and reliable trade relationship with the United States (see Lent 2001: 239).

In other words, business relations between the American animation industry and the Japanese anime industry since the 1960s demonstrate how animation industries became interconnected through global production and distribution networks, and began competing for shares in foreign media markets—some would say avant la lettre, and all would agree long before economic experts started talking about "outsourcing" (see

FIGURE 2. Footage of *Tetsujin 28-gō* (based on a manga by Yokoyama Mitsuteru, directed by Watanabe Yonehiko, 1963) was used to create the American series *Gigantor*. © Eiken Inc.

Corbett 2004: xiii), "offshoring" (Corbett 2004: 39), or "glocalization" (Robertson 1992: 173–74).

Although the U.S. animation industry was a leader in establishing global links, the growing Japanese anime industry was no passive player. Japanese animation studios started outsourcing in the 1970s: for example, Tōei Animation started a partnership in South Korea in 1977 and a joint venture operation in the Philippines in 1986 (Lent 2001: 241). Since the late 1980s, animation has surged globally as an important medium with the growing popularity of animated forms in mass-targeted and globally disseminated entertainments, such as video games, television series, special effects in features, and multimedia devices (LaMarre 2009: xxi). During the 1990s, the Japanese animation industry came to rely increasingly on subcontractors in Asian countries for both 2D animation and CG animation. Outsourcing to subcontractors in East and Southeast Asia has become a central feature of anime production. In 2010, it was estimated that approximately 70 percent of the in-between stage (tracing errors and finalizing the editing of the images) of production in the Japanese anime industry was outsourced to overseas subcontractors in China, South Korea, and Southeast Asia. Tōei Animation is even connected to its subsidiary in the Philippines via an undersea optical fiber network used not only to send and receive work but also for constant communication (Morisawa 2013: 258–69).

The global production networks of the animation industry sometimes run even beneath the radars of quarreling nations. Outsourcing to North Korea demonstrates this point well. The North Korean animation industry is supported by the national government, and productions for European studios, notably France and Italy, have become commonplace since 1983. Since the 1980s, South Korean companies also outsource to North Korea because of the cheap labor. The situation vis-à-vis the United States animation industry is different because American companies are forbidden to trade with North Korean companies. However, the Internet is full of suggestive rumors and concrete data claiming that some series—including *Teenage Mutant Ninja Turtles* (1987–), *The Simpsons* (1989–), and some Disney productions, including *Pocahontas* (1995) and *The Lion King* (1994)—were partially outsourced to North Korea via South Korea (see Kim 2010; Lee 2007). American production companies outsource to South Korea (in the late 1990s, South Korea received over half of the animation production subcontracts in the world with partners in Europe, Japan, and the United States), and South Korean companies then outsource production to North Korea, supposedly without the official consent of their American partner.

At the same time, not all players in the global arena have an equal footing in it. By selling its products to overseas distributors who approached them and who were therefore the initiators of these transactions, Japanese animation has achieved a significant presence in foreign television markets since the 1970s. Moreover, as previously described, Japan developed important outsourcing networks for the production of anime. Unlike their major U.S. counterparts, however, Japanese anime production companies did not develop independent international distribution channels for their products until the early 2000s, relying instead on local agents in various markets around the world. (This point will be discussed at length in chapter 2.)

Today, local animation industries around the world have become increasingly interconnected thanks to the mobility of talents—animators, animation directors, and producers—across the globe. The artists and producers from Europe, North America, and Israel interviewed for this book all unanimously addressed the animation industry as a global industry and saw themselves as working in a transnational field. However, Japanese artists and producers, a few exceptions notwithstanding, do not feel part of a global industry that can offer them opportunities for employment or transcultural enrichment. The Japanese professionals we interviewed were excited to hear about success stories of Japanese animation overseas and emphasized the universal appeal of anime messages, but they remained hesitant about actively expanding anime to other markets and doubted its commercial success (as we discuss further in chapter 3).

A Short History of Japanese-Made Animation in the United States: Exports, Imports, Outsourcing, Adaptation, Reproduction, and Hybridization

To better understand the creative links between local animation industries and global production networks, we propose the framework of the "local-global nexus" (Alger 1988). On a local level, each industry adapts the techniques of animation to local artistic traditions and production constraints (e.g., cultural imageries, censorship, funds). On a global level, transnational business trajectories opened by entrepreneurs, sometimes by international film festivals and fans' activities, and since the 1990s also by the Internet, enable cross-cultural artistic pollination that is exhibited in locally oriented as well as export-oriented productions.

In its emergent stage, Japanese animation was influenced and inspired by American animated films produced by Warner Bros., Max and David Fleischer, and, of course, Disney. Japanese postwar productions of animation features were inspired by Disney to the point of almost looking like imitations. As has been previously noticed, however, the diffusion of Western (in this case, American) culture, especially at the popular level, has not generated cultural homogenization but rather has promoted the revitalization and generation of new cultural forms in different localities (Patterson 1994). The emergence of anime as a distinct form of expression may be traced back to the 1960s, when the artistic creativity of Japanese anime directors had to be negotiated with financial constraints, and they developed "limited animation" techniques that used fewer frames per minute (LaMarre 2002: 335). By combining aesthetic conventions drawn from manga (e.g., emphasizing emotions with stylistic iconization, freezing movement for dramatic effect) with innovative camera effects and cost-effective techniques, such as moving the background instead of the characters, new and distinct animation styles were developed that became the signature of Japanese animation (LaMarre 2002: 336).

As with the manga industry a decade earlier (see Kinsella 2000: 48), Japanese anime producers in the 1970s expanded their audience by maturing alongside the first generation of Japanese television for children. Unlike its Euro-American counterparts, the Japanese animation industry began targeting an audience older than the Disneyesque audience of child-oriented cartoon animation (Asaba 1989: 254). The prosperous local Japanese anime market enabled the nurturing of outstanding anime directors who demonstrated their individualistic, and sometimes eccentric, styles in full-length theatrical features and animated series. The influences on Japanese animation became much more varied and included not only foreign (mostly American) animation but also live-action cinematographic and storytelling strategies, as well as thematic choices of various domestic and foreign live-action genres, such as Westerns, samurai movies, crime and gangster movies, action films, and period dramas— genres that manifest cross-cultural fertilization.

A wonderful example of this "cultural ping-pong," which highlights the way in which centers of creative industry multiply across the globe and move and overlap with one another to produce ever more complex intercultural flows, is embedded in the science fiction boom in anime since the 1970s. This trend, often interpreted as a local Japanese reaction to or sublimation of the devastation of the Pacific War (Murakami 2005), was also influenced by the postwar North American and European science fiction boom that reflected both the postwar desolation as well as the space race between the United States and Soviet Russia. The science fiction genre in the West has been iconized in television series such as *Buck Rogers* (1951), *Flash Gordon* (1954), *Space Angel* (1962), *Star Trek* (1966), and *Thunderbirds* (1965), and the groundbreaking movies *2001: A Space Odyssey* (Stanley Kubrick 1968), *Close Encounters of the Third Kind* (Steven Spielberg 1977), and *Star Wars* (George Lucas 1977).[4] *Star Wars*—a phenomenal success in Japan and a major influence ever since it was first shown in theaters in 1978—was itself a product of cross-cultural pollination with distinct Japanese/oriental influences. Beyond the Asian visual and mythical elements in the plot and the look of *Star Wars,* Lucas acknowledged on several occasions that among the many influences on *Star Wars* were Kurosawa Akira's samurai films, most notably the storytelling and cinematography of *The Hidden Fortress* (*Kakushi toride no san akunin,* 1958).[5] Kurosawa, on the other hand, often referred to the influence of John Ford's Westerns on his own work. As far as we know, Lucas has never formally recognized the influence of anime on *Star Wars,* but similarities between some of the characters and the industrial design of *Star Wars* and the anime *Star Blazers* (*Uchū senkan yamato,* created and directed by Matsumoto Reiji, 1974), suggest that, at the very least, both creations were inspired by similar sources.

1960–1980: DECADES OF INGENIOUS CREATIVE PRODUCTION AND ADAPTATION

The initial success of Japanese animated series on American television in the 1960s opened the door to new opportunities, such as innovative Japanese science fiction animated series that made it to the United States in the late 1970s. Like their predecessors, these series were heavily edited to conform to the stricter standards of American television. Violence and other storytelling elements deemed inappropriate were removed, story plots were altered, and the overall look and feel of the series was Americanized. One of the notable features of these imported anime series was that their settings and protagonists had ethnically neutral features. In other words, the settings did not look particularly Asian, and while the protagonists behaved according to Japanese sociocultural values and often had Japanese names, they did not have Asian features and were not dressed in Asian or Japanese traditional clothes.

When Japanese anime was in its emerging stages and opening up to various artistic influences, alongside indigenous cultural imagery, exotic foreign themes and heroes were also adopted uninhibitedly. Caucasian

pirates, maritime world explorers, American-style Wild West gunsling-
ers, blond beauties, multiethnic environments, European landscapes and
castles, Western folktales, and Euro-American pop music became part
of a large parcel of imaginative elements that together make up anime.
Napier (2001: 24) explains that anime is essentially context-free; it does
not stand for or even reproduce a sense of national identity. It occupies
its own space that does not necessarily coincide with Japan. According
to Iwabuchi (2002a: 94), even if Japanese animators were not consciously
drawing characters without recognizable Japanese ethnic or national
attributes for export considerations, whenever the Japanese animation
industry has had the global market in mind it was aware that the non-
Japaneseness of characters (and stories) works to its advantage in the
export market. In comparison with other media products, this visual
quality together with dubbing makes anime a product that can be adapted
easily to every market. Ōkawa Hiroshi, the first president of Tōei animation, realized this when he said in the trailer to *Hakuja den* (*The White
Snake Enchantress,* 1958), that animation (manga-eiga [manga films] as
they were called back then) has a strong advantage in the international
market compared to live action movies.

In other words, from the initial production stage, anime series based
on Japanese stories and characters were considered in Japan to be nonex-
portable, whereas culturally neutral productions were deemed good candidates for export.[6] Among the Japanese science fiction animated series
that became hugely popular in the United States after undergoing major
adaptations are the previously mentioned *Star Blazers* (*Uchū senkan
yamato*) and *Battle of the Planets* (*Kagaku ninjatai gatchaman,* created by
Yoshida Tatsuo, directed by Toriumi Hisayuki 1972; produced for American audiences by Sandy Frank Entertainment, 1978). Both series belong
to the space opera genre, with its focus on drama, and adventures in space.

The other science fiction genre that succeeded in the United States
was *mecha* animation (a word deriving from the English word "mechanical"), characterized by piloted battling giant robots. Japanese *mecha* series followed a different path of import into the United States. From the
outset, Japan's anime culture was closely tied to the toy industry,[7] and in
the 1970s the Shogun Warriors, a line of Japanese toys licensed by Mattel
Inc. and consisting of a series of robots based on popular giant robot
anime shows, entered the American toy market and became extremely

popular with American boys. In response to that popularity, five imported Japanese giant robot animated series, originally produced by Tōei Animation, were broadcasted as the cartoon anthology *Force Five* (American Way Animation, 1980).[8]

Cartoons based on successful Japanese franchises became a trend in the United States beginning in the late 1970s. In 1978, Hanna-Barbera coproduced with Tōhō Company the animated series *Godzilla,* a loose adaptation of the Japanese *Godzilla* films by Tōhō. In 1982, Hanna-Barbera produced the popular *Pac-Man: The Animated Series* based on the video game *Pac-Man* by Namco. In the 1980s, the television cartoon market in the United States grew significantly thanks to an increase in syndication initiatives (Erickson 2001: 289). In 1983, the financial opportunities in producing television shows tied to toys became even more promising in the United States when the Federal Communication Commission (FCC) relaxed its regulations protecting children from product-based programming (Erickson 2001: 289; Scott 2010: 4). In 1984, inspired by toy maker Takara's line of humanoid robots that could transform into vehicles, the American toy company Hasbro joined with Marvel comics and Sunbow Productions to create the toy-based television animated series *The Transformers. The Transformers* was written in the United States and animated in Japan by Tōei Animation and later also in South Korea by another animation studio. Another toy-inspired animated *mecha* series from 1984 was *Mighty Orbots.* What was outstanding in *Mighty Orbots* is that the series was coproduced as a highly collaborative transnational project: the story and music were created by the American companies Intermedia Entertainment and MGM television, while the Japanese company Tokyo Movie Shinsha was responsible for the character design and animation that was directed by veteran anime director Dezaki Osamu.

In 1984, following the enthusiastic U.S. response to *mecha* animation, the American company World Events Production partnered with Tōei Animation to create the American animation series *Voltron* (see plate 5). *Voltron* was not a reedit of an existing anime series nor was it an anthology of several existing series or a new franchise-based series. Rather, the footage from two of Tōei's *mecha* anime series was combined to create a new story.[9] This production pattern was thereafter repeated with two later examples: *Robotech,* and the less successful *Captain Harlock and the Queen of a Thousand Years,* which both hit the American small screen in 1985.[10] The motivation for this combination of unrelated original series by re-editing, altering dialogues, and changing plots was neither artistic nor designed to overcome potential cultural barriers. Rather, the aim was to produce a series with a minimum number of episodes in order to qualify for syndication on American television.

The presence and influence of Japanese animation in the United States during the 1970s and 1980s was not limited to *mecha* and space opera genres. Nippon Animation had been targeting foreign markets since its establishment and was instrumental in producing anime series in genres other than science fiction. Their first of many international, mainly European, collaborations was in 1975 with the Germany Kirch Media Group on the television animated series *Maya the Honey Bee.* The studio was well known for its *World Masterpiece Theater* animated series (1969–), which consisted of animated adaptations of classic world children's literature, including *Heidi Girl of the Alps* (1974), *The Moomin* (1969–70), *3000 Leagues in Search of Mother* (1976), among others. These series achieved great global success, with a few titles even making it to the United States with the intermediary of Saban Entertainment, including, for example, *Tom Sawyer* (1980; produced in the United States by Saban Entertainment, 1988), and *Little Women* (1981; produced in the United States by Saban Entertainment, 1988). In 1990, Saban Entertainment produced *Maya the Honey Bee* for American audiences.

In 1993, Saban Entertainment became globally famous for its adaptation of the Japanese Super Sentai series *Kyōryoku sentai zyuranger* (1992), which became known as *Power Rangers. Power Rangers* is a live-action series with special effects. Interestingly for our topic, the tactics used for the adaptation of *Power Rangers* to the U.S. market repeat many seen in the adaptation and reediting of anime for U.S. audiences and reflect Saban Entertainment's previous ventures. The U.S. television series *Power Rangers* took much of its footage from the original Japanese series while splicing it with scenes featuring English-speaking actors. In the editing process, new plots were created and the characters were given original American names and identities.

The aforementioned *Mighty Orbots* (1984) was an unusual example of an early American–Japanese collaborative animation project. During the 1980s, most transnational coproductions of television animated series with Japanese studios that were characterized by a high degree of collaboration—a collaboration in which all parties contribute to several aspects of the creative and production process—were with European studios: for example, *Mysterious Cities of Gold* (France-based DiC Entertainment and Studio Pierrot, 1982–83), *Sherlock Hound* (Italian broadcasting company RAI [Radiotelevisione italiana] and Tokyo Movie Shinsha, 1984), and *Around the World with Willy Fog* (Spanish Studio BRB and Nippon Animation, 1987). The primary audience of these series was Western, and this determined their thematic choices, storytelling, and visual styles.

During the 1980s, American animation studios experimented with cross genres of science fiction, fantasy, and *mecha*. Many elements in these series were drawn from Japanese animation, most prominently, the industrial design. But they also combined new and imaginative themes, and had some very American cultural traits, such as the massive build of the characters, the hierarchical relations between superhero squads (as opposed to more egalitarian relations in Japanese series), and, in some cases, local cultural references, such as wrestling or the Wild West. The script and storyboards were created by the American companies, while the animation was often outsourced to Japan. Rankin/Bass Productions was a prominent player in the niche of such cross-genre productions in the mid-1980s, with three hits: *Thunder Cats* (based on characters created by Ted Wolf, 1985), a science fiction fantasy featuring wrestler-looking humanoid cats as protagonists, with the animation outsourced to the Japanese company Pacific Animation Corporation (see plate 6); *Silver Hawks* (1986), a space-fantasy Western featuring part-human, part-bionic heroes with the animation likewise outsourced to Pacific Animation Corporation; and *Tiger Sharks* (1987), a science fiction fantasy featuring human protagonists who can transform into sea creatures, again animated by Pacific Animation Corporation.

THE 1990S: A NEW ERA FOR JAPANESE ANIMATION IN THE UNITED STATES

Although still huge in economic terms, from an artistic point of view the American television animation industry hit a low point in the 1980s. Production costs rose, which drove producers to outsource overseas more than ever before. The job market for animators was badly affected, proving impossible for newcomers. Limited budgets as well as repetitive formulaic series forced production companies to adopt standardized action and physiognomies, and to recycle previously used cells with minor modifications (Bendazzi 1995: 238). In late 1988, Otomo Katsuhiro's *Akira* (Tokyo Movie Shinsha) was released in North American theaters by Streamline Pictures, a company founded earlier in the year by film distribution veteran and animation historian Jerry Beck and television animation producer Carl Macek (script editor on *Robotech*). Streamline's mandate was to bring Japanese animation to American cinemas.[11] Although a commercial failure, *Akira* is considered a landmark in the history of anime in the United States, with a somewhat cult following, and is said to have influenced many Hollywood live-action movies in the ensuing years.

During the 1990s, young U.S.-based animators who had grown up in the 1970s and 1980s became aware of the Japanese origins of some of their favorite childhood cartoons. One such animator is Alex Orrelle, who was a California-based animation student at the time. Orrelle started his career as an animator in the special effects production for *The Matrix Reloaded* (2003). He then worked for Pixar Animation Studio. In 2005, he founded Crew 972 Animation Studio, and has since been involved in many transnational animation projects. According to Orrelle, the sophisticated industrial design in the Japanese giant robot and science fiction genres and the innovative character animation and complex storytelling in anime were seen by an emerging generation of American animators as offering compelling new possibilities.[12] These young artists became actively interested in anime and began using a wider variety of animation genres and styles as inspiration for their own creations.

One example for this mixed-inspiration mechanism was the experimental science fiction miniseries *Æon Flux,* created in 1991 for MTV Animation by Korean American animator Peter Chung. Chung has acknowledged many influences on *Æon Flux,* including *Akira*. Another American science fiction animated series that exhibited Japanese influence is *Exosquad* (1993). The show, created by Will Meugniot and Jeff Segal for Universal Cartoon Studios, is described on Will Meugniot's web page as "the first attempt by an American Studio to do a series with anime-like complexity."[13] For fans, *Exosquad* stands out among other cartoons for targeting older viewers: the story progresses as a continuing saga with many unfolding story lines rather than as a string of stand-alone episodes, the script features complex characters, and the plot is dark and violent with many scenes of death and destruction. While the script and storyboards for *Exosquad* were produced at the U.S. headquarters, the animation was outsourced. In an Internet forum from 1995, Meugniot revealed the huge influence of *Gundam* (created and directed by Tomino Yoshiyuki; Studio Sunrise, 1979) on him and his team members, to the extent that he wanted to have the Japanese company Sunrise animate *Exosquad*, but this did not work out.[14] Sunrise did eventually contribute some storyboards, but the series was animated by a South Korean studio.

By the 1990s, the influence of various anime genres and styles reached beyond experimental projects and into the very core of the American animation industry. Coming full circle from the early days of Japanese animation, Disney and Pixar animator and animation director Glen Keane, who has been involved in the production of many box office hits since the late 1980s, acknowledged the influence of Japanese animation in a 2010 interview. For Keane, Japanese animation is part of Disney's animation heritage.[15] Anecdotal yet revealing in this context is the now well-known controversy resulting from the striking resemblances of Disney's *The Lion King* (1994) to Tezuka's *Kimba, the White Lion* (1965). To make the story even more complex, it has been pointed out that *Kimba, the White Lion* was itself inspired by Disney's *Bambi* (1942) (see Peterson 2011: 176). The official response of Tezuka Productions to the alleged plagiarism was that the two stories are completely different (Kelts 2007: 45). In an interview with Kelts (2007: 45), Shimizu Yoshihiro, who worked alongside Tezuka, claimed that had Tezuka been alive and known that Disney was copying elements of his work, he would have been proud. In 1997, Walt Disney Company acquired the distribution rights of Studio Ghibli Productions, excluding movies that had previously been licensed for international distribution. In 2008, ties between Disney and Ghibli were further strengthened when Hoshino Kōji, former president of Walt Disney Japan, became the president of Studio Ghibli.

In the late 1990s, a new generation of Japanese animated series became popular in the United States. According to Shinoda Yoshihiko,[16] managing director of Fujiko Pro and longtime promoter of anime and manga, an important reason for the growth of Japanese anime on American television in the 1990s was the expansion of cable television's broadcasting time, which led to a demand for more programs. American cable companies were buying "time blocks" that they partly filled with anime, also making money by selling time for advertisements (for every 30 minutes of broadcasting time, 3 to 3.5 minutes are dedicated to advertisements and announcements).

One of the first new generation anime series that made it to the American screen in the 1990s was *Sailor Moon* (*Bishōjo senshi sērā mūn*, created by Naoko Takeuchi, directed by several directors, 1992; licensed by DiC Entertainment). Although *Sailor Moon* was first broadcast in 1995, its ratings grew only in 1998 when it was broadcasted on Cartoon Network's Toonami block on weekday afternoons. The ratings of *Dragon Ball Z* (*Doragon bōru zetto*, created by Akira Toriyama, directed by Nishio Daisuke 1989; licensed by Funimation), first broadcast in 1996, grew similarly in 1998. Most notably, *Pokémon* (based on a video game created by Satoshi Tajiri, 1997; licensed by 4Kids Entertainment), became an instant hit in 1998 when broadcasted on U.S.-syndicated television. The year 1998 thus became a tipping point in the history of anime on American television.

There are two ways to interpret the success or failure of creative products in the global market. The first argues that creative products such as animation embody cultural codes and characteristics, which may thwart global market success (see Caves 2000: 283; Condry 2013; Yoon and Malecki 2010: 263). The second contends that good marketing—including, in the case of animation, efficient advertising and promotion, favorable broadcasting hours, the timely release of merchandise, and appropriate localization measures—might play an even more crucial role (see Allison 2000). Although during interviews with television producers we heard much support for the former view, empirical data increasingly supports the latter: a good show with an excellent marketing and distribution infrastructure has a very good chance of becoming popular. As explained above, *Dragon Ball Z* and *Sailor Moon* did not do so well when first aired in the United States, but their popularity grew once they were broadcasted during prime-time slots on the action-oriented Toonami block. From the outset, *Pokémon,* which aired mornings and afternoons on syndicated television before moving to the Kids WB block, was allocated prime-time slots. It was, moreover, an irresistible marketing machine, with the launch in September 1998 of the Nintendo video game on which it was based, the collectible toys, and the trading card game. The *Pokémon* package was a masterful example of "remediation" (see Bolter and Grusin 1999) or "media-mix" (Steinberg 2012).

Like their predecessors, these new generation anime series were heavily reedited for the American market. However, they belonged to animated subgenres, based on formulas with remarkable and innovative visual styles that had never been previously seen on American television. *Sailor Moon* is a cross-genre between girls' animation, focusing on friendship and romance, and the superheroes squad genre (*sentai*), set in a magical yet recognizable contemporary Japan. In accordance with *shōjo* (young girls) manga, the young protagonists of *Sailor Moon* dress in a sexier way than young girls in conventional American cartoons and are slim with fancy hair styles and huge watery eyes. The show itself deals with sexual and gender themes that were downplayed in the English dubbed version but were not entirely effaced. *Dragon Ball Z* is a martial arts, action-packed tale of friendship and struggle, loosely based on the Chinese tale *A Journey to the West*. The epic tale takes place in a magical, fantastic, futuristic setting, with elements that disclose Asian/Japanese affinities. It develops from one episode to another, and in its complexity, targets an older audience. The design of the characters in *Dragon Ball Z*, drawing on the legacy of *shōnen* (young boys') manga stylistic conventions, was new for American television audiences: spiky and unrealistically colored hair, huge eyes, exaggerated difference in the stature of the protagonists, which does not reflect their physical or magical powers, and hybrid animal-human compositions. Lastly, *Pokémon* portrays a contemporary, familiar yet fantastic world with many Asian/Japanese characteristics. The characters tend to be cute and toy-like, in accordance with Japanese commercial design that has, since the 1970s, used innocent-looking, young, round, pastel-colored and animal-like characters (see Yano 2004).

An additional innovative element in these series was that their Japanese origins became part of their marketing. Unlike their predecessors, the media companies who licensed and distributed these series saw great potential in promoting "anime" as a brand. *Dragon Ball Z* was licensed and distributed by Funimation, a company that was established with the purpose of exploiting the commercial potential of anime. *Sailor Moon* was initially licensed by DiC Entertainment, a company that did not, as yet, focus particularly on anime but that had a long history of collaboration with Japanese studios. From its third season, however, *Sailor Moon* (2000) was licensed by Cloverway Inc., the international branch of Tōei Company (owners of Tōei Animation), which had a special interest in marketing Japanese anime. *Pokémon* was licensed by 4KIDS, which, likewise, had not been focusing solely on anime but for which anime had become a major business. In 1999, the theater feature *Mewtwo Strikes Back,* a tie-in with the *Pokémon* series, debuted in the United States and quickly became one of its highest grossing animated films ever.[17]

The popularity of these shows paved the way for more anime series that might have otherwise been seen as too "Japanese" or too "different" for the American palate. These titles were also licensed and distributed by companies established with the purpose of popularizing Japanese anime, such as VIZ media and Funimation, or by companies with a variety of children's entertainment products and a strong Japanese anime desk, such as 4Kids Entertainment, Saban Entertainment, and the Canadian Nelvana Limited.[18] Among the television anime series that became megahits in the United States are *Digimon* (*Dejimon,* based on the franchise conceived by Hongō Akiyoshi [probably a collective pseudonym], first two seasons directed by Kakudō Hiroyuki 1999; Saban Entertainment, 1999), *Card Captor Sakura* (*Kādo kyaputā sakura,* created by Clamp, directed by Asaka Morio 1998; Nelvana Limited, 2000), *Beyblade* (*Bakuten shūto beiburēdo,* created by Aoki Takao, directed by Kawase Toshifumi 2001; Nelvana Limited, 2001), *Yugioh!* (*Yūgiō,* created by Takahashi Kazuki, directed by Kakudō Hiroyuki 2000; 4Kids Entertainment, 2001), *Inuyasha* (created by Takahashi Rumiko, first 54 episodes directed by Ikeda Masashi 2000; VIZ Media, 2002), *Full Metal Alchemist* (*Hagane no renkinjutsushi,* created by Arakawa Hiromu, directed by Mizushima Seiji 2003; Funimation Entertainment, 2004), *One Piece* (*Wan pīsu,* created by Oda Eiichiro, directed by Uda Kōnosuke and others 1999; Funimation Entertainment, 2004), and *Naruto* (created by Kishimoto Masashi, directed by Date Hayato 2002; VIZ Media, 2005). In 2002, Miyazaki Hayao's *Spirited Away* (*Sen to Chihiru no kamikakushi,* created and directed by Miyazaki Hayao, 2001; Walt Disney Pictures) won the Golden Bear at the Berlin International Film Festival, and in 2003 it won the Academy Award for Best Animated Feature.

Within only a few years, there was a noticeably growing number of American-made feature-length live-action films, animated features, television cartoon series inspired by Japanese anime formulas, formats, style, and thematic choice, and even American re-makes of well-known anime series: for example, *The Matrix Trilogy* (created and directed by the Wachowski Brothers, 1999–2003), *The Powerpuff Girls* (created and directed by Craig McCracken; Hanna-Barbera for Cartoon Network, 1998), *Samurai Jack* (created and directed by Genndy Tartakovsky; Cartoon Network Studios for Cartoon Network, 2001), *Teen Titans* (created by Glen Murakami, directed by several directors; Warner Brothers Animations for Cartoon Network, 2003), *Hi Hi Puffy Ami Yumi* (created by Sam Register, directed by several directors; Renegade Animation for Cartoon Network, 2004), *Avatar: The Last Airbender* (created by Michael Dante DiMartino and Bryan Konietzko, directed by several directors; Nickelodeon Animation Studios for Nickelodeon, 2005), *The Boondocks* (created by Aaron McGruder, directed by several directors; Rebel Base for Adult Swim [an overnight block of adult animation that shares air time with Cartoon Network], 2005), *Kappa Mickey* (created by Larry Schwartz, directed by Sergei Aniskov; Animation Collective for Nicktoons Network and Nickelodeon, 2006), *Transformers* (based on the *Transformers* franchise, directed by Michael Bay, 2007), *Speed Racer* (based on the original *Mahha GōGōGō* anime series, directed by the Wachowski Brothers 2008), *Avatar* (created and directed by James Cameron, 2009), *Astro Boy* (based on the original *Tetsuwan atomu* anime series, directed by David Bowers, 2009), and *Pacific Rim* (co-written and directed by Guillermo del Toro, 2013).

There was also an unprecedented public relations celebration of co-productions with Japanese anime studios in real-life action movies as well as in animation projects: for example, *Kill Bill: Volume 1* (Quentin Tarantino's production companies Super Cool Manchu and A Band Apart, together with Production I.G, 2003), *Animatrix* (American production companies Village Roadshow Pictures and Silver Pictures, together with studios Square Enix, Studio 4°C, Madhouse, DNA, 2003), *Batman: Gotham Knight* (American production companies DC comics and Warner Bros. Animation, together with Japanese animation studios Bee Train, Madhouse, Production I.G, and Studio 4°C, 2008), and *Thunder Cats* (Warner Bros. Animation, together with Japanese animation Studio 4°C, 2011). This also extended to media coverage of the innovative experimentation of Japanese studios with American directors and artists:

for example, *Alexander Senki* (character and setting design by Korean American animator Peter Chung; Madhouse, 1999), *Tekkon Kinkreet* (directed by Michael Arias; Studio 4°C, 2006), and the television anime series *Afro Samurai* (created by Okazaki Takashi and directed by Kizaki Fuminori; Studio Gonzo, with the creative collaboration of Samuel L. Jackson and a musical score by RZA, 2007).

Cultural barriers that had once seemed unbridgeable were coming down, challenging the accepted notion that culturally specific animation products could not compete in the global arena, and suggesting that animation was more of a global transnational, transcultural industry than ever before.

Conclusion: The Complexity of the Globalization of Media Content

By positioning the anime boom in the United States on a longer time line, starting with the emergence of global animation in the 1960s, in this chapter we offered an analysis of processes related to transcultural artistic pollination and transnational commercial entrepreneurship in the creative industries. Admittedly, the differentiated analytical usage of *transnational* and *transcultural* in this context does not always sustain closer scrutiny; transgressing national borders with business initiatives such as outsourcing and imports results in transcultural interactions and influences. It is, nevertheless, productive for emphasizing the complex duality of artistry (more related to the notion of culture) and business (more related to the notion of national regulations and borders), which was debated in this chapter as characteristic of the animation industry.

Thanks to the new import and distribution channels established in the 1990s, Japanese animation on U.S. television was redeemed of its transparency, and its presence became more daring and more recognizably influential. As we have suggested earlier in this chapter, no one can determine why an animation style, or even a show, becomes a hit in one country but not in another (Bielby and Harrington 2008: 37). Cultural differences are often suggested as the reason anime has managed to acquire a devoted fan base in the United States without securing a stronger foothold in the mainstream television market (with the exception of hit kids' anime series). During interviews with professionals from animation industries around the globe, they stressed unanimously that in media content, taste and preferences are, to a significant extent, culturally specific. Sam Register, for example, explained that American superheroes never did well in Japan: "American super heroes are too robustly built for Japanese boys to identify with."[19] Berthe Lotsova, writer and producer at French Marathon Media, explained that her company hires American writers to ensure that the series they produce are exportable to the United States.[20] It is an accepted rule of thumb that media content must be adjusted to appeal to audiences of different cultures.

While we are not looking to challenge this notion, perplexing questions immediately emerge if one adheres too closely to its rationale: if cultural proximity is so crucial for ensuring the reception of media content, how is it that American media content is eagerly watched on so many television networks around the world regardless of cultural differences? And can the process of active localization completely neutralize cultural differences? In addition, refocusing on animation, some adult-oriented U.S.-made animation series, such as *South Park* and *American Dad*, which are embedded with references to American culture and society, are broadcast around the world and have acquired many non-American fans. Similarly, as previously discussed, some Japanese anime series that were previously considered "too Japanese" for American tastes made it big in the United States. It would seem that while cultural preferences are, of course, important, they do not provide a complete explanation for why and how media content gets globalized. In the following chapter, we offer a complementary explanation that stresses the importance of distribution channels in the globalization of content.

CHAPTER 2

Building Silk Roads

A Comparative Analysis of Television Animation
Industries in the United States and Japan

By rights, the Japanese industry should have nurtured by now a
company akin to Walt Disney Co., the media giant whose strength
is based on decades of excellence in animation. But behind the
fast-paced tales and rich images, there's a business that hasn't pro-
gressed very far from its roots as a cottage industry of sensitive
artists. Few anime operations have developed slick marketing
skills.[1]

According to the *Bloomberg Businessweek* article quoted above, in
2004 Production I.G, creators of Oshii Mamoru's first big international hit *Ghost in the Shell* (1995) and of the critically acclaimed anime
sequence in Quentin Tarantino's *Kill Bill: Vol. 1* (2003) earned just $4.6
million on sales of $52 million. By contrast, Pixar posted a net income of
$141.7 million on sales of $273.5 million, "achieving margins Japan's anime producers can only dream of." Rhetorically, this example is very convincing. However, not all comparisons of Japanese and U.S. animation
studios yield similarly unflattering results. Moreover, since its 1995 hit *Toy
Story,* and for at least a decade before being bought by Disney in 2006,
Pixar was seen as an outstanding phenomenon in the U.S. animation
industry as well (Price 2008). In fact, according to many of our interviewees, a near 10 percent margin, like that of Production I.G, is considered very good. What can be said, however, is that when comparing
the largest animation studios in the United States with their counterparts in Japan, their business scales, and hence their nominal sums of
net income, are of completely different proportions; the American companies dwarf the business scale of even Japan's largest and most famous

animation studios such as Tōei Animation or Studio Ghibli (see also *Anime Sangyō Repōto* 2015).

Among the terms that determine the business scales of television animation industries in the United States and Japan, the two largest television animation industries in the world, are the size of the local markets and the fact that historically the United States also targeted the global market, whereas Japan has always focused more on the domestic market. The size of the local markets is a given, but by accessing global markets, the overall business scale can be changed. Efforts to shift the locally oriented focus of the Japanese anime industry toward the global market have grown since the turn of the millennium. Many owners of anime studios, anime producers, and anime directors acknowledge (if only passively) the importance of overseas markets. This is not just a matter of a growing appetite or of seizing business opportunities following the recent global exposure of Japan's media-centered culture. Japan is a rapidly aging society. As far as the local market is concerned, the television anime industry is increasingly relying on geeky *otaku* consumers rather than on mainstream viewers.[2] To preserve the size of the television anime industry, and even expand it, it is widely acknowledged by both industry and government that new markets for anime must be developed.

At the time this book was written, however, although global exposure to Japanese television anime via television networks around the world and alternative distribution channels has increased substantially, the export of anime has not proved as financially rewarding as expected. By focusing on the export of anime to the United States, as is the aim of this book, what we see is that while the scale of the exposure to Japanese television anime in the United States has grown significantly, as described in chapter 1, anime has not become part of mainstream television in the United States, and many U.S.-based companies that concentrated on the import of anime to the United States have closed down.[3] For those professionals who took an active part in launching the anime boom in the United States, it is long since time for reflection.

In this chapter, rather than suggesting cultural explanations for the limited success of anime in the United States, we offer organizational and structural ones. We would like to propose a further exploration of the hypothesis that within the culture industry, "it is cultural distribution not cultural production that is the key locus of power and profit" (Garnham

1990: 161–62). A comparative analysis between the U.S. television animation industry and the Japanese animation industry is particularly revealing in this context.

As argued in the previous chapter, first because of outsourcing and
cross-cultural pollination and later because of the mobility of talents, the
animation industry has become a global industry, with the American and
Japanese industries as key players. As far as global distribution is concerned, however, not all key players have a similar footing. We will show
that the respective differences in the long-standing organizational structures and business models of the animation industries in the United States
and Japan, particularly their export infrastructures and export strategies,
are what has determined, and is still determining, their global reach and
profitability. We argue that the structure of each industry is one of the
main factors that determine both the global orientation of the U.S. television animation industry and the lack of similar global expansion am-
bitions on the part of Japan's anime industry. Put differently, both the
global orientation of the American industry and the local orientation of
the Japanese industry are embedded in their respective organizational
structures. At the same time, digital distribution is revolutionizing the
distribution and consumption of traditional television content. This revolution creates new risks, but also new opportunities. It remains to be
seen whether the Japanese anime industry will be able to tap into these
opportunities and influence the terms of media consumption in the years
to come.

The Structures of the Animation Industry in the United States and Japan

American television content was readily available for local public broadcasting networks around the world from the very first days of television
broadcasting, becoming even more abundant when commercial broadcasting began booming in the 1980s. To some extent, the global success
of American (mostly entertainment) content reflected the number of
hours of airtime that needed to be filled in national television systems
(Bielby and Harrington 2008: 38). American television content and

American formats thus became the medium standard for many local television industries around the globe, even where cultural differences were significant.

In his introductory remarks to the 1999 seminar "How We Do It: A US Television Market Primer at NATPE [National Association of Television Program Executives (United States)]," Ron Alridge of *Electronic Media* said, "America is to television what Switzerland is to clocks and banking" (cited in Bielby and Harrington 2008: 40). This is the underlying reason for the American ethnocentric self-confidence that asserts the belief that media content that succeeds in the United States will likewise spark the interest of the rest of the world, as we were told in snatched whispers during our interviews. In addition, since the 1990s a small number of American media conglomerates have, through mergers and acquisitions, come to dominate the global media distribution infrastructures by owning cable television networks and satellite dishes around the globe. Today, the United States remains the world's most dominant television exporter. It has been estimated that 85 percent of all children's programming sold in the global television market is made in the United States (Bielby and Harrington 2008: 39–40). The case of television animation particularly reflects the domination of U.S. media conglomerates over the global distribution of content, as there are American television networks that specialize in children's animated programs that have acquired a global reach, such as Nickelodeon and its sister channels, the Disney Channel and Cartoon Network.

As far as the many television genres other than animation are concerned, audiences generally prefer local programs, and hence the percentage of programming hours filled by imported programming (from the United States and elsewhere) translates into a smaller percentage of audience viewing hours. However, television animation is different, because most countries don't have a local, well-developed animation industry and their television broadcasters are therefore dependent on imports. In countries where a well-developed animation industry exists, such as Japan or France, audiences often prefer local products.

In contrast to all of the above, as the potential of Japanese television anime has unraveled since the 1990s, entrepreneurs have had to create new "silk roads" to enhance its global distribution beyond the international pull of anime to international shores, and the few proactive initiatives by

Japanese companies (Leonard 2004). They have also had to, and still need to, look for viable business models to make their efforts worthwhile.

To understand the system that enables the financing, production, and distribution of animation locally and globally, we examine the organizational arrangements (both formal and informal) that underlie the animation industries in the United States and Japan. By stressing the importance of organizational structure and distribution channels in the globalization of media content we hope to provide a complementary explanation for the commercial rise and fall of the anime boom in the United States.

THE UNITED STATES: THE CONGLOMERATION OF THE TELEVISION ANIMATION INDUSTRY

The structure of the television animation industry in the United States is a by-product of the media's centralized industrial ecosystem. Due to weak regulations and neoliberal policies, since the 1990s the American media industry has seen the rise of sprawling media giants headed by Walt Disney Co., News Corporation (renamed 21st Century Fox), Time Warner, CBS Corporation, Viacom, and NBC Universal. These companies have become powerhouses of integrated communication, media, and entertainment across all platforms. Through mergers, acquisitions, and a strategy of convergence, they have concentrated their control over what people in the United States, and to a significant extent, around the world, see, hear, and read. These companies are vertically integrated, controlling everything from initial production to final distribution. They often partner with each other, lend money, and swap properties when mutually advantageous (Fellow 2010: 390). It is true that since the early twenty-first century, an opposite strategy of spin-offs, split-offs, deconsolidation, and deconvergence is being pursued by the same media behemoths: Viacom, Time Warner, News Corporation, and many other significant players. This is due to plummeting stock prices, feeble content, and the fact that synergies are not as easily achieved as the "visionaries of convergence" had hoped (Jin 2011). Nevertheless, the ownership structure of the American media has not yet been decentralized. What we see today is more of a horizontal convergence, with an emphasis on core businesses.

This industrial ecology also affects the animation industry, although, like every media sector, the animation industry has its own unique characteristics and changes dynamically in accordance with economic and technological developments. According to Internet sources, there are about 160 animation studios and production houses in the United States. Although there are also small- and medium-size animation studios, the U.S. television animation industry is dominated by a few major animation production companies that are subsidiaries or divisions of huge media conglomerates or that have partnered with other media giants. When discussing large television animation production houses in the United States, primary examples are Nickelodeon, Warner Brothers Animation, Cartoon Network Studio, Disney Television Animation, and DreamWorks Studios. These production houses have their own in-house facilities to create animation from the initial idea right through to production. They either fully finance or cofinance the animation they produce. The animation production houses that produce original content outsource the labor and spread the service work throughout animation studios all over the world. Through mergers and acquisitions, they own some of the largest IP libraries in the world: Warner Brothers Animation, for example, owns the Hanna-Barbera library, the Ruby-Spears library, and the MGM library; Disney Animation owns the Marvel library as well as the Pixar library; DreamWorks owns the Classic Media library.

Apart from DreamWorks Studios, all of these production houses distribute their shows in the United States using television networks that are divisions or subsidiaries of their holding companies. Cartoon Network Animation, for example, is a subsidiary of Turner Broadcasting, itself a subsidiary of the multinational media conglomerate Time Warner Inc. Turner Broadcasting operates several television networks as in-house divisions: TBS (Turner Broadcasting System), TNT, Cartoon Network, Boomerang, Adult Swim, and more. Another example is Warner Brothers Animation, which is a direct subsidiary of Time Warner Inc., and hence is also directly connected to Turner Broadcasting and its television networks. These networks also broadcast animation made by other studios.

In recent years, they have been more open to broadcasting international content and international coproductions. But animated programs made by the animation studio owned by their holding company have a secured prime-time spot. As for DreamWorks Studios' television animated series, they are distributed domestically by DreamWorks Television (not a network but a distribution and production division of DreamWorks Studios) and CBS television distribution. This is a shortcoming of Dream-Works Studios and perhaps the reason that it is the least profitable among the other big names. As we will see shortly, it is at least one of the reasons that DreamWorks Studios has been restructuring and trying out new distribution models. In other words, for most major production houses, all or most of the profit from broadcasting stays "in the family," whether it is through commercials, cable and satellite subscriptions, or sales to syndicated television.

Today, merchandising is the most important revenue source in animation (for both television animation and animated theatrical releases). Toy experts are consulted during the storyboard stage, and changes in the design of the characters are made according to their specifications.[4] Merchandising deals are signed during the early stages of production. The big animation production houses have major licensees. In 2012, it was rumored that Disney, the most vertically integrated and successful in cross-promotions among all (television) animation production houses in the United States, was trying to acquire Hasbro, the multinational toy and board game company. As of early 2017, the acquisition had not yet happened, but Hasbro, a major licensee of Disney since the early 1950s, has extended its licensing deal with Disney until 2020.[5]

The individual animator and the smaller animation studios in the United States must team up with a strong animation production house, a television network, or a distribution firm to get an outsourced production job, not to mention to produce an original television series. The latter happens very rarely because most service-driven, small or medium U.S. animation studios are not looking to produce original content. If a deal is signed for producing original content, the coproduction firm(s) will finance and distribute the show and will own most or all of the copyrights. According to Michelle Orrelle, managing director of the transnational animation studio Crew 972, one most often gets a job in the U.S. animation industry through personal connections: "You need to be schmoozing all the time, or have your agent schmooze for you, and if you are lucky you might be at the right place at the right time." To have your original concept produced, you need to go "from door to door."[6] Media content festivals are another venue to approach decision makers and impress them.[7] Orrelle added that, "Eventually, if the show is produced and becomes successful, it will be the distribution company or the television network who will make the money. The [small- or medium-size] animation studio will be happy to have had a chance to prove itself for the sake of getting another future job opportunity."[8]

A well-known example of a hugely successful American cartoon that began as a concept outside the established scene of the large television animation studios is the series *South Park*. Trey Parker and Matt Stone created two experimental shorts based on their own original concept. The second short was designed as a Christmas card and became one of the first viral videos on the Internet.[9] Parker and Stone began looking for a coproduction broadcasting network to turn their concept into a television show, which was not easy due to the show's lack of inhibitions.[10] *South Park,* the television series, would probably have never become the world-famous series it is if Comedy Central executive Doug Herzog had not watched the short and commissioned it to be developed into the series we have known since 1997.[11] Comedy Central was still a relatively young cable and satellite television channel that did not attract much attention. It was, however, owned at the time by Viacom and Time Turner (as of 2017, it is owned entirely by Viacom). *South Park* became "a mini phenomenon" for Comedy Central, whose ratings grew significantly thanks to the series.[12]

The Simpsons, created by the independent artist Matt Groening, is another example of a successful animated show. *The Simpsons* began as animation shorts during *The Tracey Ullman Show,* a comedy produced by 20th Century Fox (a film studio and television production company), and Gracie Films (a television production company) since 1987. According to Internet sources, the idea to include animation shorts in *The Tracey Ullman Show* was initiated and developed by producer James L. Brook who worked on *The Tracey Ullman Show* and who is the founder of Gracie Films. He approached Matt Groening. Following their popularity, in 1990 *The Simpsons* shorts were adapted into a half-hour series for Fox Broadcasting Company, a commercial broadcast television network owned by the Fox Entertainment Group. They were originally animated by the then small Klasky Csupo animation house. *The Simpsons* is today distributed by 20th Television, the syndication arm of 20th Century Fox Television.

In sum, animation production in the United States is bound within larger organizations, which maintain core control over the various stages of production and distribution. Individual creativity and small-scale animation production is possible, albeit rare, and must be tied to larger American media conglomerates that control the market.

JAPAN: THE FUNCTIONAL STRUCTURE
OF THE ANIME INDUSTRY

Unlike the American television animation industry, the anime industry in Japan is fragmented and decentralized, and could be characterized as having a "functional structure" in which every set of tasks is handled by a different specialized business entity (Nakamura 2003). With a population of less than half that of the United States, in 2015 there were 419 registered anime studios in Japan (*Anime Sangyō Repōto* 2015). Some are very small, with less than ten employees; others are medium- or large-size enterprises. About 120 are registered as large, full-production animation houses known as prime contractor production companies (*motouke seisaku gaisha*). According to Shichijō Naohiro, a senior research fellow at the National Institute of Science and Technology Policy and a Professor at Tokyo University of Technology who has closely surveyed the work of Japanese anime studios and knows many of the people in the industry, only about twenty of these are dominant players in the television animation industry.[13] While the largest animation studios in the United States are a part of huge media conglomerates, in Japan the number of anime studios that are affiliates, subsidiaries, or divisions of larger media conglomerates is small. Animation studios in Japan are either independent studios or stock companies owned by multiple shareholders.

The western part of the Tokyo metropolitan area is the hotbed of Japan's anime industry. Eighty to ninety percent of the domestic production capacity is concentrated there, with almost all major production companies clustered along the three parallel railway lines that run from Shinjuku and Ikebukuro stations westward (into the cities of western Tokyo) and other cities of Saitama Prefecture (Morisawa 2013: 258–69). The fragmentation of the Japanese animation industry into several hundred anime studios is part of a larger industrial structure that includes anime full production houses, anime studios, publishing houses, television networks, media distributors, broadcasting sponsors, companies involved in the merchandising business, advertising agencies, and companies that produce media packages such as DVD and Blu-ray discs.

Anime full production houses handle everything related to the production of anime shows, from planning to production. There are many cases in which the anime production house subcontracts the entire production or parts thereof to subcontractors, that is, to smaller studios in Japan or abroad (mostly Asia) that specialize in such things as the drawings, background art, and shooting. The anime production house that undertakes the production also collaborates with voice and music studios. As explained in chapter 1, in 2010 it was estimated that approximately 70 percent of the in-between stage (tracing errors and finalizing the images) of production in the Japanese anime industry was outsourced to overseas subcontractors in China, South Korea, and Southeast Asia. Tōei Animation is connected to its subsidiary in the Philippines via an undersea optical fiber network used not only to send and receive work but also to enable ongoing communication (Morisawa 2013: 258, 268). As a result, successful coordination has become a key aspect of the animation production flow.

Securing funds for a new show is the first step toward production. Anime production houses, even the biggest ones, do not self-finance their projects. Although anime production houses may come up with an idea for an original show, they are more often commissioned to produce a show. In either case, they will not produce a show unless it is commissioned by a second party who will also sponsor it. Anime production houses and anime studios are still largely viewed in Japan as professional providers of artistic "talent." This way of thinking has had a crucial impact on the accepted way of sharing profit in this industry, even during the anime bubble years when the industry was particularly lucrative. As expressed by Toyonaga Mami, who at the time of our 2012 interview was a director in charge of overseas market research at JETRO: "anime artists are doing what they love doing. Isn't that good enough?"[14] Similarly, industry insider Tanaka Eiko, the founder and president of Studio 4°C, also explained, "what the *anime gyōkai* [anime industry] people need is just enough money to keep doing what they love doing."[15] In other words, the big money in the industry is not going to the anime production houses, anime studios, or the talents they nurture.

In the past, the most common way of financing television animation was by selling commercial time during the show. The key player was the television network, which put together a plan for a show, commissioned it to an animation production house, and financed the production by selling commercial time. It wasn't long before advertising agencies began buying television time. Advertising agencies thus began playing a vital role in producing anime by coordinating between television networks, sponsors, owners of original stories (publishers who own the copyrights to interesting stories, novels, and manga, and in more recent years, developers of game software with successful hits), and anime production houses. The advertising agency plans the animation show and entrusts the production to an animation production house. It then sells commercial time to sponsors, thereby recuperating the money it paid for the broadcasting time as well as a commission fee. The commission pays for the anime production together with a profit for the advertising agency.

Television advertising in contemporary Japan is nearly entirely controlled by the three advertisement giants: Dentsu, Hakuhōdō, and ADK. Among these three big names, ADK (Asatsu-DK), which began focusing on television animation very early on, handles a very large number of anime television shows. It is responsible for many hits since the 1970s, including *Majingā zetto (Mazinger Z,* 1972), *Doraemon* (1973), and *Kureyon shin-chan (Crayon Shin-Chan,* 1992). According to Kogake Shintarō, executive producer at Dentsu Entertainment, the anime market in Japan was historically not so big.[16] It thus attracted medium-size advertising companies such as ADK and Yomiuri Advertising. Dentsu entered the market only around the year 2000, at the peak of the anime bubble.

Further developing the business model for anime productions, today about 80 percent of anime productions are produced with funding provided by "production committees" *(anime seisaku iinkai).* The television production committees system first emerged in the 1980s but came to prominence in the late 1990s and early 2000s (Steinberg 2012: 172). Television networks or advertising agencies organize a production committee of sponsors for each show, including, for example, publishers such as Shūeisha and Shōgakukan; DVD makers such as Bandai Visual and King Record; producers of game software such as Sony Computer Entertainment, Sega, and Konami; toys makers such as Takara-Tomi and Bandai;

music companies such as Victor Entertainment and Sony Music Entertainment Japan; television channels such as Fuji Television and NHK (Nippon Hōsō Kyōkai); and advertising agencies such as ADK and Dentsu. It is only in recent years that more anime production houses to which the actual anime production is entrusted (especially those with a more business-oriented management such as Studio Gonzo, Tōei Animation, Madhouse, Studio Ghibli, and Sunrise Studio) have also become members of production committees.

In return for investing capital in the production, the members of the production committee receive copyrights. Investing in anime production through a production committee is a lot like putting up venture capital. There are no guarantees that any anime product will do well, as in the saying "nobody knows anything" regarding the unpredictability of success or failure in the motion picture industry (Goldman 1984: 39). Once the production is finished, the production committee members share the copyrights of the final product and earn money from television advertising, cable television, the DVD version, derivative game software, merchandising, overseas sales, and so forth. The economic advantage of working as a production committee rather than as a sole investor is the division of financial risks among all the players. The downside is that production committees prefer risk-averse plans, which result in a proliferation of sequels, prequels, spin-offs, and franchise reboots.

This industrial structure dictates who plans an animation show in Japan. Whereas business enterprises such as television channels or advertising agencies open up the opportunities for producing a television anime show, the idea for an anime show can come from publishers who own the copyright to interesting stories, novels, or manga (such as *Brave Story, Doraemon*); producers of successful game software (such as *Pokémon, Street Fighter II*); and artistic people from the *genba* ("the real place"—namely, the studios where animation is actually produced) who come up with an original story (such as *Neon Genesis Evangelion* and *Mobile Suit Gundam*).

Television anime series are broadcasted on a fixed day every week, or even every day. If the series becomes a hit, one or more feature-length anime inspired by the series are produced for movie theaters or for the OVA market (original video [DVD] animation that is released directly to the video [DVD] market without first going through a theatrical release or television broadcast). Some mostly young adult anime shows are aired late at night. There are no commercial breaks during late-night television, so there is no income, but late night broadcasting fees are relatively cheap. Some anime production houses, such as Studio Gonzo, as well as some production committees, buy late-night broadcasting time for the purpose of self-promotion. The money invested in buying broadcasting time is recuperated by selling some of the time to other anime production houses that are similarly interested in self-promotion. Moreover, in Japan the target audience members of late-night television anime are strong buyers of merchandise, collectibles, and, in particular, DVDs, all of which are referred to in Japan as "secondary uses" of anime. Money is thus recuperated through this secondary use. According to the *Anime Industry Report 2012* by the Association of Japanese Animation, the number of television anime titles broadcast in 2011 was 220, up 20 percent from the previous year. One of the reasons for this boost was an increase in the number of anime titles broadcast during the late-night time slot.

Organizational Structure and Organizational Culture in the United States and Japan

The centralized organizational structure of the television animation industry in the United States, on the one hand, and the decentralized organizational structure of the anime industry in Japan, on the other, has an impact on their respective organizational cultures. In the United States, the most famous animation production houses are known as a brand: Disney, Pixar, DreamWorks, Cartoon Network Studio, the now-defunct Hanna-Barbera (bought in 1991 by Turner Broadcasting System, which later merged with Time Warner), Warner Brothers Animation, and Marvel Animation (a subsidiary of Marvel Studio, itself a subsidiary of Marvel Entertainment, which was bought by the Walt Disney Company in 2009). These animation production companies employ many anime directors, some of whom are celebrities in their professional milieu but not as famous outside their milieu as their colleagues from the motion picture industry.

Likewise in Japan, the names of some anime production companies are known as brands (definitely among anime aficionados and less so among the general populace): Tōei Animation, Studio Ghibli, Madhouse, Sunrise, Production I.G, Studio Gonzo (GHD), Gainax, and so forth. Unlike the American industry, most of these studios are also strongly associated with well-established and well-known directors who have become identified with specific productions—thus becoming a brand unto themselves, and for many in Japan, even cultural heroes. Gainax, for example, is the home studio of Anno Hideaki; the late Kon Satoshi used to do a lot of work for Madhouse; and Watanabe Shinichiro works at Sunrise Studio. Some anime production companies in Japan are even associated with one specific director who often founded them (although they usually employ more than one director), such as Studio Ghibli with Miyazaki Hayao and Takahata Isao, and Tezuka Production with Tezuka Osamu. This is not merely a strategic choice for self-promotion. In the United States, animation products are *studio-driven,* although they are signed by specific directors and creative producers; in Japan, however, animation products are more often *director-driven,* although they are, of course, created through the collaboration of several contributors, including scriptwriters, animators, coloring stylists, background layout artists, music writers, voice actors, timing directors, producers, and many others.

According to animation director Alex Orrelle, risk management is the reason many studios in the United States prefer emphasizing the studio's brand rather than specific directors. They prefer a game that does not become a "one-man show." Orrelle recalled Miyazaki Hayao's visit in the 1990s to Pixar Studio, where he had a friendly discussion with Pixar animators on the differences between U.S. and Japanese animation methods. Miyazaki was very impressed with the number of storyboard artists who work for one director on each project. The Pixar animators, for their part, were fascinated to learn that it was Miyazaki himself who drew all the storyboards for his movies. In the American animation industry, Miyazaki's films would be called "very personal films." Orrelle explained that in the American animation industry, Pixar is well-known for giving its directors unusual license to express their creativity as compared with, for example, Disney Studio, where directors have to constantly market their ideas to their executive producers, who are often neither scriptwriters nor directors. But even Pixar is not a one-director studio, boasting the motto: "No one person is the source of all good ideas." Pixar animators, while impressed by the eccentricity and individualism of Miyazaki's movies, argued that these would never pass Pixar's executive board. American production teams are more concerned with estimating the capability of their audience than allowing room for the director's creativity and avant-gardist innovations.

In television animation production in the United States, the most influential person on the set is usually the creative producer, especially if this person is both the creator of the series and the show runner. The creative producer then becomes the supervisor of both the writing and the shooting of the series. The director of an animation series in the United States is more of a coordinator. In Japan, the labor division between the creative producer, the producer, and the director is more complex.

According to anime director and professor at Osaka Art University Takahashi Ryosuke (2011: 54–56), two approaches to anime production have developed in Japan, which he calls the Tōei Animation system and the Mushi Production system. Tōei Animation, established in 1956 as a division of Tōei Company, was designated by its first president, Ōkawa Hiroshi, to become Disney's Far East rival, and its management organization is thereby similar to that of a film production company. Tōei has been home to a large number of creative personnel, including character designers, production designers, and animation directors, some of whom have become celebrities in their field. But the products of Tōei are mostly associated with the studio. Mushi Production was established in 1961 as a rival to Tōei Animation by the manga and animation artist Tezuka Osamu. At Tōei, the producer, both in name and practice, had the greatest responsibility over the product, thus holding the highest authority on the set and beyond. At Mushi, however, while the producer held responsibility and authority on the set, the creative producer and director (Tezuka himself) could at any time come up with a new creative idea that would hold up or alter the entire project. The production process was director-driven and the director was the only one who knew the whole narrative of the unfolding story. For as long as Tezuka was at Mushi production, the anime produced by Mushi Productions were associated with him. As explained by Wada George, president and CEO of Wit Studio, in Japanese animation studios today a lot of negotiation takes place during the production process under the supervision of the director, and many significant changes are made on site.[17] The legacies of these two approaches can be seen in various combinations in different studios. Both managerial strategies have their advantages and disadvantages, reflecting the tension inherent in any creative industry between artistry and business.

Another noticeable difference between Japanese and American animation production is the participation of fans, who in Japan are often not only on the receiving end of the production but are also sometimes part of the production cycle. The inclusion of fans in the considerations of production is enabled by the more intimate ecosystem of the Japanese anime industry. *Otaku,* the most avid consumers of anime, provide a safety net for the release of new anime production, and more important, send in their feedback on new anime productions, which the industry takes into consideration. These fans are not only consumers but, given their special interest in anime, they speak their mind in various forums. Anime studios release information and images of anime even before the completion of a series to gauge the market and sometimes make subsequent adjustments.[18] Many Japanese animators were themselves fans who unofficially engaged in anime drawing or editing without formal education and were recruited by the established industry. In other words, the interaction between the industry and the consumer audience and creative amateurs is more intense, and is viewed as beneficial to the production process for measuring and extracting creativity from below.

The American animation production process, on the other hand, is closer to the so-called Hollywood model, which typically features groups of professionals working in large-scale production houses and creating media products for a wide global audience. This "Hollywood model" has changed over the years, gradually loosening the tight control the industry used to exert over the production of popular culture before the 1970s (Ryan 1992; Storper 1994). Yet in animation production in the United States, there is a clear differentiation between "professionals" and "fans," whereas in the Japanese anime system there is closer proximity and an attempt to constructively co-opt the fans' input into the production process.

From Domestic Production to Global Outreach

The global market of television syndication is like a spider's web that spans borders and government regulations. It is made up of numerous organizations and institutional actors: from production firms and media conglomerates to advertising agencies, law and government regulatory agencies, ministries (which set quota policies), and rating companies. The buyers in this multiplex world include national and privately owned broadcasts, satellite and cable networks, cable systems, digital broadcasters, pay-per-view operators, station group owners, and independent television stations (Bielby and Harrington 2008: 45–46). Like other sellers of media content, large American animation production houses play in this complicated system, but they also have a built-in advantage, as we are about to demonstrate. This is in contrast to the Japanese anime production houses, which were (and still are) very much domestically oriented and have not developed their own global distribution links, aside from occasional teaming with global players and entrepreneurs.

THE UNITED STATES

To understand the ready-made global distribution infrastructures of the large animation production houses in the United States, we must remember that in America animation is primarily regarded as a child's medium, and then take a glimpse into the history of American children's television channels and how they became a global phenomenon. Nickelodeon was launched as the world's first children's channel in 1979. It soon grew to become the most popular American channel among child viewers (Kodaira 2005: 105). Following the domestic success of Nickelodeon, there was an influx of U.S. children's channels and cartoon channels throughout North America and Europe in the 1980s, which, by the end of the 1990s, had spread all over the world. There are also European children's channels that have acquired a global reach, but the global market of children's channels has been dominated by the American channels ever since. U.S.-produced children's channels, such as Nickelodeon, Cartoon Network, Disney Channel, and the now-defunct Fox Kids, give limited airtime to local programs but have always tended to be dominated by American programs.

Moreover, research conducted in the early 1990s showed that due to American influence, non-American children's channels often increased the number of American and American-style programs, predominantly cartoons. The response in many countries was to launch local/national public children's television in an effort to deliver more diversified, educational, and less Americanized television for children (Kodaira 2005: 105). Nevertheless, the popularity of American programs, particularly cartoons and American-style programs, has remained overwhelming. In other words, due to its precedence, powerful presence, and quality, and because only a few countries have an independent animation industry that produces original television animation, American television animation has, to a large extent, determined the shape and character of children's television animation culture around the world.

Let us now reconsider the advantageous position of major animation production houses in the United States regarding global distribution. Nickelodeon Animation Production Company, owned by Nickelodeon Channel, demonstrates the solid bond between the conglomeration of American anime production and its global outreach. Nickelodeon is owned by media conglomerate Viacom Inc. Through a subsidiary, Viacom International, Viacom Inc. operates approximately 170 media networks around the globe. As of 2013, the Nickelodeon brand included several Nickelodeon sister channels in different parts of the world, including Europe, the Middle East, Asia, South America, and Canada. Nickelodeon programs are watched in over 160 countries and regions around the world. Television animation made by Nickelodeon Animation Production Company has therefore secured global distribution channels.

Another example is Warner Brothers Animation, which is owned by Time Warner Inc. Time Warner distributes programming in more than two hundred countries through its Warner Bros. Television Group. Its subsidiary, Turner Broadcasting System Inc., manages several domestic and overseas cable networks and television channels, including Cartoon Network and Adult Swim. As in the case of animation series produced by Nickelodeon Animation Production Company, products made by Warner Brothers Animation are immediate candidates for global distribution.

As a last noteworthy example, Disney Television Animation is the television animation production arm of Disney Channel Worldwide. Disney Channel Worldwide is a subsidiary of Disney-ABC Television Group, which operates various children's channels around the world: Disney Channel, Disney XD, Disney Junior, Disney Cinemagic, and Hungama TV. Disney Channel Worldwide is a subsidiary of Disney Media Network, which comprises a vast array of businesses from content development to marketing and distribution. All of these (as well as other subsidiaries) work under the larger umbrella of Walt Disney Company.

DreamWorks is an interesting comparative example, because although it is a major studio, it does not, as mentioned earlier, own distribution arms. DreamWorks has been restructuring since 2013. It was rumored that DreamWorks might launch its own television channel.[19] Meanwhile, whereas in the past DreamWorks made deals for individual series with different networks, since 2013 the studio has signed broad-ranging content deals with both Netflix and the German children's channel Super RTL, Europe's leading children's channel. Super RTL had a limited partnership with Disney since 1995. In 2013 it was ready to sign new agreements with competitors such as DreamWorks because Disney prepared to launch an independent version of Disney Channel in Germany.[20]

Smaller studios, American or otherwise, can count on global distribution if they have an agreement with one or more strong (often American) global distributor(s) of television animation. Berthe Lotsova, writer and producer at French Marathon Media, explained that broadcasting regulations in France determine that a certain proportion of all programs must be produced in France. Nevertheless, securing funding for animation is still difficult. Provided they meet certain criteria, French animation enjoys a subsidy from CNC (Centre nationale du cinéma) for local and international coproductions. The French market is small, and therefore the strategic approach at Marathon Media is to produce for the global market, beginning with the American market. As Lotsova explains, "Distribution with even a small American television network secures more viewers than with the largest French television network." After developing a concept for a new series (always with American writers, as mentioned in chapter 1), the first step is to secure Nickelodeon or Disney as coproducers. They invest money in the production and are thereby committed to the distribution of the product.[21]

One result is that the global market for children's television anima-tion is, as mentioned above, dominated by American animation. Another is that a mediocre series produced by strong American animation studios has a better chance at global distribution than a better series made by a non-American studio. If an American less-than-hit television series does not become popular or bring in extra money from merchandising and tie-ins, it at least fills airtime.

As for the less common American young adult animations, the same mechanism of global distribution applies, albeit using different infra-structures. The previously mentioned example of *South Park* and Com-edy Central is revealing in this context as well. Since late 2006, Comedy Central has expanded globally. The international channels of Com-edy Central are operated by Viacom International Media Networks. As of this writing, *South Park* is broadcast internationally on channels that are divisions of Comedy Central and MTV Networks, both subsidiaries of Viacom, and on other independent networks that have distribution deals with Comedy Central.

JAPAN

Unlike the animation industry in the United States, the Japanese anime industry has throughout its history been domestically oriented, and most anime titles were considered unexportable. It is true that Tōei animation was established in 1956 to become a world leader in animation. It is also true that Tezuka Osamu made *Tetsuwan atomu* (Astro Boy, 1963) with the specific intention of selling it overseas (Schodt 2007: 77). The series was indeed licensed by American NBC (National Broadcasting Com-pany) for the American market almost as soon as it hit the airwaves in Japan. Nevertheless, this has not become the standard strategy in the industry. The domestic orientation of anime was repeatedly emphasized in our interviews, as will be further discussed in chapter 3. The Japanese television anime industry led by television networks, advertising agen-cies, and production committees has not developed proactive strategies for global distribution.

There are six nationwide television networks in Japan: NHK, Nippon TV, TBS, Fuji Television, Television Asahi, and TV Tokyo. These television networks have several local affiliated stations. There are children's channels in Japan as well, including American channels such as Nickelodeon and Cartoon Network and Japanese channels such as Kids Station and Animax. But as the general channels have, since the 1970s, devoted relatively long hours to children's programs, predominantly anime and television dramas with special effects, demand for distinct children's channels has not been particularly high (Kodaira 2005: 110). As producers of content, the Japanese nationwide television networks are also involved in international content and format sale, but NHK is the only Japanese network to have provided an international broadcasting service known as NHK World since 1998. In Japan, anime is broadcast daily on NHK, but as of 2017, NHK World had one program, *Imaginenation,* in which Japanese pop culture is highlighted, including the latest trends in Japanese anime, and in April 2017, NHK began broadcasting a new show *Anime SuperNova* that focuses on promising anime directors.

While the focus of television networks in Japan is domestic, since the 1970s Japanese advertising agencies have developed a growing presence in the global market by opening local branches or by merging and forming partnerships, sometimes with other huge global players. As of 2012, Dentsu, the largest advertising firm in Japan, ranked fifth globally among advertising agencies in terms of revenue (*Ad Age* 2012). In recent years, Dentsu has established itself as a global player with the acquisition of strong advertising companies around the globe. In 2013, Dentsu's acquisition of London-based AEGIS attracted great attention. Hakuhōdō, the oldest advertising company in Japan, established in 1895, and its second largest firm, became part of the Hakuhōdō DY Holdings in October 2003 after merging with Daiko Advertising and Yomiuri Advertising. In 2012, Hakuhōdō DY Holdings ranked seventh globally among advertising agencies in terms of revenue (ibid.). ADK, the strongest player among advertising agencies in the anime market, is the third largest firm in Japan and also ranks in the global top ten companies in terms of revenue for 2012 (ibid.). Asatsu-DK has been active for several decades in developing an international network. In 1999, Asatsu-DK formed a partnership with the British WPP group, the world's top advertising company in terms of revenue for 2012 (ibid.). In addition, Asatsu-DK has set up alliances with a number of other leading global agencies to provide services to the international operations of its largely Japanese clientele.

Nevertheless, the global presence of Japanese advertisement companies was not used as a lever for starting global content distribution infrastructures, or even for looking actively for global distribution opportunities. As put by Kogake Shintarō, when Dentsu entered the anime market at the turn of the century, first by buying television time and then by becoming a member of production committees, they did not initiate the sale of anime overseas but served as liaisons or agents (*madoguchi*) to global/American distributors: "As Japanese we cannot actively and directly sell anime to foreign [American] broadcasters. We sell copyrights to distributors with a minimum guarantee (MG) system."[22] Minimum guarantee is the upfront license fee. According to Kogake, in 2003, at the height of the anime bubble, fifty-two episodes were sold for around JPY 100 million (then equivalent to US$1.1 million, or US$20,000 per episode). The transaction was between Dentsu and an intermediary (often a U.S.-based company such as Funimation or A.D. Vision), which then sold the property to international/American networks. As the liaison for this transaction, Dentsu received a 30 percent commission. Once this transaction was completed, the Japanese side had no further business or financial claim on the distribution and broadcasting of the product overseas. As many of our interviewees concluded, when selling anime to overseas distributors, until a few years ago the Japanese party was happy to recuperate some of the capital invested in the production of the anime show and make a nice, one-off profit.

This locally oriented business mentality is still characteristic of production committees. In reference to production committees, Kogake explained, not without criticism: "Japan has a huge local market [for anime]. For us, the international market is 'plus alpha.'"[23] The overseas anime market has not grown consistently and has therefore provided no further stimulus for investing resources in the initiation of international adventures. The overseas anime market in 2014, for example, brought in about 10 percent of the entire revenue of the anime industry (*Anime Sangyō Repōto* 2015). However, a look behind the scenes reveals that the general lack of enthusiasm for pursuing the international market is not just because the overseas market for anime doesn't seem lucrative enough. METI executive Mihara Ryōtarō and his colleagues from the creative industry division[24] explained that the Japanese shy away from negotiating more sophisticated international contracts with global/

American distributors due to language and cultural barriers: "problems with the language" (*kotoba no mondai*) in the words of Sonobe Yukio, senior director of the International Department of Fuji Creative Corporation.[25] Similarly, Shinoda Yoshihiko of Fuji Pro argued: "Japanese have very little experience abroad dealing with other companies. . . . [Japanese] have little understanding of global markets, especially when it comes to intellectual property related issues."[26]

Toyonaga Mami from JETRO explained that the Japanese representatives and holders of copyrights found themselves more than once too naïve and trusting, thus being tricked into signing bad contracts.[27] Although for many years selling anime for a minimum guarantee was considered a good enough opportunity, Japanese businessmen began to think that this arrangement was less attractive when *Pokémon* became a 1 trillion yen business in the United States (then US$10 billion), and only a fraction of that came back to Japan. Kogake was even more explicit when he described cases in which, intending to sell broadcasting rights only, the Japanese owners of the property ended up selling de facto merchandising rights as well. In some cases, copyrights were sold without the awareness of the Japanese owners of the property. There is no trust, and economic transactions, including international commerce, are embedded in social relations and trust (DiMaggio and Louch 1998: 634, cited in Bielby and Harrington 2008: 61–62).

Negotiating media content production and distribution contracts with U.S. distribution companies is seen as a very intimidating hurdle for everyone, as we were repeatedly told by our non-Japanese informants as well. It is interesting that the Japanese entrepreneurs we met tended to interpret this as a problem that characterizes them (as Japanese) in particular. One of the work-in-progress suggestions raised in an interview of the creative industry division at METI was that METI should offer intermediary legal services to Japanese companies that struggle and are intimidated by the idea of going international. This important issue of cross-cultural negotiations will be discussed in chapter 3; policies geared to amplify the globalization of anime will be examined in chapter 5.

Instead of relying on foreign/American distributors of content, an obvious though daring solution is buying into/buying out existing distribution channels or creating Japanese-owned global distribution channels for anime. After all, Japanese media companies have already done something similar before, when they bought into Hollywood in the late 1980s and early 1990s. As nicely expressed by Iwabuchi (2002a: 29) regarding the late 1980s: "Japan has become one of the main players in the development of media globalization by virtue of the fact that its manufacturers of consumer technologies extended their reach into the software production business during the 1990s. It was Sony's purchase of Columbia in 1989, and Matsushita's purchase of MCA (Universal) in 1990 which dramatized the ascent of Japanese media conglomerates through the merger of hardware and software."

Iwabuchi continued further (2002a: 37): "the purpose [of these buyouts] was to construct a total entertainment conglomerate through the acquisition of control over both audiovisual hardware and software." It is interesting to note that the role division between the Japanese companies and the American companies was reversed at the time: Japanese consumer technologies were to work as distribution systems for American entertainment products. In the case of anime, it is Japanese anime that is in need of better distribution systems and the Americans who control worldwide distribution channels for television content and who have a good grip on worldwide television markets.

An early outstanding and highly interesting attempt at creating a Japanese-owned global distribution infrastructure for anime is Animax, an anime satellite television network launched in Japan in 1998. The majority shareholder of Animax is Sony Picture Entertainment Japan Inc., a movie and anime distribution company also involved in the production of anime (not to be confused with Sony Picture Entertainment Inc. [formerly Columbia Pictures Entertainment Inc.], the American television and film production and distribution unit of Sony Corporation). Other co-owners are prominent business-savvy anime studios: Sunrise Studio Animation; Tokyo Movie Shinsha (TMS); and the anime production and character merchandising company Nihon Ad Systems (NAS), a subsidiary totally owned by the advertising agency Asatsu-DK. In other words, all shareholders were major players in the more proactive efforts at overseas expansion by the then (1998) emerging global field of anime.

As of 2017, Animax operates in Japan, Taiwan, Hong Kong, South Korea, India, Pakistan, several countries in South East Asia, Europe, as well as in South Africa and Australia. For a few years, it operated as an anime network in Latin America as well, but low ratings forced Sony to drop it. Apart from operating its programming as a television network, Animax has also operated since 2007 as mobile television in Japan, gradually expanding the service to Australia, Canada, Latin America, South East Asia, and Singapore. In 2012, Crackle.com, the American Sony Picture Entertainment–owned, U.S.-based streaming service, added Animax to its lineup for the North America region, marking the network's first launch in the United States (although not on television), but toward the end of 2013 the Animax branding was dropped. As of 2017, Animax operates as a satellite network, mobile television, and streaming channel.

The popularity and profitability of anime series such as *Pokémon* and *Dragon Ball Z* in the United States, and the ensuing early 2000s anime boom on television networks in the United States (see chapter 1) drove some entrepreneurs with specific interests in the American anime market to launch anime channels for the local market: in 2004, the 24/7 Anime Network Channel was launched by the now-defunct A.D. Vision; in 2005, Funimation launched Funimation Channel, broadcasting anime around the clock; and Toonzai was a Saturday morning block, created by 4Kids Entertainment and Saban Brands, which specialized in anime and aired on the CW Television Network from 2008 to 2012. Disappointingly, Anime Network Channel abandoned its 24/7 operation due to low ratings and became a video-on-demand service. Meanwhile, Toonzai was sold to Saban Brands due to financial problems. It was renamed Vortexxx and had a more diverse lineup of programs, which also included anime. In 2014, Vortexxx was also dissolved. For a while, the only anime-exclusive television network that was still operative 24/7 or on-demand in the United States was Funimation Channel. In December 2015, Funimation Channel stopped broadcasting. The struggles of all-anime television channels reflect that while anime has acquired a devoted fandom, it has not become part of American mainstream culture.

Familiarizing U.S. audiences with the "acquired taste" of anime is one challenge, but beyond this, the business model for distributing anime on U.S. television is also not working. This business model dictates that broadcasting copyrights are bought by a U.S.-based distribution agency (e.g., Viz Media, Funimation, A.D. Vision, etc.). This agency sells the anime to broadcasters with profits, and the broadcaster recuperates the money from subscription fees or commercials, or both, during the shows. In the case of the all-anime channels, the distribution agencies assume the broadcasting fees and enjoy the revenues from subscriptions and commercials. If merchandising copyrights were included in the copyrights deal, the U.S.-based distribution agency and (pending the deal) the broadcaster can also profit from merchandising. If, because of low ratings, the subscription fees do not cover distribution/broadcasting expenses, DVDs and merchandising provide another source of revenue.

In Japan, DVDs and merchandising sales are an important revenue source for anime producers. According to the *Anime Industry Report 2015*, from the point of view of anime-related enterprises, sales of DVDs, merchandising, and anime-related music in Japan consistently exceeded the sales to television broadcasters from 2002 to 2009. This shifted in 2010 and 2011 in favor of sales to television broadcasters, but DVDs and merchandising sales were still very important in the overall distribution of sales per category. From the point of view of users' expenditures on anime, from 2002 to 2011 merchandising and DVDs were by far the biggest expenditure category (*Anime Sangyō Repōto* 2012: 53). In the United States, however, the DVD market is dead, and American teen or adult fans do not buy collectibles. "Anime fans outside of Japan turned to the Internet long ago to feed and fuel their habit, and the prospect of them returning to overpriced, hard-to-find, and long-delayed DVD releases is not in anyone's rational vision of anime's future" (Kelts 2011). As a result, it is only hugely successful child-oriented anime series that sell toys that repay their distribution on television.

According to Ishikawa Shinichirō, founder and representative director of Studio Gonzo, at the height of the anime boom in the United States, Japanese licensors charged increasingly high sums for content and flooded the market with mediocre shows.[28] Sam Register explained that at first distributors were ready to pay any sum of money, hoping for another *Pokémon*. After they got burnt once or twice, they did not try again. Something was wrong in the value chain of anime.[29]

The question remains, however, why Japanese companies have been so slow to adopt the seemingly easy-to-adopt, lower operation costs, online streaming options that have become a common Internet feature in recent years, leaving this alive-and-kicking market to non-Japanese start-ups (e.g., Crunchyroll, Anime on Demand, Hulu, and Netflix).[30] Online streaming would seem the perfect solution for niche markets, allowing the implementation of the long-tail model (Anderson 2004). This reluctance indicates that media convergence does not work seamlessly and similarly in all contexts. The first and most common answer to this question is, as mentioned above, that the Japanese anime industry still relies on the lucrative domestic market and local hard-core fans who are ready to pay handsomely for collectors' DVD editions of their favorite shows and other tie-ins. Japanese companies are, therefore, not too interested in potentially risky overseas adventures. In 2011, Kun Gao, cofounder and chief executive officer of Crunchyroll.com, was quoted as saying: "The conventional way of watching anime in Japan is still TV. There's no platform like ours [CrunchyRoll.com] in Japan. . . . One of their [licensors'] fears is that a title be leaked online before its domestic TV broadcast" (Kelts 2011).

METI official Mihara Ryōtarō suggested to us another less common interpretation of the Japanese lack of enthusiasm for entering the online streaming market, namely, that payable streaming services are not the great source for anime revenues that some would like to think they are; the target audiences for anime in Europe and the United States are teens who need their parents' approval and credit card to subscribe.[31] In 2012, rumors suggested that the user base of Crunchyroll, for example, was not growing fast enough to keep up with the increased operation costs.[32] Patrons of streaming sites pay a small flat fee to watch as much anime as they want; in other words, streaming distribution may have lower costs, but it still has expenses while not generating significant enough revenue. Online advertising, as another business model, still pays little because web advertising is dependent on a consistent increase in viewers. In 2013, Crunchyroll was bought out for reasons that will be examined shortly.

An illuminating discussion regarding the downside of streaming services was published in early 2012 on the fan site Anime Review:

> There are so many streaming services, and most require you to sign up and pay a monthly fee. Netflix, PSN, XBL, Hulu, Crunchyroll, FUNico, ANN, Amazon Instant Video . . . so many services to decide from. What happens when you have three series you like but each is on a different service? . . . Streaming is just not popular yet outside of the US. . . . Streaming is almost unheard of in Japan. . . . Streaming hasn't taken Europe by storm either, because each streaming company has to ask the Japanese anime companies for permission to air their licensed series in Europe, and then

receive permission to air the content from the TV authorities in the European country they wish to air the series at. In short, it's a bureaucratic hell which will probably amount to nothing in the end. And streaming anime in the Middle East? Don't make me laugh. Neither the Japanese companies nor the American distributors care for such a small market.[33]

Particularly painful for anime producers is the fact that many non-Japanese anime fans who might have used payable online streaming options are in fact using fans sites where watching and downloading anime is free. There has been an ongoing debate on whether fan sites are supporting media industry by promoting exposure to new products or rather causing tremendous damage by killing the potential business revenues (see Condry 2004 on Internet music sites). One of the strongest proponents of media fans and fandom, and the ways in which they have been transforming cultural production and cultural consumption, is Henry Jenkins. In the afterword he contributed to the edited volume *Fandom: Identity and Communities in a Mediated World* (Gray, Sandvoss, and Harrington 2007: 357–64), he describes how the "web 2.0" has given birth to a discourse about a new kind of consumer, who, very much like a fan, is empowered, socially connected, and creative. Jenkins praises these new fanlike consumers for bringing on a democratization of culture. He also argues that fandom practices, which were seen as geeky and weird, have become part of the normal way that the creative industries operate, and that media fans were, in fact, an avant-garde that preceded its times. However, nowhere in this manifesto is there mention of media piracy and its effects.

The digitalization and convergence of media, and particularly the rise of social media, have given rise not only to fanlike savvy consumers but also to unprecedented media piracy that can be (and is) lethal for many media producers. Nevertheless, the plausible solution to enforce legal measures against infringement of copyrights (as in the case of derivative works) and piracy is seen by many netizens as going against the uninhibited creativity and sense of freedom that has been driving cyber culture for the past twenty years. For them, the enforcement of legal measures is transforming the liminal space of the Internet into something similar to the old corporation-dominated mediascape. A reconciliation between these two stands is presently not in view. Returning to our topic, it would

probably be most accurate to say that fans are responsible for both promoting unprecedented exposure to anime as well as for unprecedented
damage to businesses.

There are some U.S.-based Japanese distributors who encourage limited free online distribution in order to cultivate an international market
and create brand name recognition and who are moving into paid
streaming platforms. Funimation (1994–), Sentai (2008–), and Viz Media (1986–), in particular, utilize streaming distribution to attract traffic,
generate brand loyalty, and advertise physical media releases. As well as
being one of the most outspoken fighters against the online pirated distribution of anime,[34] Funimation has also been quite innovative in the
realm of alternative distribution. In 2006, Funimation created a designated YouTube channel where they upload advertisements for box sets
and clips, and preview episodes of their licensed series. In 2008, Funimation began distributing full episodes of series on Hulu, also adding a
video section to their main website with preview episodes of various series. In 2009, they began distributing full episodes of series on Veoh.
Full episodes of anime series licensed by Funimation are also available
on Netflix, the PlayStation Network Video Store, and Xbox Live/Zune
Marketplace. In 2011, Funimation announced that it will begin coli-
censing anime for streaming and home video release overseas with the
Japanese video-streaming service Niconico. The two companies have
formed a joint venture called Funico. Niconico streamed Funico-licensed
titles, and Funimation released Funico-licensed titles on home video.
Shortly after being launched, the venture was ended.

Despite the huge reluctance in Japan to move to online streaming,
in 2013 Asatsu-DK, Tōei Animation, Aniplex, Sunrise, TMS Entertainment, Nihon Ad Systems, and Dentsu (all names that should be familiar
to readers by now) joined together to provide Daisuki, a free online
streaming service of anime content with some premium content that is
watched for a fee. The service is provided worldwide, with some content
restricted due to the previous sale of exclusive copyrights. Revenues are
mostly earned from the online store. This service was a declaration from
Japan about the need to be more attuned to development around the
world and to gauge new opportunities abroad. In 2014, the operation of
Daisuki was taken over by the joint venture Anime Consortium Japan
Inc., and Japanese game maker Bandai Namco; publishers Kodansha,

Shūeisha, Shōgakukan, and Kadokawa; merchandise firm Good Smile Company; and the government's Cool Japan Fund joined the founders of Daisuki. In March 2017, it was announced that Bandai Namco will buy out its partners in Anime Consortium Japan Inc. (Chapter 5 will provide more discussion on Daisuki.)

In the past few years, it has been widely acknowledged that viewing content online is replacing, and will continue replacing, traditional television-viewing practices. In late 2013, despite Crunchyroll not generating enough profit, the Chernin Group bought its majority stake. The Chernin Group estimated that anime is a genre with a broad fan base but a mixed profit record. The rationale for the buyout was that the group would use the Crunchyroll platform as an anchor to launch new channels in different genres, as web video is growing faster than any other media sector.[35]

With the changes in the consumption of television content, American Amazon Instant Video (through Amazon Studio) and Netflix, both video-streaming services, ventured into the production of original content. In 2013, Netflix revolutionized the market by producing the highly acclaimed *House of Cards* television drama series and making the whole series instantaneously available to viewers. More relevant to our discussion, in June 2013 Netflix announced its decision to run original television series from DreamWorks Animation. An official at Netflix said that the multiyear agreement with DreamWorks Animation is their biggest deal ever for original first-run content and includes more than three hundred hours of new programming. It expands on an existing relationship between the two companies. For DreamWorks, the transaction was part of the aforementioned major initiative to expand its television production and distribution worldwide. DreamWorks has since been running with Netflix shows inspired by characters from its hit franchises and upcoming feature films, as well as the Classic Media library that DreamWorks Animation bought in 2012.[36] This initiative is another indication that the rules for television production and distribution are shifting.

In January 2016, Netflix and DreamWorks Animation expanded their film and television rights agreement. Among the series that Dreamworks Animation developed for the Netflix platform is a remake of the Voltron franchise.[37] Returning full circle to anime, since 2015 Netflix began offering its subscribers "Netflix original" anime series, that is, series licensed for streaming exclusively by Netflix, such as *Knights of Sidonia* (created by Nihei Tsutomo, produced by Polygon Pictures, seasons 1–2, 2014–2015) and *Deadly Seven Sins* (created by Suzuki Nakaba, produced by A-1 Pictures, seasons 1–2, 2014–2016). These Netflix original series became available on Netflix after they had been aired in Japan. In 2016, Netflix announced its investment in another Netflix original anime series, *Perfect Bones*, this time to be produced in collaboration with the Japanese studio Production I.G and debuted in 190 countries simultaneously on the Netflix platform. Again, the business leadership is American rather than Japanese.[38] It still remains to be seen if and how the anime industry will tap into these unfolding opportunities.

Conclusion: Cashing in on Opportunities in the Global Animation Market

Anime production in both Japan and the United States is embedded in a coercive set of organizational conditions that by and large determine the sort of productions each industry engages in, the scale of risks they are ready to take, the division of labor within the system of production, the relationship between domestic consumption and global expansion, and their business expansion direction. We emphasized two central features: the corporatization of animation production in the United States, which is taking place within large production houses and their sister companies, with a clear division between the teams of professionals working in big companies and the receiving audience; and the more decentralized, target-oriented, and collaborative anime cottage industry that is prevalent in Japan. Given the scale and the transnational expansion of American conglomerates, it is natural that they are actively seeking global marketing, whereas Japanese producers, which are smaller in scale, lack knowledge of foreign markets, fear infringements of their copyrights, and are generally risk-averse, remain constrained by the domestic market and do not, for the most part, pursue a global strategy.

Since the 1990s, new initiatives have made anime more available than ever in the United States through local broadcasters and new media silk roads. Aside from a few booming years, however, the results of these efforts have not been as financially rewarding as was hoped. It now seems that many in the anime industry are turning inward, finding solace in the domestic market, and resigning from the global market competition. But the truth is that these could be very exciting times for anime producers who are willing to think outside the box, that is, producers who will take risks, unleash and enlist the bountiful pool of creativity and innovativeness that exists in the anime *gyōkai,* and leave behind the rules and practices of the Japanese ecosystem to play in the global arena by rules set in the global arena, in the lingua franca of the global arena, and according to the tempo of the global arena.

The global animation industry is growing every year. The global market of animation today is increasingly characterized by multinational coproductions and joint ventures. Several countries (predominantly in Asia) have prioritized their national media industries and are subsidizing their film industries, including their animation industries. For this reason, multinational coproductions today seem a good model for exploring global market opportunities and production subsidies, not to mention the beneficiary cross-cultural pollination of talents and ideas. However, as we were told by Ishikawa Shinichirō, Japanese media industries are not leading this transformation. At most, he lamented, they follow behind.[39]

In the next chapter, we explore both the history and the present-day reality of the entrepreneurial dimensions of anime inroads in the United States. We will show how a handful of producers built the first bridges between the Japanese anime industry and the U.S. animation industry, and how producers today are increasingly directing their efforts toward overcoming cultural differences and creating viable business models with new modes of distribution and collaboration.

CHAPTER 3

Entrepreneurs of Anime

The warm reception and interest in anime in the United States during its heyday (1998–2008) has drawn wide academic attention. As discussed in the introduction, the focus of the literature on the topic is often directed toward interpretation of the sociocultural "meanings" of anime, and more generally of Japanese popular culture; the way it is consumed abroad; and the images it projects. There are also studies that emphasize its international fandom, its "cultural strength," or the artistic qualities that have made it especially appealing to postwar Japanese society and to the global "Internet generation" of young people interested in transnational culture and lifestyles (recent examples include Brown 2008; Pellitteri 2011; Salkowitz 2012; and Shiraishi 2013). In the case of the transnational movement of anime and other media and cultural commodities between Asia and North America, to the best of our knowledge there are no studies that directly analyze and conceptualize the condition and impact of entrepreneurship in paving new marketing routes and creating fresh markets for cultural commodities.

On the other hand, studies of entrepreneurship—rooted in economic and business management—tend to overlook anime and, more generally, the pop culture sector, or refer to it only in passing (e.g., Kuratko and Audretsch 2009; Morris, Kuratko, and Kovin 2008; Munoz and Javier Otamendi 2014; and Sharma and Chrisman 1999). Attention is typically directed toward the individual or group of individuals who have used their ability to recognize opportunities and take calculated risks to initiate change in existing organizations and overcome institutional rigidities by implementing new ideas and creative solutions. Although the study of entrepreneurship has expanded in recent years to include the fields of governance and technology, the literature on entrepreneurship lacks conceptual and empirical evidence from other fields where entrepreneurship is of consequence.

The expansion of anime to the United States provides an interesting perspective on the role of entrepreneurs who have been central in the process of identifying an opportunity, experimenting with new products and productions, developing new marketing routes, and bridging the organizational and cultural differences between Japan and the United States. This chapter focuses, therefore, on the least studied aspect of anime: the actors and the "actorhood" that have driven the marketing and localization of anime in the United States, with particular emphasis on the period from the mid-1990s until today, when anime started to occupy a sizable market share. It attempts to show that we can better understand the spread of anime in the United States by looking at the mechanisms designed by industry professionals to commercialize, market, and distribute anime, and by examining the work of the people who initiated and led these operations. In other words, this chapter emphasizes the role of entrepreneurship as a central feature in the process of transnational penetration, distribution, reproduction, and consumption of cultural and media commodities.

We begin our exploration by examining the business trajectories developed by Japanese and American companies and entrepreneurs for domesticating, marketing, and profiting from anime in the American market since the 1960s. We then discuss two levels of entrepreneurship—company-led entrepreneurship and individual entrepreneurship—by referring to specific cases. We analyze the current state of Japanese–American corporate relations in producing and marketing anime, and describe the various difficulties that hinder or even prevent further collaborations. Finally, we offer an overview of some of the recent creative attempts and experimental strategies used to enhance and invigorate the marketing of anime in the United States and to further transnational associations in the post–anime boom years. The conclusion of this chapter draws wider lessons from the case of anime in the United States about the role of entrepreneurship in the globalization of the media and cultural industries.

Entrepreneurs of Anime: Bridging Cultures and Markets

Entrepreneurship in the cultural industries is understood as the process by which entrepreneurs identify market opportunities and convert innovations, culture, fashion, and the like into commercialized products (Otmazgin 2011: 261–64). Entrepreneurship in anime is essentially the process of identifying potentially successful anime series and movies or anime-related products, localizing them to suit local tastes and needs, and marketing them to a specific group of potential consumers. It also includes embedding cultural innovations in local productions and forming new organizational arrangements (e.g., outsourcing, collaborating with local firms, working with local agents) to support and manage these operations. Even in an era of intense cultural globalization, when ideas and images are supposed to circulate freely and easily, entrepreneurs play a pivotal role as mediators bridging between cultures and markets.

A SMALL PROFESSIONAL MILIEU RESPONSIBLE FOR THE GLOBALIZATION OF MEDIA

The import and export of anime to the United States, as well as its adaptation, reproduction, and hybridization with local styles and thematic choices—debated at length in chapter 1—have never been the result of unrelated and random artistic sprees or unsystematic economic opportunities. Rather, they are the product of the efforts of a relatively small number of companies and studios, and within them, of a small group of entrepreneurs and artists-turned-entrepreneurs who see an opportunity and create a new business milieu with specialized know-how and personal connections.

Long before the anime boom in the United States, a few animation production companies on both sides of the ocean had been particularly instrumental in initiating the import/export of anime to the United States. In the early years, the Japanese side was dominated by Tōei Animation, Tatsunoko Productions, Mushi Production, Tezuka Productions, and Nippon Animation. On the American side, the names of NBC Enterprise, American Way Entertainment, and Harmony Gold recurred throughout the 1960s and 1970s, with Saban Entertainment and DiC

PLATE 1. *Tetsuwan atomu* (*Astro Boy*, created and directed by Tezuka Osamu, 1963). © Tezuka Productions.

PLATE 2. *Hakuja den* (*The White Snake Enchantress*, also titled *Panda and the Magic Serpent*, directed by Yabushita Taiji, 1958; released in the United States, 1961). © Tōei.

PLATE 3. *Shōnen sarutobi sasuke* (*The Magic Boy*, directed by Yabushita Taiji, 1959; released in the United States, 1961). © Tōei.

PLATE 6. American-style Cheetara, *Thunder Cats*, 1985. © Warner Brothers Animation.

PLATE 7. *Dragon Ball Z* protagonists differ in body proportions; their size does not reflect their powers (created by Akira Toriyama and directed by Daisuke Nishio, 1989–1996). Note the spiky hairdos. © Toei Animation.

PLATE 8. Anime-inspired American cartoon: *Teen Titans* (created by Glen Murakami, 2003). © Warner Brothers Animation.

Entertainment becoming very strong in the late 1980s and early 1990s. As described in chapter 1, to meet American television standards and technical requirements for domesticating the series they imported from Japan, the American companies showed great creativity with heavy editing, creative translation, dubbing, and music reproduction with English lyrics. They sometimes recreated the series altogether by combining them into new sagas. Their creativity extended to early capitalization on the great potential of tying in animation with toys, whether by importing ready-made media-mix packages (anime and toy lines) from Japan or by creating original American animation based on popular Japanese toys and other Japanese IPs (e.g., *Godzilla, Pac-Man*).

Acknowledging the opportunity and the special efforts required to introduce and distribute anime in the United States, a number of U.S.-based Japanese and American companies were established from the mid-1980s for the sole purpose of importing, adapting, and managing the distribution of Japanese anime in the United States. These companies became the sales agents of anime. Some of the entrepreneurs who established these companies were themselves fans of anime, manga, and other forms of Japanese popular culture. Others were offered an opportunity by partners in Japan. Some, as savvy businessmen, saw the potential in this venture in an era when VHS had already set off a revolution in consumer entertainment, soon to be followed by another even greater revolution, namely, the 1990s digitalization of media. Among the most well-known companies are Streamline Pictures (1988–2002), VIZ Media (1986–), U.S. Renditions (1987–mid 1990s), AnimEigo (1988–), Central Park Media (1990–2009), A.D. Vision Films (1992–2009), Funimation Production (originally Funimation Entertainment) (1994–), Urban Vision Entertainment Inc. (1996–currently inactive), and Geneon Entertainment USA (2003–7; originally established as Pioneer Entertainment, renamed in 2003). The Japan connection was very important for all of these companies: some of them had strong business partners in Japan, others were founded by Japanese Americans or cofounded by Japanese and American partners.

There were also companies founded as an international branch or international affiliate of a Japanese publisher or media company. U.S. Renditions, for example, was established as the special projects division of Books Nippan, itself the American branch of Nippon Shuppan Hanbai. VIZ media was coestablished by Japanese-born American Seiji Horibuchi and the Japanese publishing company Shōgakukan. They were later joined by Shūeisha and by Shōgakukan's licensing division, Shōgakukan Production. As a last example, Geneon Entertainment USA was the North American division of Geneon Universal Entertainment Japan.

As a result, the number of Japanese anime releases on American television, as well as on VHS and later on DVD, rose significantly. These companies also introduced titles that were previously deemed unsuitable for American audiences as well as new anime genres that had not been considered for export until then. Some of these companies pioneered the distribution of anime for adult audiences in the United States. Others made a name for themselves by introducing a new policy of prioritizing original anime versions and minimizing editorial changes during the adaptation to American audiences.

Similar to the small number of companies responsible for the import/export of anime since the 1960s, the number of studios in Japan and the United States engaged in transnational outsourcing services (such as ordering or providing the service), transnational collaborative projects, and transnational coproductions, was also limited. On the Japanese side, the most prominent examples are Tokyo Movie Shinsha, Pacific Animation Corporation, Tōei Animation, Sunrise Productions, and, in more recent years, Madhouse, Studio 4°C, and Production I.G, and on the American side, DiC Entertainment, Rankin/Bass Production, Marvel Comics during the 1980s, and Warner Brothers Animation since the late 1990s. It is thus a relatively small professional milieu of creative people and entrepreneurs that was and still is responsible for carving out new transnational trajectories of cultural production and distribution.

By mapping the social networks among the professionals who work in these companies, we gain valuable insight into the social infrastructures that lie behind the global animation industry. It seems that personal connections are indeed crucial. This is not specific to animation or to "doing business in Japan"—a market notorious for its dependence on personal connections and long-term relationships. Evidence shows that the importance of social networks characterizes local television industries and the international television trade in general. Bielby and Harrington (2008: 63) emphasized the importance of personalized relationships in rationalizing the chaotic and unpredictable business of international television trade. Their research showed that the business of buying and selling television content in the global arena is inextricably linked to relationships among the key individuals involved in the process. The intimate professional milieu ultimately ensures trust among the players, and there is, of course, also the issue of know-how, experience, and cultural capital accumulated by those who pioneered the market or who presently dominate it.

A look back at the earliest days of the import of anime into the United States can provide some useful anecdotal examples. In the first American adaptation of *Astro Boy* (1963) by NBC Enterprise, television and film writer and producer Fred Ladd, who already had some experience in localizing foreign television programs, played a vital role in determining its final look (Schodt 2007: 80–87). Ladd, together with Al Singer and voice actor Peter Fernandez (with whom he worked on *Astro Boy*), then cofounded the production company Delphi Associates (1964), which produced the American adaptation of *Gigantor* (1964). Ladd was later hired again by NBC Enterprise to work on *Kimba the White Lion* (1966). He was still in the business when he was hired by DiC Entertainment as creative consultant for the adaptation of *Sailor Moon* in the mid-1990s. Peter Fernandez, his once business partner, writer, voice actor, and producer, gave his voice to the main protagonist of *Speed Racer* (1967) and, in the ensuing years, to many other anime protagonists. In 2007, Fernandez was given a special award for life achievement by the American Anime Awards. Likewise, *Robotech* (1985) and *Captain Harlock and the Queen of a Thousand Years* (1985) were produced on behalf of Harmony Gold by writer and producer Carl Macek, who later, in 1988, cofounded Streamline Pictures.

If we fast-forward many years to 2010, the then–executive vice president at Warner Bros. Animation, Sam Register, was looking for a Japanese studio to collaborate (as executive producer) on his new project, the remake of *Thunder Cats* (2011). He auditioned several studios and ended up choosing Tanaka Eiko's Studio 4°C. Register recalled that it was a hard choice but that he felt that Tanaka would deliver the best quality in order to maintain her reputation: "It is very hard to work with the Japanese. They want to do things only their way. With Tanaka it is different."[1] It should come as no surprise that by the time Register decided to work with Tanaka, she had already made a name for herself and her studio in high-profile transnational collaborative animation productions, including *The Animatrix* (2003), *Batman: Gotham Knight* (2008), and *Halo Legend* (2010). Based on her portfolio and our interview with her, it is our impression that Tanaka stands out among her peers for her openness and proactive willingness to explore transnational forms of collaboration.[2] While working on *The Animatrix,* Tanaka cooperated with then-producer Michael Arias. Japan-based Arias, who is also a visual effects artist and animation software developer, made his debut as the first non-Japanese director of a major anime film with *Tekkon kinkreet* (Steel Reinforced Concrete, 2006), which was produced and animated by Studio 4°C.

TWO FORMS OF ENTREPRENEURSHIP
IN THE ANIME TRADE BUSINESS

It is possible to recognize two forms of entrepreneurship in the anime trade business. The first, which is relatively overlooked in the existing literature, is "company-led entrepreneurship." This refers to companies and organizations whose success ultimately depends on a form of cultural creativity that must be packaged, marketed, and localized in the form of products or services. "Company-led entrepreneurship" does not only amount to initiating marketing and distributing new anime productions but also to recognizing, co-opting, localizing, and then commodifying cultural creativity. The second form is "individual entrepreneurship," which refers to initiatives undertaken by individuals directly engaged in innovating, producing, reproducing, adapting, and marketing anime and its related accessories and spin-offs, as well as founding new silk roads for the distribution of anime.

There are a few companies that demonstrate the spirit of "company-led entrepreneurship," among them Japan's biggest advertisement company, Dentsu. While it is a large and highly institutionalized company, Dentsu still manages to maintain a strong entrepreneurial drive by constantly looking for ways to support new creative initiatives using staff who often work in small teams on ad hoc projects. Dentsu is one of the few Japanese companies that actively markets Japanese contemporary culture commodities abroad on a wide scale, employing a proactive marketing campaign rather than just sitting and waiting for local demands to emerge. Recognizing the limitations of existing distribution channels of Japanese anime to global markets, in 2008 Dentsu established Dentsu Entertainment USA to develop opportunities for Japanese anime and toy manufacturers.[3] Equally creative, Dentsu forms "tie-up"[4] alliances between advertisement and anime content, and organizes anime fairs in various countries. Also in 2008, Dentsu initiated the Anime Fair Asia (AFA), first in Singapore and later in Malaysia and Indonesia. In these high-profile events, attended by tens of thousands of fans, Dentsu attempts to profit from the overseas popularity of anime and promote business opportunities by mediating between the Japanese anime companies who are invited to the fair and local media distributors.[5]

But even in successful companies (both large and small), it is often one imaginative and creative individual who makes the difference. In fact, many of the companies established in the United States since the mid-1980s to license, domesticate, market, and distribute anime were established by one or two visionary entrepreneurs. These founders often ran or are still running the companies; some of them are still working hard today, in the post–anime boom era, to find new ways to reinvigorate anime presence in the United States and find new business models to justify their efforts.

One famous entrepreneur responsible for bringing anime and other Japanese media products to the United States is Haim Saban, previously president of Saban Entertainment (e.g., *The Adventures of Tom Sawyer*, 1988–; *Huckleberry Finn*, 1992; *Power Rangers*, 1993–; *Masked Rider*, 1995–96; *VR Troopers*, 1994–96). Saban is a talented entrepreneur who not only predicted that the Japanese child-oriented television programs he saw in a Tokyo hotel would appeal to American kids but who also knew how to reduce costs by buying in cheaply, adapting to American tastes, distributing to various television channels, and tying in with toys and merchandising. Saban had acquired expertise in the European music and television industries under the brand Saban International Paris before launching Saban Productions in the United States. Already in 1978, he had produced the French version of the theme song for the hit anime series *Goldorak* (*UFO robo Gurendaizā* or *Gurendaizā*, created by Go Nagai, 1975–77). *Goldorak* became something of a milestone in the media culture of French and Italian kids (Pellitteri 2011: 295–300; Toyonagi 2010). Saban was neither an animator nor an expert in Japanese culture, but a gifted intermediary with knowledge of the global media industry and a sense of timing who licensed media products and repackaged them to suit different audiences, first the French, then the American, and eventually the global market.

The work of Japanese-born American Gen Fukunaga also illustrates the importance of individual entrepreneurship. Fukunaga, founder of Funimation, began his business by licensing the *Dragon Ball* franchise in the United States. Apparently Fukunaga was assisted by his uncle, a producer at Tōei, in concluding the deal. Ishikawa Shinichirō, founder and representative director of Studio Gonzo, still remembers his first meeting with Fukunaga in 2001 at the annual NATPE (National Association of Television Program Executives) international market and conference for the global television industry. Ishikawa recalls that in 2001 there were two outstanding companies leading the growth of anime in the United States: A.D. Vision, led by John Ledford, and Funimation, led by Gen Fukunaga. Ishikawa found common ground with both Fukunaga and Ledford, who, he believed, shared his vision of the future and gambled on the same things. The three of them were subsequently responsible for the anime boom. Ishikawa sold them many anime titles at very high prices; according to Ishikawa, at its peak Gonzo sold its anime properties to Funimation and A.D. Vision for 50 percent of their production costs. These selling prices were unprecedented, and probably went some way to precipitating the eventual collapse of the anime boom. According to Ishikawa, Funimation and A.D. Vision never recovered that money.[6] In 2009, after the subprime crisis in the United States, A.D. Vision went out of business, selling whatever it could to several smaller companies. Fukunaga, however, proved a very shrewd businessman. In 2005, Funimation was sold to Navarre Corporation for over US$140 million, with Fukunaga remaining as CEO. In 2011, Navarre Corporation, facing a major financial crisis after two years of recession and nonprofitability, sold Funimation to a group of investors that included Fukunaga for a mere US$24 million dollars. Funimation is still one of the strongest players in the American anime market, showing exceptional company-led entrepreneurship in innovative distribution trajectories (as discussed in chapter 2).

Gonzo, led by Ishikawa, also suffered significant financial problems following the 2008 global economic crisis and the end of the anime boom in the United States. But the story of the company, and particularly the story of its then-CEO (Ishikawa himself), is, like that of Saban and Fukunaga, an example of innovative and daring entrepreneurship. Another example of that spirit is Gonzo's high-profile transnational production of the miniseries *Afro Samurai* (2007). *Afro Samurai* is based on an amateur manga installment (*dōjinshi*) drawn by the then anonymous artist Okazaki Takashi. At the beginning of the three-year-long production process, Gonzo created a trailer and managed to interest Samuel L. Jackson in the *Afro Samurai* project, which was to be produced in English and released in the United States and Japan simultaneously. Jackson became executive producer of the series and also dubbed the main character, Afro. American rapper RZA (Robert Fitzgerald Diggs) composed the soundtrack. Unsurprisingly perhaps, Funimation bought the distribution rights to the series. The script had to be Americanized to better suit global audiences, and two scriptwriters, Christine Yoo and Derek Draper, were hired by Gonzo to rewrite the dialogues and other parts of the story to sound authentic.[7] Great fanfare heralded the debut of the visually striking series, with viral trailers on the Internet and Jackson himself promoting it on various media platforms.

In video clips from the premiere party that were shown on the website of Spike TV, Jackson said conclusively that anime is "the real thing today" and that "anime is about emotions, it is sexy and full of action." Such praise from someone of Jackson's stature seemed the final seal of approval that anime had indeed become a part of mainstream culture (although, in retrospect, we know that things didn't quite work out that way). The series premiered on the Spike TV website in January 2007—an enterprising and original marketing ruse for the time. In the ensuing months, Funimation did an outstanding job of promoting the series with special gadgets and high-profile public screening events, and distributing it on DVD, the iTunes platform, Xbox, and Blu-ray Disc. The project as a whole had mixed success; the series was criticized for its weak plot but praised for the quality of the animation and music. A made-for-television movie sequel entitled *Afro Samurai: Resurrection* was released in 2009 and won an Emmy for outstanding individual achievement in animation that year. At the time of this writing, Gonzo, led by Ishikawa, was still looking for new innovative business models, as will be discussed toward the end of this chapter.

Corporate Differences: Japanese–American Anime Collaborations

Despite their shared interests, Japanese–American collaborations often lead to conflicts; their different corporate cultures make it difficult for them to work together. Sasaki Hiroshi is vice president of Aniplex, a Japanese company specializing in anime production and marketing that established an American subsidiary in Santa Monica, California, in 2005. According to Sasaki, the "work cultures" in Japan and in the United States are different: the Japanese seek long-term commitment and the preparation process (*nemawashi*) takes time, whereas the Americans look for short-term profits and always seems to be in a hurry.[8]

This point about cultural differences came up in other interviews as well. According to Fujisaku Junichi, director of the previously mentioned Production I.G, one of Japan's biggest anime production companies (e.g., *Ghost in the Shell*, 1995; *Psycho-Pass*, 2012–13; *Kuroko's Basketball*, 2012; *The End of Evangelion*, 1997; *Patlabor*, 2002), Japanese and American companies see the development and marketing of anime very differently. He believes that Production I.G's collaborations with American companies through its Los Angeles branch were hampered by disagreements and sensitivities about funding and marketing. For this reason, argued Fujisaku in 2014, Production I.G's strategy was to no longer pursue an active marketing strategy in the United States, but to sell its distribution rights to different companies in various countries according to local demand.[9] As we saw in chapter 2, however, the company did sign an agreement in 2016 with Netflix, attesting to the dynamic changes in the market and to companies' efforts to cope with these changes.

The lack of English language skills is very often blamed for the difficulties in Japanese–American collaborations. But it seems that "English" is regarded not simply as a language of communication but as a wider cultural barrier that creates unbridgeable differences between Japan and other parts of the world. According to Karasawa Ted of Gonzo animation,[10] studios and movie companies in Japan lack good "English communication skills" and thus prefer to concentrate on the Japanese market. Ishikawa elaborated on the different ways of doing business in Japan:[11]

The Western way of doing business—how you can "influence" others?—is very obvious in the communication style. In Japan it is not how to "influence" but how to communicate, discuss, and find a solution. Because of our culture, Japanese people want you to understand without us saying it. If you say something ridiculous, I won't tell you that what you are saying is ridiculous. I'll just ignore it. That is why American producers get frustrated. Japanese companies say "OK, I am listening to you" and if their English skills are bad, those guys will say "I understand." The Westerners think that the Japanese have heard and will do as told, but the Japanese only mean to say "I understood."

At the same time, some Japanese companies, frustrated that their products have not sold more in global markets, blamed both cultural difficulties and a lack of effective marketing. The importance of market knowledge and not only cultural or linguistic know-how but also the necessary know-how in the opening of new routes to fresh audiences was emphasized repeatedly in our interviews, highlighting the need for intimate knowledge of the local market and the organizational skills necessary for mediation. According to Kogake Shintarō, executive producer at Dentsu,[12] creativity and technology are not enough; you also need to actively create new business opportunities. Talking about toys, he commented: "We [in Japan] have many good toys but having them is worthless without effective marketing. . . . it is not only a question of raising money [for expanding manufacturing] but in expanding the reach of our marketing." A similar frustration about the difficulty of marketing Japanese productions was voiced by Amagi Yukihiko, executive vice president of NHK Enterprises:[13] "I make good documentaries, so why aren't they selling around the world?!" He recognizes that making and selling visual productions are two separate things and that Japanese companies are not good at marketing their products abroad because they concentrate their efforts on the production side alone.

Elsewhere on the Asian continent, Chinese-born Anthony Kang, former CEO of Dentsu Singapore,[14] responsible for organizing annual anime-related events in Asia, expressed his frustration with the Tokyo headquarters. This was particularly revealing because, as previously stated, Dentsu is considered a model of entrepreneurship in local and global markets. According to Kang, Japanese companies have not adjusted themselves well to the global market. For example, their decision-making processes take too long, which is especially destructive in the world of media marketing, where timing is of the essence and fast decisions are often needed. By the time Japanese companies reach a decision, the momentum is often lost. Kang calls it a "hindering decision making process." If he wants to get something done, he explained, he needs to press hard and have a capable insider to get the process moving. He gave the example of Dentsu's investment review committee, which meets only once a month, and by the time it meets and gives its approval, the moment might easily have passed. He recalled that he had once wanted to buy one of Singapore's most successful creative companies and the owner, a friend of his, wanted to sell to Dentsu because she liked Japan and the company. For three whole years he tried to get the company to reach a decision. Finally, she gave up and sold the company to one of Dentsu's biggest France-based rivals.

Another example Anthony Kang gave is the Anime Festival Asia (AFA) event. According to him, even though most of the preparations were completed, it took him no less than two years to convince Dentsu to go ahead with it. "How can they expect me to succeed if I don't get answers on time," he complained. He identified as another problem the fact that although many Japanese companies talk about the global market and express their wish to expand their businesses, they remain too passive. Rather than waiting for global players to come to you, you have to be proactive and actually go and open their doors, or, in his words, "embed globalization within your company rather than wait for globalization to come to you." The problem, he believes, is not so much linguistic or cultural but instead relates to the different modes of work within a Japanese corporation. Since in the anime business the marketing stage is relatively short (see, e.g., the marketing period of a new anime movie) and new ideas and fashions constantly crop up, companies and promoters need to react swiftly to new market trends.

According to Sasaki of Aniplex, Japanese and Americans target different audiences. While American anime companies and promoters tend to concentrate on massive audiences, looking to appeal to the widest range of potential consumers, the Japanese believe that specifically applied targeting is more effective—for example, anime for children, for young women, or for basketball fans. In Sasaki's opinion, "you need to invest more in recognizing a designated audience and focus on targeting specific groups of fans."[15] According to him, the key to success in the anime business is finding a direct link to the right groups of consumers, especially the most dedicated and obsessive fans, the so-called *otaku*. This can be achieved by active market research, such as going to various events and gatherings, organizing booths at anime conventions, and conducting on-line market research with *otaku* communities. In other words, Sasaki advocates cultivating a close relationship between the fans and the estab-lished industry as an integral part of the production and marketing of anime.

The differences between Japanese and American marketing strategies, and their implications, also came up in other interviews. In the opinion of media expert Daryl Surat, the anime industry in Japan is used to ap-pealing to a relatively small number of ardent fans who are ready to pay high prices for their products, but they thus rule out many other potential consumers. The American marketing system, on the other hand, works on the masses and attempts to appeal to a larger audience by marketing products at a low price.[16] This difference in the pricing system makes the purchasing of anime from Japan too expensive, which prevents fur-ther expansion of the business. Similarly, JETRO official Toyonaga Mami emphasized that Japanese anime companies do much more to tar-get and preserve small groups of fans, tending to separate "hard-core fans," who obsessively consume anime, from "light fans," who are inter-ested only in certain productions. Holding on to the "hard-core" fans is important for anime companies, especially in hard times when produc-tions do not prove successful and revenues are low. In this sense, "hard-core fans" provide a minimum safety net.[17]

It should be noted, however, that the importance of the *otaku* and other highly passionate fans is not only in providing this safety net for new productions, but perhaps more important, *otaku* serve as a channel to a wider consumer market. Being die-hard fans with a deep understand-ing of anime, the *otaku* communities serve as a kind of filter for bad productions. Their feedback at anime and manga events (such as the Komiket) or during the launch of new anime productions is acknowl-edged by the established industry to the extent that anime productions are sometimes revised if criticized strongly by the *otaku*. In this sense, the *otaku* serve as the gate-watchers of anime and as an "insurance agency" against bad industry decisions.

Another related difference between Japanese and American anime production and marketing, as discussed at length in chapter 2, is the cre-ative relations between the established industry and the amateur market. According to METI executive Mihara Ryōtarō,[18] the relation of the anime industry to amateurs and anime fans is what distinguishes most clearly between the work of Japanese and American animation promoters. He claims that, in the United States, animation producers make very limited use of the creative power of fans, whereas in Japan the established industry is far more receptive to the voices and ideas coming from below. This sort of participatory fandom is a pattern of involvement dubbed by Roland Kelts as the "do-it-yourself" factor (2007: 47), in which an integral part of the fandom includes generating new anime-related ideas from below. In fact, since as early as the 1970s, anime fans in Japan have been engaged in inventing interactive fan practices. These practices, which are often based on intertextual play and "derivative works" (Azuma 2009: 25), including costume play and the drawing of *dōjinshi* (work by amateur manga artists), have allowed fans to experience immersion, participation, and communal interactivity with their objects of desire and passion. In other words, practices of Japanese anime fandom highlight the blurring of lines between production and consumption. Fans are enabled, and even encouraged, to produce endless simulacra of their favorite mode of consumption and to offer it to the established industry.

At the same time, however, not everyone agrees that dedicated fans are so constructive for Japan's anime industry. According to media scholar Marco Pellitteri,[19] while *otaku* are ready to spend a big part of their disposable income on anime and frequently attend anime events, their number is actually smaller than they appear, and the fact that they are ready to pay more raises dramatically the prices of anime, thus making it inaccessible to others. Based on his long-term observation of fan gatherings, Pellitteri claimed:

> Fans are a noisy minority that led many observers in the industry (and in academia!) to think that they are more numerous, representative, and important than they actually are. . . . today, the targeting of narrow audiences [by the industry] is a self-fulfilling prophecy in terms of total economic failure: you make a series for a very tiny specific audience, then you want to sell it [overseas] for a higher price, because you want to make abroad the money you failed to make in your own country.

In this sense, while in the short term the *otaku* provide a buffer for the anime industry, in the long term they make the industry too attuned to their specific needs and eventually cause the prices of anime to go up and make them less relevant to other, less dedicated audiences.

One last problem that was emphasized in our interviews relates to intellectual property (IP). According to many of our interviewees, Japanese companies demand too much for their IP rights, not only for anime movies/series but also for the related accessories and spin-offs. This increases the price dramatically and makes collaborations and marketing extremely expensive, and hence highly unprofitable. (It should, however, be noted that American companies, most obviously Disney, are vehemently protective when it comes to their own IPs.) In interviews with the American side, we heard constant accusations that Japanese companies are too strict about the usage of image rights, which creates a problem for promotions and collaborations. Sam Register, who worked with the Japanese pop idol duo Puffy in producing the anime-inspired cartoons *Teen Titans* (2003) and *Hi Hi Puffy Ami Yumi Show* (2004), recalled an episode when Puffy came to the United States for a press conference and their agents asked photographers to refrain from taking pictures of them—a demand that ran counter to the promotional logic of their American hosts. The Japanese producer inexplicably refused an offer for the duo to open a Britney Spears performance, even though this could have given the *Hi HiPuffy Ami Yumi Show* a major boost.[20]

The issue of IP is a serious problem that obstructs more Japanese–American collaborations. According to Roland Kelts, this starts with the industry in Japan; Japanese anime artists and often the studios themselves are "paid pennies" by the production committees they work for. As explained in chapter 2, the studios often own no copyrights. Once the production committees hold the copyrights of the productions, they go on a rampage of commercialization and spin-off products. Shichijō Naohiro, a senior research fellow at the National Institute of Science and Technology Policy and a Professor at Tokyo University of Technology, pointed out that from a Japanese point of view (and his for that matter), American companies are far shrewder than Japanese companies, who are too honest, or even foolish (*shōjikibaka*). In the automobile industry, he explained, deals are much simpler than in the anime industry: "a car is sold and that's it, but profit in anime and in other forms of the media industry is on-going in a very complex and fragmented way, and the profit is also divided among many hands."[21] Due to bad past experiences in which

Japanese owners of anime IPs signed unfair contracts, unreasonably high prices are asked today from companies who are interested in licensing anime for the global market. As a result, American companies do not want to deal with Japanese companies, and these days fewer Japanese anime series are distributed in the United States.

New Business Models in the Post–Anime Boom Years

With, on the one hand, an overwhelming feeling of creative stagnation in the Japanese anime industry, and on the other, the ongoing destabilizing effects of the digitalization of media, the shrinking of the global market by illegal Internet downloading, the death of the DVD market in the United States, a lingering economic malaise in post-2008 America, and much suspicion among players on both sides of the ocean, it seems that reinvigorating and thus also profiting from the transnational Japanese–American anime business today has become quite difficult, if not impossible.

For one, the tension inherent in anime as a creative industry, which is propelled by both creative artists and industrial entrepreneurs who do not always see eye to eye, has become very clear from the responses to this crisis. Regarding the criticism that contemporary Japanese anime productions have become formulaic and *otaku*-oriented, Makihara Ryōtarō, anime director at Wit Studio, said quite emotionally after a public screening of *Hal* (2013), a movie he directed, that he strongly believes in what they (at studio Wit) are doing. Makihara was reluctant to discuss the end of the anime boom from a financial point of view. Instead, he said that as long as the stories he tells relate to universal humanistic themes, implying a return to what anime was once about, he is sure that anime lovers around the world will continue to appreciate them. In the same interview, however, Wit studio's CEO Wada George indicated that "although he was delighted beyond words to see that the works of Studio Wit have fans around the world, he would be very happy if the studio could at least make some money in the global market."[22] Unlike artists, entrepreneurs are in the anime business for its financial potential; the cultural impact is merely a (welcome) by-product.

While conducting our research, we encountered other examples of outstanding entrepreneurs exploring new business models. Gonzo's tireless entrepreneur Ishikawa told us in 2012 of a new strategy for the global market that he plans to adopt in the near future. He is thinking of selling anime IPs to Hollywood producers for live-action movies. For an established studio with a distinguished IP library, focusing on licensing IPs is not an entirely innovative strategy. For example, the only business line today of Tezuka Productions, the animation studio founded by Tezuka Osamu in 1968, is selling copyrights of Tezuka's IPs. Since these are IPs based on the works of the great Tezuka Osamu, the company does not have to search too hard for a local or global market; interested parties usually look for them.[23] In 2014, Bloomberg News announced that the international production and creative management company Cross Media International (CMI, established in 2004 with the support of JETRO), headquartered in San Francisco, had entered into an agreement with Tezuka Productions of Japan to develop distribution opportunities for Tezuka's extensive portfolio of popular properties and characters within North America.[24] Ishikawa, on the other hand, needs to be more proactive than Tezuka Productions. He sees Marvel Studios as a model. Marvel Studios was on the verge of bankruptcy in 1998, and Ishikawa believes that beyond the restructuring and merging with ToyBiz, the growth engine that pulled Marvel Studios out of financial disaster was their new focus on selling IPs to live-action productions such as *X-Men* (2000) and *Blade* (1998).[25] Nine years later, the (by then) Marvel Enterprises was sold to Disney for over US$4 billion.[26] In Ishikawa's words: "Going from geeky to mainstream is a transformation that could happen to Japanese anime because of the current movement [production of live-action movies based on comic characters]. Because Hollywood doesn't have enough content, they are actively looking for Japanese content. This has become possible because during the early 2000s, anime in the US went beyond geek status."[27] Ishikawa looks at Hollywood projects based on Japanese anime IPs, such as *Astro Boy* (David Bowers, 2009), *Speed Racer* (Wachowski Sisters, 2008), *Akira* (underway), and *Death Note* (underway), and would also like to mine this opportunity.

Another entrepreneur who is actively looking for opportunities in the global market is Tanaka Eiko of Studio 4°C. As previously mentioned, Tanaka earned a good reputation for herself and her studio in the global market, where she is engaged in collaborative projects as well as in outsourcing jobs. Tanaka said quite bluntly that although she has had the opportunity to be involved in some high-profile and creative projects, it is not easy to survive in the anime industry, and thus she is not very picky about the projects she chooses; she cares, first and foremost, about having work. Studio 4°C makes animation for television, theatrical releases, video games, and commercials. As discussed in chapter 2, the financing system of the anime industry is very similar to raising venture capital from several investors who then become a production committee. Tanaka explained that her dream is to raise money for an original production from an international group of investors.[28]

When we conducted our interview with Kogake of Dentsu in 2012,[29] one particularly fascinating anime series production project was underway that was implementing an innovative business model. This media project, *Monsuno* (2012–14), which has since been launched and already boasts three seasons, was designed by Dentsu for the American market. Using its Dentsu Entertainment USA office, Dentsu has acted as main copyright holder, controlling production, global distribution, and merchandising. The series is child-oriented (in Kogake's words, "not too geeky") and American writer Mike Ryan, who was involved in the writing of *Speed Racer, Transformers, Ben 10,* and *Generator X,* was hired to supervise the writing. Dentsu then approached several American toy makers—including Mattel, Hasbro, JAKKS Pacific, Spin Master, and Bandai U.S.A.—and concluded a deal with JAKKS Pacific. Because of different ideas about toy design and to ensure the sale of toys in Japan as well, some of the design was done in Japan, where, according to Kogake, they produce much more interesting toys.

Another deal was concluded with the American company Topps to produce collectible cards, with Fremantle Media North America signed off as distributor. All of these companies became deeply involved in the project because they were not only service providers but also investors and coproducers. The U.S. children's television network Nickelodeon has picked up the worldwide broadcast rights. While JAKKS Pacific was responsible for producing and distributing the toys in the United States, Bandai Japan distributed the imported toys in Japan, Giochi Preziosi in Europe, and Hunter Products in Oceania. Kogake expressed great excitement when he explained that this is probably the first time ever that an animation product (television series and toy line) will hit the whole world at once.

Instead of focusing primarily on North America, some anime artists and producers as well as media companies in Japan are looking carefully at creative and business opportunities in emerging markets in Asia, particularly in China. In the 1990s, Japanese anime entrepreneurs swept the Chinese market but saw little financial profit because they could not protect their copyrights. The Chinese government, for its part, occasionally bans Japanese anime series that it considers to be inducing violence and depicting content that endanger public morality. China thus remained largely a site for outsourcing some of the labor-intensive parts of anime production as a way of reducing costs rather than a market to generate revenues from sales.

In 2004, China launched a fully fledged promotion of its animation sector supported by government subsidiaries and protectionism that pushed non-Chinese animation series out of domestic prime-time television. There has since been unprecedented expansion in Chinese animation production, but the results are heavily criticized from both an artistic and creative point of view. Today, there are two ways of entering the Chinese market: the first is collaborating with local companies in projects for the Chinese market, a collaboration enabled only if foreign investment of funds and transference of know-how are provided; the second is Internet delivery of anime products, which is advantageous due to laxer government regulations. Both of these options, however, carry risks.

In 2013, media researcher Yamada Kenichi (2013) published a report on market opportunities for the anime industry in China. In this report, he explained the conditions summarized above and highlighted TV Tokyo, a major television station that has been making considerable inroads into the Chinese animation market since 2011 through collaboration with Chinese productions and a streaming deal with a leading Chinese file-sharing website in which TV Tokyo offers same-day streaming of a wide variety of genuine anime programs. In 2014, *Yahoo! Finance* announced that TV Tokyo had signed a licensing agreement with iDreamsky Technology, China's largest mobile game publishing platform. iDreamsky will create mobile games for China and other Asian countries based on TV Tokyo's anime IPs and has, in addition, obtained the rights to distribute each game it creates in mainland China, Taiwan, Macau, Hong Kong, Korea, Philippines, Malaysia, Thailand, Indonesia, and Singapore.[30] Unfortunately, as of 2017, Internet sources do not attest that much has come out of the original fanfare around the signing of the licensing agreement.

Nevertheless, this perhaps anecdotal episode tells us that in spite of the financial risk and regulatory impediments, the anime industry has become aware that the Chinese market is just too big to ignore.

Conclusion: Anime Entrepreneurship in Global Markets

The transnationally embedded entrepreneurship described in this chapter has obvious implications for the global animation industry. Entrepreneurs exploring new opportunities and creating new ventures—motivated by the search for new products to localize and distribute—are paving new marketing routes, gauging new materials, and encouraging the establishment of transnational mechanisms for delivery across regional and cultural boundaries. Given the shrinking of the anime market in the United States, aside from greater creativity and closer integration between various media forms, entrepreneurship is the only hope for the future of the industry.

Literature on the transfer of cultural commodities in an age of intense globalization processes has concentrated on the dialectical relations between global and local forces, emphasizing the abilities of the supplier (usually American media conglomerates) or the localization and submission of the receiver. However, very little emphasis has been placed on the mediating mechanisms, especially the active mediation undertaken by entrepreneurs. The role of entrepreneurship and the companies that actively mediate and deliver content is generally overlooked in favor of a cultural and textual analysis of the anime itself. But this process, as discussed in this chapter, is crucially important since anime does not simply "appear" on television or computer screens but is rather the product of the mediation and the efforts of entrepreneurs.

So what makes a good entrepreneur in the transnational market of anime? As seen in the cases examined in this chapter, successful entrepreneurship in the global anime business depends, as with any other business, on persistence, passion, open-mindedness, resourcefulness, creative thinking, good communication skills, and of course, timing. As pointed out in chapter 2, in the content business very little is predictable, and it is always about taking risks and venturing into new grounds. We can nevertheless highlight some acquired skills of successful media entrepreneurs in the global anime arena. Entrepreneurs must have good knowledge and strong intuition about the market(s) in which they work. To our great surprise, Sam Register, for example, said plainly of himself that while he is an expert on what American kids want and need, he cannot say much about other markets.[31] Thanks to their knowledge of the local media market and its demands, successful entrepreneurs are able to tailor specific strategies—bringing in the right productions, adapting them to suit local tastes, and marketing them to designated audiences.

Anime distributors in the United States need to be attuned to the fluctuations in the American market and the rapid changes in consumers' tastes, and react with haste. As became evident from the interviews we conducted, to succeed in promoting anime nowadays, one must choose the right products. According to Dentsu producer Kogake,[32] when marketing anime in the United States today, a "delicate localization" must be applied: the anime should not look too foreign to American kids, but at the same time, it should keep its ostensibly "Japanese" features. For example, some Japanese features, like the surrounding neighborhood and the house where the plot takes place, should be retained, but not the mother calling "*okaeri*" (welcome home) when the child comes home or the removal of shoes on entering the house; these things might look too strange to American kids. For this reason, local knowledge of the market is an essential component of connecting Japan-made animation to foreign audiences. Not everyone would concur with the specific examples provided by Kogake, but the general notion of domestication as critical for the favorable reception of media content is widely agreed upon. As discussed earlier, in the production of *Afro Samurai*, American scriptwriters were hired to ensure its positive reception among American viewers. Likewise, as mentioned in chapter 1, Berthe Lotsova, writer and producer at French Marathon Media, emphasized how her company hires American writers to guarantee that the series they produce are exportable to the United States.[33] Bielby and Harrington also advocated doing cultural homework:

> To operate successfully in the international export market for television, sellers need to adapt their product for use in other locales, and they need to understand how audiences engage television's cultural attributes, deriving pleasures and constructing meanings through aesthetic valuation.

Industry participants understand this, with varying degrees of insight and accountability, and formulate a wide range of arrangements that seek to retain creative control and ownership over products while simultaneously adapting them sufficiently to transcend cultural differences. (2008: 59)

Another important trait of the successful entrepreneur in the media market is the ability to adjust to organizational arrangements in foreign markets. Flexibility and adaptability to foreign markets and cultures are key to enable transnational transactions of all kinds. Kogake also elaborated on this: "For example, if an Israeli or a Filipino approaches TBS or Nippon Terebi [Japanese television stations] and asks [them to broadcast Israeli or Filipino content], this will certainly not work. It must be a local person who approaches the television stations. This is why *Pokémon*, even though it is a Japanese production, was distributed in the US by Americans."[34] In other words, entrepreneurs who wish to extend their business overseas must understand and comply with local organizational structures, often tying up with local agents. Carrying culturally biased presumptions into business transactions can be very damaging.

Lastly, entrepreneurs in the anime business today cannot ignore the fierce competition from emerging animation industries. In his 2013 report on the market competition in the animation industry between Japan and China, Yamada (2013) warned about the shortsightedness of the anime industry that adopts a condescending attitude toward Chinese animation. According to Yamada, this is exactly how Japanese automobile makers fell behind German and other automobile companies in increasing their share of the Chinese car market. While we do not necessarily concur with Yamada's pessimistic prediction, we think that in today's media market, some of the most interesting opportunities are in international collaborations; the worst strategy for Japanese anime entrepreneurs would be to condescendingly shut themselves off and withdraw to the safer grounds of the Japanese islands.

CHAPTER 4

The Legacy of Anime in the United States

Anime-Inspired Cartoons

T he anime boom years in the United States were another chapter in a history of cross-cultural pollination during which the rise of Japan as a global center of animation became overt. A few years' perspective suffice to show that while the anime boom years may be commercially over, the normative impact of anime has continued providing an innovative tool kit for animators in the United States. As we showed in chapter 1, American animation has been a primary influence on Japanese animators since the beginning of the medium in Japan. Animators in the United States were similarly inspired by Japanese anime themes and styles long before the late 1990s and early 2000s. But it was during these years of anime boom that a new animation category emerged labeled anime-inspired cartoons or anime-influenced cartoons. This category includes non-Japanese animation that consciously emulates visual styles and thematic ideas that have been developed by and are closely associated with the anime industry over the years.

It has been argued that through various forms of hybridization and creolization, "the meaning of externally originating goods, information and images are reworked, syncretized and blended with existing cultural traditions and forms of life" (Featherstone 1995: 117). Put in this context, anime-inspired cartoons offer a wonderful case study for exploring how the adaptation and subsequent displacement of ideas, images, and representations into new animated contexts may (and indeed often do) change their symbolic meanings.

This chapter is a study of cross-cultural flows and adaptations. It describes the indirect and overwhelmingly unintended consequences of anime in the United States, not as a commercially driven consumer product but as a creative force made up of a recognizable set of images, sounds, and narratives that has generated different responses from the American animation industry. In this sense, the presence and influence of anime in the United States should be valued according not only to sales records and other commercial factors per se but also to the cultural processes initiated, the response of the American anime industry, and its overall influence on anime production and appropriation in the United States.

The Penetration of Anime into Mainstream American Cartoons

As seen in chapter 1, the moment that signaled the beginning of the anime boom in the United States was the unprecedented success of the *Pokémon* series with its related products and merchandise in 1998. American animators' reactions did not lag far behind. Soon enough, acclaimed American satirical animated series for adult audiences, which may well be regarded as compasses of American mainstream consciousness, referred to this somewhat overwhelming phenomenon.

The Simpsons and *South Park* had something to say about these cultural developments almost as soon as they were happening (see table 2). In May 1999, the Simpson family all went to Japan in an episode called "Thirty Minutes over Tokyo" (season 10, episode 23). For those in the know, the title of the episode alludes to a 1944 war film called *Thirty Seconds over Tokyo* (directed by Mervin Leroy). *Thirty Seconds over Tokyo* tells the story of the first American retaliatory airstrike against Japan four months after the attack on Pearl Harbor in December 1941. In the film, the leader of the mission, while on an aircraft carrier en route to Japan, assembles his volunteer task force and invites a certain Lieutenant Jurika, who spent several years in Japan, to tell them what he learned about the Japanese. In response to the question, "Just what should we do, Mr. Jurika? How should we conduct ourselves in case we are forced

Table 2

Examples of References to the Japanese Popular Culture Boom
in American Satirical Animated Shows for Adults

American Dad

Season	Episode	Episode title	Original air date
7	3	"Best Little Horror House in Langley Falls"	November 7, 2010

Billy and Mandy

Season	Episode	Episode title	Original air date
6	4	"Modern Primitives/Giant Billy and Mandy All-Out Attack"	January 27, 2006

Drawn Together

Season	Episode		Original air date
1–3	All episodes	Ling-ling is one of the eight housemates (all caricatures of well-known cartoon characters) who are the focus of this satire. It is a violent and homicidal parody of Pikachu.	2004–7

Family Guy

Season	Episode	Episode title	Original air date
8	1	"Road to the Multiverse"	September 27, 2009

The Simpsons

Season	Episode	Episode title	Original air date
10	23	"Thirty Minutes over Tokyo"	May 16, 1999

South Park

Season	Episode	Episode title	Original air date
3	11	"Chinpokomon"	November 3, 1999
8	1	"Good Times with Weapons"	March 17, 2004
13	11	"Whale Whores"	October 28, 2009
15	6	"City Sushi"	June 1, 2011

down over Japan," Jurika answers: "My advice is, see that you are not forced down over Japan." In other words, the Japanese are depicted as frightening brutes in the movie, and the Americans are here to teach them a lesson.[1]

The Simpsons, however, who get to Japan by mere coincidence on a cheap last-minute flight, are hoping to have a lovely vacation. It could be that in referencing the war film, the creators of the show were actually implying that it is the Japanese who should be aware of "the troubles" arriving in Japan. In fact, according to Long,[2] the original title of the episode was "Fat Man and Little Boy," an unambiguous reference to the nicknames given to the American atomic bombs that were dropped on Nagasaki and Hiroshima in August 1945. The episode's nonsensical plot parodies unrestrainedly (as always in *The Simpsons*) the American working class as well as several aspects of Japanese culture. As the Simpsons arrive at their Tokyo hotel, viewers are reminded of the cultural backdrop and the reason for making the episode—namely, the surging U.S. interest in contemporary Japanese culture in reaction to the *Pokémon* craze. In a parody of the 1997 broadcast in Japan of the *Pokémon* episode "Dennō senshi Porygon" (Electric Soldier Porygon) (season 1, episode 38), which due to certain repetitive visual effects caused hundreds of Japanese viewers to experience epileptic seizures and rush to emergency rooms, the Simpsons watch a television cartoon called *Battling Seizure Robots* in their hotel room and immediately drop to the floor with dilated pupils and epileptic seizures. References to the Imperial Gardens, the Meiji Shrine, and the Hello Kitty factory are all made in the ensuing scenes. In one particularly amusing scene in which Homer Simpson takes his family to eat in an American-themed restaurant, the creators ridicule both the Americans for wanting to feel at home when they go abroad and the Japanese for trying hard and unsuccessfully to emulate Americanness. The episode lingers the longest on the participation of the Simpsons, who have no money left, in a Japanese television game show to earn tickets to go back home. The "Happy Smile Super Challenge Family Wish Show" is a satirical rendition of Japanese television game shows. The Japanese host of the show explains the difference between American game shows and Japanese game shows by saying: "American shows reward knowledge. We punish ignorance!" As the Simpsons finally leave Japan, their plane is held up midair by four Japanese megacelebrity science fiction monsters, including Godzilla. They are reassured by the pilot that this often happens and that the plane will soon be released, as indeed happens—a metaphor perhaps of the grasp of Japanese anime/popular culture and their commodified paraphernalia on American mainstream culture. The title "Thirty Minutes over Tokyo" mocks implicitly the resurgence of post–World War II anti-Japanese sentiments. In other words, the episode itself ridicules the provinciality of the American working class while simultaneously reviving the long-standing Euro-American orientalist view of Japan as the land of the weird, the nonsensical, and the grotesque (see Daliot-Bul 2007).

When compared with later animated parodic commentaries on the Japanese popular culture boom in the United States, what stands out in "Thirty Minutes over Tokyo" is that Japanese culture is depicted in Japan and not yet in the United States. The creators of *South Park* went one step further with their episode referring to the Japanese popular culture boom released just a few months later in November 1999. The plot of the *South Park* episode "Chinpokomon" (season 3, episode 42) revolves around the young American protagonists' fascination with *Chinpokomon*, a fictional Japanese television anime series aired on American television, and its related products (an obvious parody of *Pokémon*). Their zeal does not abate even when Kenny suffers seizures as a result of playing the *Chinpokomon* video game (a reference to the previously mentioned *Pokémon* episode "Electric Soldier Porygon"). Unbeknownst to them, *Chinpokomon* is actually part of a Japanese plot to conquer the United States by brainwashing American kids and turning them into soldiers of the Japanese emperor in preparation for a new attack on Pearl Harbor. *Chinpokomon* merchandising products use undetectable brainwashing techniques to transmit anti-American sentiments. As parents become concerned about their children's commitment to the silly series and its Japaneseness (which includes them talking Japanese among themselves), they are mollified by the Japanese managers of the *Chinpokomon* company, who point out that Americans have "huge penises" compared to the Japanese with their "microscopic penises." (The word *chinpo* is, in fact, Japanese slang for penis.) This childish diversionary tactic works like a charm, particularly on the American fathers, and even on Bill Clinton, then president of the United States. But when the kids ready themselves to pilot Japanese fighter jets, the parents, in line with Stan's mother's cunning plan, all declare their love for *Pokémon,* and soon *Chinpokomon* and all surrounding it lose their magic, and the kids lose their interest in it.

Like all other episodes of *South Park,* this episode, which was nominated for an Emmy award in 2000, is primarily about the total lack of self-awareness of the American middle class. The adults in the series, although well-meaning, are always off-target. In this particular episode, adults on both sides of the ocean just don't get the picture. The euphoric nationalistic sentiments unleashed in Japan in reaction to the global success of Japanese popular culture (see Iwabuchi 2002b) are ridiculed. Similarly, anti-Japanese sentiments are mocked in a narrative outlining a Japanese plan for revenge over their loss in World War II in one form or another of neo-imperialism. Such sentiments were indeed unleashed in the late 1980s as a reaction to Japanese global economic exploits (Morley and Robins 1995) and were expressed in the late 1990s in articles that depicted how Japanese border-crossing consumer hit products were pre-engineered by psychologists and marketing specialists who had identified the ways in which children could be successfully manipulated and who thus plan to conquer the world (see, e.g., Samoha 2002). But at the end of the day, the episode concludes, *Pokémon* is nothing but another consumer fad.

What Are Anime-Inspired Cartoons?

Anime-inspired cartoons are a different cultural phenomenon from animated satirical commentaries on the popularity of Japanese (popular) culture in the United States. The term "anime-inspired cartoons" suggests an effort by non-Japanese studios to produce an animated show that refers to, reproduces, and even emulates that particular (rather elusive) something found in anime that attracted so many fans around the world. Considering that anime has long been an influence on American animators, the neologism "anime-inspired cartoons" should be understood, first and foremost, as a marketing tactic developed during the heyday of anime's global popularity. Although motivated by different things, animators, producers, and fans are complicit in the creation and enhance-

ment of the concept of anime-inspired cartoons. Among the first cartoons to be marketed in the United States as inspired by anime were *The
Powerpuff Girls* (created by Craig McCracken, 1998)³ and *Samurai Jack*
(created by Genndy Tartakovsky, 2001). *Teen Titans* (created by Glen
Murakami, 2003) and *Xiaolin Showdown* (created by Christy Hui, 2003)
were among the first cartoons to be marketed and received by fans as
anime-inspired cartoons.

It seems that the label "anime-inspired cartoons" was always mean-
ingless and unimportant for most viewers of television animation who
lack a particular taste for anime. For non-Japanese committed fans of anime, however, it became a favorite topic of discussion in various Internet
forums. From defining the style by deconstructing the constituents of anime in terms of artistic and visual styles and themes to creating devoted
websites, making databases of anime-inspired cartoons, and ranking
anime-inspired cartoons, the topic has sparked indefatigable emotional
exchanges among anime fans. Anime fans seem consistent in their belief
that a good anime-inspired cartoon should be indistinguishable from anime, suggesting the purist approach characteristic of die-hard fans in
general. Accordingly, there is not much leniency with artists who use
anime inspiration to create something new. In a 2013 animation aficionados' roundtable podcast, the discussants were very critical of most anime-
inspired cartoons. One of them concluded the debate by saying that
there is a difference between "being a fan and being a stalker," meaning
that if you have no idea about anime, do not try to emulate it; in other
words, if you do it, do it right.⁴

At present, the use of the label "anime-inspired cartoon" by producers to promote new television animated series in the United States has
become practically obsolete, reflecting the commercial end of the anime
boom. One of the last examples of anime-inspired cartoons was *RWBY*
(created by Monty Oum, 2013), a web animated series (i.e., a series created for web distribution), and an effort to capitalize on the emerging medium of web animation/web television. A few years later however, it is
clear that the marketing category "anime-inspired web cartoons" has not
become a lasting trend.

There are several patterns of cross-cultural interactions that are exhibited repeatedly in anime-inspired cartoons. Each of these interactions
reveals something about the potential and possibilities in cross-cultural

hybridism and about the cross-cultural politics of identity. Following is an analysis of three such patterns: emulation of visual styles and narration themes, playing with Japaneseness as fetish, and the transformation of meanings when symbolic forms migrate between cultures.

EMULATION OF VISUAL STYLES
AND NARRATION THEMES

Although they have multiple sources of inspiration, some anime-inspired cartoons closely emulate Japanese animation genres as cultural experimentation. One prominent example is *Avatar: The Last Airbender* (created by Michael Dante DiMartino and Bryan Konietzko, 2005–8). An adventurous quest set in an expansive world that draws on an Asian setting with mythology and storytelling, where humans, animals, and mystic powers mingle, this show follows the adventures of teenage Aang and his friends, who must defeat evil with their special powers that enable them to bend and manipulate the elements. The creators of the show explained that their love for Japanese anime, Hong Kong action and kung fu cinema, and yoga and Eastern philosophies was the initial inspiration for *Avatar*. In particular, they emphasized Miyazaki Hayao's work and the character design, storytelling, and animation of *Fooly Cooly* (written by Enokido Yōji and Tsurumaki Kazuya, directed by Tsurumaki Kazuya, 2000–2001). The result attracted the warm attention of anime fans, to whom the creators responded by saying, "America—us included—has a long way to go to catch up with the animated work being done in a handful of countries, namely Japan."[5] In the previously mentioned 2013 animation aficionados' podcast on anime-inspired cartoons, *Avatar: The Last Airbender* ranks among the most accomplished anime-inspired cartoons. This raises the question: What is it in *Avatar* that resonates so well with anime, and thus so pleases anime enthusiasts?

In chapter 1, we described how anime developed between the 1960s and the 1970s into a medium quite different from Euro-American animation, with particular visual styles, storytelling techniques, and very broad—in fact unlimited—thematic interests. It is impossible to offer a singular definition of anime due to the numerous styles and storytelling techniques, which differ according to the age and gender of the target audiences. Moreover, anime styles and storytelling techniques are continuously evolving and changing as they respond to new technologies, current cultural circumstances and concerns, and changing aesthetic sensibilities. A science fiction anime series from the 1970s, for example, looks very different from a contemporary one, and often addresses different philosophical issues.

Nevertheless, when trying to understand what makes a contemporary anime-inspired cartoon look like anime, at the risk of generalization and oversimplification we suggest one way of limiting the scope of investigation. Anime-inspired television cartoons of the late 1990s and early 2000s were largely influenced by representative products of three contemporary anime genres for television that are available on American and European television: *shōnen* anime, which targets preteens and early teen boys (e.g., *Pokémon, Digimon, Dragon Ball Z*); *shōjo* anime, which targets preteen and early teen girls (e.g., *Sailor Moon, Card Captor Sakura, Fruits Basket*); and a genre which, for want of a better name, we have called the *pseudorealistic genre,* which is interpreted variously by different anime artists but can nevertheless be characterized by the great emphasis it places on visually detailed and realistic settings and character design (characteristic of late-teen and adult-oriented anime shows such as *Serial Experiments Lain, Death Note, Black Lagoon,* and all full-length anime movies that are not merchandizing spin-offs from *shōnen* or *shōjo* anime). It is thus possible to articulate some shared characteristics of anime that have become particularly influential in the global television animation sphere since the late 1990s.

One of the least discussed characteristics of anime, which is most important in differentiating anime from cartoons, is the sophisticated use of colors. Cartoons often use the bright basic colors of the color wheel (i.e., hues) deemed appropriate for children. Generally speaking, anime shows use a much more subtle palette by toning (adding black and white), tinting (adding white), and shading (adding black) the basic colors of the color wheel and their derivatives and combinations. In anime shows targeting a younger audience, hues are used for the characters, as in cartoons, but a much more nuanced color palette is used for the settings and backgrounds. The overall result is more realistic. All anime genres put great emphasis on detailed and artistic shadowing. The effect ranges from realistic to dramatic and emotive. Further enhancing this artistic use of colors and shadowing is the creative use of camera angles and cinematographic shots.

Anime has borrowed from manga, its printed counterpart, iconic visual symbols of emotions (called *manpu* in Japanese) that work well with techniques of limited animation, which use fewer cells per minute and which have become the signature of Japanese anime (LaMarre 2002: 335). This technique is often used in anime genres for television. To portray anger, for example, the image may freeze on the character's facial expression, which is exaggerated by a suddenly and disproportionally inflated head with large eyes and a large mouth replete with a ridiculously large set of teeth. Knitted eyebrows are completed with iconic cruciform markers of anger on the forehead, and lightning is sometimes projected around the character's head (see fig. 3).

Shōnen anime. In *shōnen* anime in particular, human or humanoid characters are usually drawn with realistic anatomical proportions; however, unlike in many cartoons, there is no connection between physical size and stature, on the one hand, and the magnitude of physical or magical powers, on the other. Male characters in *shōnen* anime are often more muscular and robust than in other genres of anime but rarely as tall, muscular, and robust as in American superhero cartoons. Two other recurring stylistic elements of contemporary *shōnen* anime are relatively large and emotive eyes, and for the male character, often spiky hairdos, sometimes with unrealistic colors. *Shōnen* anime, like all other anime styles, uses physical features (unrealistic stature, incredibly large eyes, fantastical skin and hair colors, etc.) to convey feelings rather than to mark ethnicity (see plate 7).

Plot settings in *shōnen* anime range from realistic contemporary athletic clubs or schools, technologically enabled alternative realities, futuristic worlds, ancient worlds, or any combination of the above and more. However, the storytelling always revolves around a group of early teens who are endowed with special powers or abilities (athletic, magical, technological, martial arts, etc.). They operate as a group, autonomous of adult supervision, and are embarking on some quest (to win the championship, to save the world, etc.). The lead protagonists are male, but there are also important female protagonists who are active and opinionated. Early buds of romance spice up dilemmas regarding friendship, group

FIGURE 3. An iconography of emotions (*manpu*) has migrated from manga to anime. We would like to thank Netta Weiss for her lovely drawings of *manpu* and the permission to use them.

collaboration versus individual competitiveness, self-discovery, and self-fulfillment. In stark contrast to American cartoons, anime plots and action scenes can take a dramatic turn and become quite violent. Good and evil are portrayed as essentially dialectical. Each episode ends with a cliff-hanger that leaves the viewer in suspense until the next episode.

Shōjo anime. Moving on to *shōjo* anime, this genre shares some characteristics with *shōnen* anime, particularly regarding the use of colors, shadowing, camera effects, often unrealistic physical features to portray emotions, iconic manga-inspired markers to display emotions, and a storytelling structure in which every episode ends with a cliff-hanger. As an underlying aesthetic principle, characters in *shōjo* anime are drawn with somewhat realistic proportions that are slightly altered to enhance cuteness or notions of beauty. Male and female characters are significantly leaner than Western animated characters. Moreover, male characters are rather effeminate in appearance in comparison with their Western counterparts; they are slim and delicate with long hair. The hair of both female and male characters is especially elaborate, lively, and full of movement.

Plots in *shōjo* anime tend to be anchored in realistic settings that are nevertheless magical and fantastical. They are driven by female protagonists who are proactive, lively, and endowed with a unique skill or gift. Romance and coming-of-age struggles excite the main adventures; it could even be argued that the adventurous plots are nothing more than backdrops to this playing out of emotions.

In the plots of both *shōnen* and *shōjo* anime, the liminal stage of teenage years is often represented by forms of hybridism, such as animal-human, male-female, alien-human, and technological-organic. The protagonists often go back and forth through physical transformations (sometimes painful) from one appearance to another; it is in this way that they transform and evolve.

Pseudo-realistic anime. The so-called pseudo-realistic anime genre is the most director-driven and idiosyncratic of the three styles, and hence the least formulaic. It shares with *shōnen* and *shōjo* anime a sophisticated use of colors, shadowing, and camera effects, as well as a dialectical nature of good and evil, and a permissiveness toward violent scenes and depictions of young people crossing the boundaries of the allowed and the socially accepted. Episodes similarly often end in cliff-hangers. Characters are drawn with realistic anatomic proportions and are often more sexually suggestive to appeal to a more mature audience.

From quantitative research we conducted on anime-inspired cartoons,[6] it transpired that there are more non-American anime-inspired cartoons that set out to emulate anime than there are American attempts. Examples include *Winx Club* (Rainbow S.p.A. [Italy], 2009–15), *Huntik: Secrets and Seekers* (Rainbow S.p.A [Italy], 2009–12), *W.I.T.C.H.* (Sip Animation [France], 2004–6), *Totally Spies* (Season 1–2, Marathon Media [France], 2002–3), *Code Lyoko* (Antefilm, Moonscoop [France]

2003–7), and *Tai Chi Chasers* (KBS [Korea], 2011–12)—all obvious attempts to produce a show with the look and feel of anime. There are other anime-inspired series that were created to look like anime (script, character design, and storyboard) by non-American animators who even turned to Japanese studios to ensure a final "Japanese touch," such as *Ōban Star Racers* (Sav! The World Productions [Canada], Pumpkin 3D [France], Hal Film Maker [Japan], 2006), *Cybersix* (original concept developed for comics by Argentineans Carlos Meglia and Carlos Trillo for the Italian comics magazine *Skorpio,* anime produced by NOA [Canada] and TMS [Japan], 1999), and *Time Jam: Valerian & Laureline* (Satelight [Japan], Dargaud [France], Europacorp [France], 2007–8).

When reviewing the list of anime-inspired cartoons made in the United States, however, most use anime as inspiration only. This can be seen in visual details—such as the eyes of the *Teen Titans* characters that are disproportionate to their general physique—that are inspired by anime and yet are quite different from the animesque style (see plate 8). It is, likewise, evident in narratives, such as *Samurai Jack,* in which the plot is set in an anachronistic future inspired by samurai mythology and anime action but which does not follow the formula of *shōnen* anime. In that sense, *Avatar: The Last Airbender* stands out among other American anime-inspired cartoons as exhibiting an unusually straightforward emulation of anime style and storytelling techniques.

Within the scope of this book, the answer to why more anime-inspired productions by non-American studios tended to closely emulate anime rather than use it only as an inspiration will have to remain a speculation. It is presumably related to issues of risk management in an industry whose every production depends on the successful recruitment of risk capital. Anime-inspired cartoons are a marketing effort to capitalize on the warm global reception of Japanese television anime series that was expressed in huge revenues from broadcasting and merchandizing. Creators and producers must convince investors that their investment stands a good chance of making a profitable return. The largest American studios, those with stronger production and distribution infrastructures (as discussed in chapter 2) that control both U.S. and global television animation markets, must of course also practice care and caution when choosing productions. Nevertheless, given their dominant position in the industry, they can afford to take greater risks and be more experimental. By comparison, according to Berthe Lotsova of Marathon Media (France), for a few years Marathon Media made great efforts to produce animation that would look Japanese: the so-called Franime. At the time of our interview in 2013, however, they too were investing more energy in finding the "French touch."[7]

JAPANESENESS AS FETISH

An interesting play with otherness in anime-inspired cartoons is the exploration of cool, contemporary "things Japanese," almost as a fetish. This is a reference to or a take on the contemporary juxtaposition of Japanese and American popular cultures. The number of animation series that exhibit the early 2000s Cool Japan global wave is small but they are revealing.

One fascinating example of this genre is the 2004 *Hi Hi Puffy Ami Yumi Show*. The production history of *Hi Hi Puffy Ami Yumi Show* goes back to the production of *Teen Titans* in 2003. According to Sam Register, president at Warner Bros. Animation and Warner Digital Series, who coproduced *Teen Titans* for Cartoon Network,[8] *Teen Titans,* which is based on a DC Comic series, was created by Glen Murakami, who wanted to recreate the Japanese anime *Fooly Cooly,* which he held in very high esteem. As a producer, Register felt that his first obligation is to be an amplifier of talents, and he very much wanted to give the show his approval. DC Comics were not thrilled, but Register got his way. The visual style appropriated from Japanese anime and expressed in *Teen Titans* is mostly evident in the characters' disproportionate and unrealistic physical attributes, including the large eyes mentioned earlier. While *Teen Titans* was under production, Register happened to hear the Japanese female duo *Puffy* on an independent radio channel (NRG), and he liked their sound; to his ears, they were Japanese singing American pop. As a result of Register's eagerness to work with them, *Puffy* ended up doing the theme song for *Teen Titans,* which Register believes gave the series some of its "Japanese" flavor.

Register subsequently came up with the idea for the anime-inspired cartoon *Hi Hi Puffy Ami Yumi,* his own concept and creation, which he also produced for Cartoon Network (2004–6). *Hi Hi Puffy Ami Yumi* follows the real-life duo Onuki Ami and Yoshimura Yumi travelling with their manager Kaz on their tour bus and performing around the world. Each episode features animation, inspired visually by Japanese anime, as well as short clips shot in Japan of the real Ami and Yumi giving a childish commentary (in English and nonsubtitled Japanese). The real *Puffy* duo perform the cartoon's theme song, and in many of the episodes their songs are playing in the background. The characters in the show speak English interspersed with interjections in Japanese. The writing on the bus and often elsewhere in the background is in English but using a font that is clearly inspired by the Japanese katakana script. The show was broadcast on prime time on Cartoon Network and signaled (intentionally or not) the height of the embrace of cool Japanese popular culture by mainstream American culture. Targeting girls between the ages of six and eleven, viewers were even learning Japanese interjections. According to Register, although the show seems to have acquired a kind of cult status over the years, particularly among fans of the real-life duo and fans of Japanese popular culture, it was not a financial success when first screened in the United States. One reason for this was that the show was broadcasted on Cartoon Network, which is mainly a boys' channel, and boys were not interested in watching two Japanese girls. There were, in addition, problems negotiating the tie-in merchandising with the duo.

Kappa Mikey (created by Larry Schwarz, directed by Sergei Aniskov, 2006–8), is another example of the exploration of cool, contemporary "things Japanese" fetish. It aired on Nicktoons and was marketed not as an anime-inspired cartoon but as "the first anime" to be produced entirely in the United States. In the show, American citizen Mikey Simon, a nineteen-year-old actor, goes to Japan where he stars in a live-action series called *Lily Mu* that is presented in the series as anime. Thanks to Mikey, the once popular show goes back to the top of the ratings, and Mikey becomes a star in Japan. In calling the show *Kappa Mikey*, the creator reveals his acquaintance with, and perhaps fondness for, Japanese culture. It is not common knowledge among non-Japanese that in Japanese mythology *kappa* are mischievous and prank-loving water demons who find themselves in trouble whenever they leave the water, much like Mikey, who in Japan is like "a *kappa* out of water." On a different level, the script idea that an American intervention in an otherwise Japanese production is responsible for the best "anime" ever is intriguing, particularly as it was conceived by an American (Larry Schwarz) involved in producing anime-inspired cartoons. The Japanese characters in *Kappa Mikey* are drawn in anime-inspired style (thin outlines, big and detailed eyes, small mouths, and ten fingers), while Mikey and the other American characters are drawn in American cartoon style (thicker outlines, single black-dot pupils, large mouths, and only eight fingers). This show too became popular among only a niche audience.

Established Forms, New Meanings

Anime-inspired cartoons offer several perspectives on the "cultural ping-pong" phenomenon in which symbolic meanings change dynamically when cultural forms (i.e., symbolic vehicles of meanings) cross back and forth over cultural boundaries. A particularly interesting perspective on this process is the symbolic transformation of ethnic and racial representations during the crossover. While images of Asian ethnicity in American anime-inspired cartoons would also make an interesting case study of this dynamism, here we will focus on an even more complex game of ping-pong, namely, the active crisscrossing of the imagery of blacks between anime and American popular culture, including cartoons.

One example of this in anime-inspired cartoons is the young adult–oriented series *The Boondocks* (created by Aaron McGruder, directed by several directors, 2005–14). This animated series is a social satire of African American culture and its racial relations with White America that follows the lives of two young African American brothers who move from inner-city Chicago to their grandfather's home in the suburbs. It joins other animated social satires on American society and culture, such as *The Simpsons* (1989–), *King of the Hill* (1997–2010), and *South Park* (1997–), as well as other African American–centered cartoons, which have become less of a rarity since the turn of the millennium, such as *The Proud Family* (2001–5), *Static Shock* (2000–2004), and *Hey Monie!* (2003). However, *The Boondocks'* visual style is, as attested by McGruder himself,[9] noticeably influenced by anime, particularly *Cowboy Bebop* (1998) and *Samurai Champloo* (2004), both created and directed by Watanabe Shinichirō. Both series are structured around various multicultural and cinematographic references: for example, both series allude to black American music (jazz in the case of *Cowboy Bebop* and hip-hop in *Samurai Champloo*). Watanabe's influence on *The Boondocks* is discernible in the design of the main protagonists, the realistic settings, and the battle sequences. It is also evident in the opening sequences that pay homage to the visual style of the opening of *Cowboy Bebop,* with hip-hop music reminding viewers of *Samurai Champloo*. According to McGruder, from the second season the production team of *The Boondocks,* not entirely satisfied with the visual look of the series, tried to work with the Japanese animation studio Madhouse, but these efforts did not produce results for reasons unexplained. The two animators subsequently responsible for bringing the visual look of the series closer to McGruder's imagining were U.S.-based South Korean Seung Eun Kim and African American Carl Jones.

In response to the question, "Why anime?" McGruder replied: "It's a better type of art for animation. I designed the characters [in the original comic strip] that way because I wanted it to be animated one day, and I knew that was the direction I wanted to go way back then."[10] It could thus be argued that McGruder used an "anime package" to tell a story that could have only been told in the United States. But there is more to it than that. For many viewers, the visual style of *The Boondocks* may not be very meaningful, but for those who notice the references to Watanabe's work in particular and to anime in general, the consideration of ethnic and racial representation in anime is most apparent.

Ethnic and racial representations in anime have attracted much attention from non-Japanese fans as well as scholars. Most notably, several have pointed out that many of the characters do not look Japanese. Schodt was perhaps the first scholar to point out how non-Japanese are puzzled when they notice that characters in manga more often resemble Caucasians with their non-black (often blond) hair, long limbs, and big "saucer" eyes, although according to the story line, they are Japanese (Schodt 1996: 59). Character design in anime follows suit. Many anime plots happen in foreign lands, away from Japan or in a futuristic alien world, which may partly explain this lack of Japanese (or Asian) ethnic characteristics. However, it is similarly true that in many anime series, which take place in contemporary or historical Japan, the characters don't necessarily look very Japanese.

Two explanations for the lack of Japanese ethnic characteristics in anime are accepted among scholars. The first explanation is that while anime characters may not look very Japanese, neither do they look white or Caucasian; they look like anime characters. Their multicolored hair and celebrated giant eyes are not so much an imitation of Caucasian traits as expressions of the graphic conventions of anime, which, as stated earlier, use physical features to convey feelings rather than mark ethnicity. The result is that although they do not look ethnically Japanese, they are recognized by Japanese and non-Japanese anime fans as "Japanese." The second explanation, which was also discussed in chapter 1, is that the non-Japaneseness of characters, the so-called *mukokuseki* (statelessness), works to the advantage of the manga and anime industries in the export market (Iwabuchi 2002a: 94; Schodt 1996: 62), and hence it is consciously manipulated by animators and producers who are thinking about the global market.

Unlike American cinema and animation in which skin color is always political, in anime's nonspecific and lenient platform of images, ethnic/racial identification is a fluid process shaped by the storytelling and, to a significant extent, the readers of the texts (or more accurately, the viewers of anime) and their societal notions of skin color and what it represents. Japanese viewers may thus interpret what they see on the screen differently from, for example, their American counterparts. Arguably, however, unlike other characters in anime, black characters are more often used as an ethnic/racial marker of otherness, even for Japanese viewers. We would even argue that the presence of black characters in anime may transform the ethnic/racial identity of other characters into more meaningful representations.

The genealogy of the Black Other in Japanese culture has been described with great insight by scholars such as Russell (1996) and Yano (2013). Russell demonstrated how literary and visual representations of blacks in postwar Japan reveal the persistence of racial stereotypes, which ascribe to blacks characteristics such as infantilism, primitivism, hypersexuality, bestiality, athleticism, mental inferiority, psychological weakness, and emotional volatility (Russell 1996: 20). Beyond these racial stereotypes, Russell also found a tendency, particularly in literary works, to employ the Black Other as a reflexive symbol through which Japanese authors deal with their own ambiguous racio-cultural status in a Eurocentric world. In other words, in terms of the racial polarization between black and white, the Japanese as Asians view themselves as occupying a liminal state between the civilized white and the barbarous black (Russell 1996: 21). According to Yano (2013: 508–9), this is further complicated by a clear distinction, which was made early on, between African blacks and African Americans, who became, in a sense, an example of a fellow people of color who could nonetheless belong to a modern and Westernized nation. Russell also pointed out that after the Vietnam War and the subsequent rise of counterculture and the influx of black popular music and culture into Japan, disaffected Japanese youth came to identify African Americans as an image with which to counter the values of the Japanese establishment, and the Black Other was adopted as a symbol of their defiance and alienation from the Japanese mainstream (Russell 1996: 35).

Since the 1990s, the adoption of popular African American "performative" behaviors (most notably in fashion and music) by Japanese youth in various popular subcultures has become more conspicuous than ever, from the *ganguro* (black face) girls of the late 1990s to youth who structure their identity around reggae, rap, and hip-hop rhythms, fashions, and countercultural stances (Wood 1997). For most youths, adopting these performative styles is not anchored in a self-conscious and well-articulated ideology. As argued by Althusser, "Ideology is a system of representations, but in the majority of cases these representations have nothing to do with consciousness; they are usually images and occasionally concepts, but above all it is as *structures* that they impose on the majority of men" ([1965] 2005: 233). Following the same line of thought, Hebdige posited: "Ideology by definition thrives beneath consciousness. It is here, at the level of 'normal common sense,' that ideological frames of reference are most firmly sedimented and most effective" (1979: 11). Likewise, Newton and Rosenfelt suggested that ideology is "a complex and contradictory system of representations (discourses, images, myths) through which we experience ourselves in relation to each other and to the social structures in which we live" (1985: xvii).

There are various anthropological interpretations that map the power structures within the social worlds of Japanese youth who adopt African American performative behaviors and the relations between these social worlds and mainstream Japanese culture. They range from suggestions that these are a means of identifying with other people of color at least in style (Condry 2006; Sterling 2010; Yano 2013: 509) to implications of an all-out war against mainstream Japanese notions of Japaneseness that are based on blood ideology (Kinsella 2005). It is against this backdrop that the exploration of the representations of blacks in anime and the way in which they were influenced by American popular culture and eventually returned to influence American popular culture is so fascinating. Following are a few select examples of such representations discussed according to chronology.

One of the first representations of blacks in Japanese anime was in the 1966 film *Cyborg 009* (directed by Serikawa Yugo), which was based on a 1964 manga by the same name (created by Ishinomori Shotaro) and which became a prequel to another film completed a year later (directed by Serikawa Yugo) and a 1968 series, both with the same name (also directed by Serikawa Yugo). The anime series had two remakes: in 1979 (directed by Akehi Masayuki) and in 2001 (directed by Kawagoe Jun). In 2012, Production I.G produced the film *009 Re: Cyborg* (directed by Kamiyama Kenji). In other words, *Cyborg 009* is a well-known franchise. *Cyborg 009* tells the story of nine people who have been kidnapped from various locations around the world and turned into cyborgs by the evil, warmongering Black Ghost Organization. As the story begins, the cyborgs, led by their creator Dr. Isaac Gilmore, break free and swear to combine their enhanced abilities for the greater good of human society. Cyborg 009, the last to be created and the most powerful among the cyborgs, becomes their leader. Cyborg 009 is Shimamura Joe, a young man whose mother was Japanese and whose father was an American GI stationed in Japan. Like Shimamura, who is a *hāfu* (half Japanese) in a very ethnic conscious and foreigner-shunning Japanese society, all the other cyborgs had been outsiders in their countries of origin. 001 is a very sick, pacifier-sucking Russian baby who was dumped by his parents. 002 is an American with a beak-shaped nose who used to be a gang member. 003 is a French war-orphaned ballerina. 004's girlfriend was killed when the couple tried to escape from East Germany. 005 is a Native American who couldn't find work in the United States due to widespread racism. 006 is an impoverished Chinese farmer who tried to commit suicide before he was kidnapped. 007 is an alcoholic ex–stage actor from Britain. And finally, the focal point of our attention, 008, whose name is Pyunma, is a runaway slave from Africa.

The multiethnic, multinational cyborg unit that is here to save the world embodies a strong political statement about the importance of international and interracial collaboration. This is particular noteworthy if one considers the lack of a civil rights movement in Japan and the strength of the homogeneous blood and culture ideology in Japan. Confusingly, however, it is somewhat tainted by the openly racist visual depiction of the characters, especially (but not only) the characters of color: the Chinese, the Native American, and the African.[11]

In both the original movie adaptation and the first anime series, Pyunma is drawn with the "darky"[12] iconography of blackface, that is, googly eyes, inky skin, and exaggerated, thick pinkish lips. Despite his ridiculous and caricatured appearance, 008, who is a secondary character among the cyborgs, is a very serious, no-nonsense fighter. "Darky" iconography was imported to Japan from the West and became standardized at the turn of the twentieth century (Russell 1996: 33). It is probably safe to assume that in a series that calls for collaboration among the races, this representation was chosen less from malice and more from ignorance and a deeply embedded endorsement of racist imagery that becomes so commonplace that the history and beliefs it carries go completely unnoticed by most people.

In light of a growing awareness of the problematical aspects of this iconography and as a result of foreign criticism, "darky" iconography became delegitimized in Japan in the late 1980s (Russell 1996: 38n4). In the subsequent animated adaptations of *Cyborg 009*, Pyunma's blackface was dropped in favor of a more natural appearance, and in the 2001 adaptation he is no longer an escaped slave but a guerilla fighter. "Darky" iconography lingered, however, in Japanese anime: the *Dragon Ball Z* series boasts Mr. Popo, a genie depicted as a caricature of a black African (1988, episode 124); *Pokémon* has Jynx, a large female blackface character (1998, episode 65); *Shaman King* features Joco, a recurring sidekick who is an African American shaman drawn with blackface. This inconclusive list of black characters designed with blackface suggests that awareness of the embedded racism in it is still not universal in Japan.

Moving forward more than fifteen years from the original *Cyborg 009* movie, the anime television series *The Super Dimension Fortress Macross* (*Chōjikū yōsai makurosu*) (created by Kawamori Shōji, directed by Ishiguro Noboru, 1982), the first series in the *Macross* franchise, became a

milestone in the history of the Japanese space opera anime genre, combining *mecha* elements with wartime romance.[13] Relevant to our current
discussion is Claudia LaSalle, a black female American bridge officer
on the SDF-1 Macross Space Fortress in charge of weaponry and naviga-
tion. Although not one of the main protagonists, she makes her debut in
the very first episode as a capable officer and a good friend to Hayase
Misa, a fellow female officer of Japanese descent and a main character.
Claudia has the look of a black American but does not display the often
accompanying racial attributes discussed by Russell. She gives the show
a sense of ethnic diversity, echoing our earlier argument that it is the appearance of black characters in anime that gives meaning to ethnic depictions and that African Americans are favored in anime as people of
color who have modernized and Westernized. The ethnic diversity on
the deck of SDF-1 Macross Space Fortress closely resembles—probably
not by coincidence—the ethnic diversity of contemporaneous American
science fiction television series and movies, particularly the Starship Enterprise of the *Star Trek* live-action series and franchise (1966–). Aboard
the Enterprise, the black character Nyota Uhura is an able communications officer and an important part of a multiethnic crew, reflecting the
backdrop of the African American civil rights movement (1954–68), and
in particular, the Civil Rights Act of 1964.

In chapter 1, we described how the science fiction boom in 1970s' anime was inspired by a similar upsurge in Euro-American science fiction,
with the *Star Trek* franchise (particularly the original live-action series
and the ensuing animated series) as a canonical television landmark. The
creators of *Macross* produced an original (and well-made) animated story
that corresponds to the style of the genre, with (perhaps unintentionally)
a good chance of selling overseas due to its non-Japanese look and its use
of the well-proven American space opera formula that was in vogue. Du-
plicating the political statement on multiethnicity by creating a multiethnic crew may have been just a by-product. Indeed, a 1985 American
adaptation titled *Robotech,* which combined the footage of two *Macross*
series and another of Tatsunoko's anime series, was produced by Harmony
Gold (USA) and Tatsunoko Productions, proving that the *mukokuseki*
strategy worked.[14]

Nothing could be further away from this strategy than what is found
in *Crying Freeman* (created by Koike Kazuo and Ikegami Ryoichi, released

in six volumes of OVA, each directed by a different director, 1988–94). *Crying Freeman* is meant for a mature audience and was not meant to be broadcast on television. It may therefore be considered an unexpected choice for this discussion, but the depiction of the black female character in this manga-based series is worth some consideration. The story revolves around a potter named Hinomura Yō, turned by force into an assassin and the leader of the Chinese mafia organization 108 Dragons. His upper body is tattooed with a magnificent dragon, and he is given the Chinese name Lóng Tài-Yáng (Dragon Sun) as well as the nickname "Crying Freeman" because he cries each time he kills someone. The action-packed thin-plot series shows Crying Freeman in close combat with his opponents, demonstrating his prowess in martial arts, particularly his unique method of killing using a blade held between his toes. Crying Freeman fights either half naked, in just a loin cloth, or completely naked, displaying a virile body.

In the third volume of the anime miniseries, three women take part in the action. Two of them are familiar to the viewers from previous volumes: Bái-Yá Shàn (White Ivory Fan), whom Crying Freeman defeated as the upcoming leader of the 108 Dragons, is an unattractive, obese giantess who initially antagonized Crying Freeman but later became his devoted bodyguard after he nearly killed her but chose instead to spare her, and Hino Emu, Crying Freeman's beautiful and smart Japanese wife, also known by her Chinese name Hu Qing Lán (Tiger Pure-Orchid). Both women are fierce fighters, have bodies tattooed with tiger images, and fight stark naked. The third female fighter who debuts in this volume is the African beauty Bugnug (Anteater). A dangerous assassin, Bugnug is the head of an African crime organization known mostly by the name the African Tusk, which engages in an all-out war with the 108 Dragons. Unsurprisingly perhaps in the context of the series, Bugnug also fights naked. One of the climactic scenes in this volume is the hand-to-hand combat between Bugnug and Freeman after he kills her two devoted officers.

Both the nudity of selected characters when fighting and the way in which they always or easily succumb to crying is a reflection of the creators' fantasies; there is an eroticization of the act of fighting that becomes very close to a sexual act. The blunt depiction of this metaphor in different fighting scenes suggests more than eroticization; it may even be read as martial art pornography. It is therefore significant that whereas among the male characters only Freeman fights naked, all three female fighters in this volume fight naked. The fight between Bugnug and Freeman is particularly interesting. Unlike the repulsive and freakish nudity of Bái-Yá Shàn or the refined and cultured nudity of Hu Qing Lán, Bugnug's black nudity is as formidable as that of an Amazon. She is savage, wild-eyed, and magnificent, and fights Freeman with death in her eyes, until he pulls her to the ground where, instead of killing her, he licks her nipple, arousing her to the point of winning her over. At that moment Bugnug falls for Freeman, and the animosity between the 108 Dragons and the African Tusk is transformed into an alliance. It may be the woman in Bugnug who is so easily subjugated, but it is impossible to ignore her race (as explained earlier, blackness is a marker of ethnicity in anime). Her athletic prowess, deemed so befitting for a black Amazon, feeds into the creators' imaginations, alongside other attributes of the Black Other, namely, an easily aroused sexual appetite that supersedes rational decision making, strength of character, and the determination to stand up for a cause. Within this fantasy, it is not insignificant that it is a Japanese man who sexually overcomes a fantasy trope of sexual impetus such as the deadly black Amazon. Bugnug may also fulfill a structural requirement of the story as a counterimage to Hu Qing Lán, Freeman's wife, who is ready to nobly sacrifice herself for his sake toward the end of the volume and who eventually wins her battle by the sheer strength of spiritual force and fidelity (although she too undresses in the process).

The anime series *Cowboy Bebop*, the acknowledged inspiration for *The Boondocks,* takes us back to the *Macross*-like realm of anime as an "amorphous media territory that crosses and intermingles national boundaries" (Napier 2001: 23), with a global audience as its target. Watanabe explained on several occasions that in addition to being heavily inspired by *Lupin III* (created by Monkey Punch, directed by Ōsumi Masaaki, Miyazaki Hayao, and Takahata Isao, 1971), *Cowboy Bebop* was largely his tribute to his favorite American movies and television series, which were shown in Japan during the 1970s and 1980s. These included *Butch Cassidy and the Sundance Kid,* anything with Bruce Lee, anything with a blues or jazz soundtrack, and lots of Blaxploitation movies.[15] The tribute is performed in style, with many references to specific movies and songs. The plot revolves around an unlikely multiage group of penniless cowboy-like bounty hunters who travel in the space vessel Bebop through a futuristic world where humans reside in outer space and travel in spaceships through space gates; in other ways, it closely resembles our contemporary world had it become a reincarnation of the Wild West. Unlike other adult anime series that are plot driven and develop from one episode to the next, *Cowboy Bebop* is motivated by action and character, and thus each episode can be watched independently. Viewers are kept interested by the campy experimentation with movie genres and styles, as well as the wide range of references in each episode. Most pertinent to our present topic, the series pays homage to Blaxploitation movies.

In episode 17 of *Cowboy Bebop*, titled "Mushroom Samba," the crew of Bebop are hungrier than usual. The episode is a particularly nonsensical tale of how Ed, the youngest crew member, and Ein the dog are sent to look for food after their spaceship crashes in a sparsely inhabited desert that looks a lot like Utah. Ed and Ein soon meet three different characters: Coffee, an ultrasexy bounty hunter modeled on the black beauty Coffy played by Pam Grier in the movie *Coffy* (Jack Hill, 1973); Shaft, an allusion to Richard Roundtree's John Shaft of the Blaxploitation movie *Shaft* (Gordon Parks, 1971) and at the same time a reference to the protagonist of the 1966 Spaghetti Western *Django* (Sergio Corbucci, 1966); and Domino, a dealer in illegal mushrooms. Movie critic Simon Abrams is correct in arguing that there is very little philosophical meaning to this episode beyond the absurd off-the-cuff tone that playfully reinforces the show's central ethos: "to live an improvised life, one must be willing to roll with the punches, no matter what strange new form they may take."[16] The episode works particularly well for those who recognize the campy intertextual references. *Cowboy Bebop*'s self-reflexivity, unconventional structure, eclectic dialogues, ironic mix of humor and violence, nonlinear story line, and cinematic allusions and pop culture references in the form of homage and pastiche turn it into a formidable example of postmodern cinema.

Within this artistic framework, the original cultural baggage of Blaxploitation movies as a genre is nonexistent. Blaxploitation movies emerged in the early 1970s, the post–African American civil rights movement era. Until then, blacks had stereotypical roles in American movies that confirmed the supremacy of white America. Blaxploitation movies, on the other hand, fumed with anger, portraying similar black stereotypes

but interpreting them more provocatively and assertively. Their protagonists, who were overly sexualized and machoized, presented an image
that was offensive to many African Americans. They were, however, dominant, charismatic, and ready to fight their oppressors. Blaxploitation
movies thus paved the way for later black films in the United States to
depict the African American experience more realistically and to con-
front ethnoracial issues of the time. None of this sociopolitical baggage
remains in *Cowboy Bebop*. We are left with a frivolous, teasing play with
globally circulating cool images.

In 2004, Watanabe directed *Samurai Champloo*—the other openly
declared influence on *The Boondocks*. *Samurai Champloo* is an outrageous
comedy adventure that features Tokugawa-era rappers, ink-brush tagging,
Hiroshima homeboys, and sword fights using break-dance moves.[17] In
this character-driven anime, viewers are transferred to an uninhibitedly
anachronistic past in which the worlds of hip-hop and samurai blend
(Fitzgerald 2008: 172). The story revolves around three main characters.
There are two young sword masters: Jin, a masterless samurai raised in
the old Bushidō way (the way of the warrior), and Mugen, a young thug
raised among criminals in the Ryukyu Islands whose fighting style is an
undefined blend. The third lead character is a young woman named Fuu
who goes through considerable efforts to recruit Jin and Mugen in her
search for a samurai who smells of sunflowers (who is, as the viewers discover much later, her father). If there is one common attribute among
the three main characters, it is that they are all strong individuals who
challenge any form of authority.

In the context of the present discussion about the shifting representations of blacks in anime, an examination of this anime series, which
lacks black characters, may seem strange. But what the series offers in
abundance is a contemporary adaptation of black American culture: hip-
hop, rap, break dancing, and fashion. As argued by Fitzgerald (2008:
172), *Samurai Champloo* invites viewers to contemplate the applicability
of historical situations to modern Japanese culture. That is, although it
takes place in an anachronistic yet not entirely invented Tokugawa Japan, it presents sociocultural issues of present-day Japan and, even more
pronouncedly, of contemporary Japanese youth, thus creating a fascinating web of conceptual possibilities (Fitzgerald 2008: 171). Two questions
run throughout the series and its imagery: the first is the question of

cultural identity in an intensively globalizing world where cultural practices migrate uninhibitedly (Fitzgerald 2008: 171); the second (which is
related to the first) is an exploration of the heterogeneity of Japanese
culture that "ultimately questions the oneness of the Japanese people"
(Condry 2006: 85).

Returning to the adaptation of black American culture to this samurai tale, Watanabe stated: "One of the things that makes samurai and
hip-hop very similar, is that in the old days samurai felt very strongly
about representing themselves . . . with their one sword, and rappers today
are also the ones who take one microphone and represent who they are"
(cited in Fitzgerald 2008: 172). In other words, this blending of seemingly
incongruous elements suggests a search for a personal as well as a cultural identity that may have taken place once upon a time in Tokugawa
Japan, particularly among masterless samurai, and is certainly taking
place today among young Japanese. The character that best parallels the
hip-hop ideal is Mugen (Fitzgerald 2008: 174), with his loosely hanging
Japanese clothing that resembles hip-hop fashion; his unruly hairdo,
which brings to mind hip-hop styling; and his battle style, which evokes
break dancing. More important, he is defiant and proudly uncivilized,
with a blatant disregard for rules—all qualities deemed to embody black
counterculture imagery. As argued earlier in this chapter, for contemporary
young Japanese, black counterculture has become a cultural vehicle that
carries the festivity of defiance and stresses an individuality and subjectivity that celebrates friendship and bonding with others while shunning
conformity and institutionalism.

This short overview of representations of blacks in Japanese anime
cannot be concluded without mentioning *Afro Samurai* (created by Okazaki Takashi, directed by Kizaki Fuminori and Jamie Simone, 2007),
although this series was produced after *The Boondocks*. As mentioned in
chapter 3, this fan comic–based anime series has a very thin plot and is
driven mostly by action and character. A collaborative production between Studio Gonzo and Spike TV, with Samuel L. Jackson voicing the
protagonist and RZA doing the music, gave it remarkable marketing
exposure, and the series set off a franchise that includes collectibles, a
movie, and two video games. The plot is set in an anachronistic displaced
futuristic Japan that still retains some feudalistic characteristics and where
the fighter who earns the Number 1 (*ichi ban*) headband by vanquishing

all other fighters comes to possess godlike powers. Only the bearer of the Number 2 headband can challenge the bearer of the Number 1 headband. The story begins when Afro, the young black son of the black Number 1 fighter, watches his father defeated and killed by the bearer of the Number 2 headband. From this moment on, Afro's life is devoted to overcoming formidable opponents to become the Number 1 fighter and to avenging his father's death.

Style, design, and music compensate for the thin story line, and peak with the lead character of Afro. A rather tall and gaunt figure, Afro is dressed in a samurai outfit complete with wooden *geta* clogs and a samurai sword, and at the same time boasts a huge afro hairdo, golden earrings, and bracelets. He is a scrupulous assassin who barely speaks, never smiles, and never swerves from his life mission. The hip-hop music that comprises much of the coolness and appeal of the series gives Afro his extra edge and unconcerned individuality.

There were times when the idea of casting a nonconformist black man as the ultimate samurai fighter would have appeared to some as blasphemous. The samurai is the ultimate image of traditional, homogenous Japan. In reality, however, the actual meaning of the samurai "has always been very much contested," and for this reason, "battling samurai can be seen as evoking a contest over the meaning of Japaneseness" (see Condry 2006: 52 [on *Samurai Champloo*]). From a Japanese point of view, the notion of a black Samurai in a Japanese–American anime production calls into question the meaning of Japaneseness in a world where Japanese culture is warmly embraced by fans around the globe. From an African American perspective, the "samuriness" of Afro may provide him with the irresistible odds needed to fight the world. From a different, perhaps global, perspective, the fusion of a samurai and an African American in a transcultural production targeting a transcultural audience fleshes out how the two sets of imageries (of blacks and of samurai) that occupy a marginal position in global power structures merge in one symbolic vehicle of individualism, subjectivity, and nonconformism, thereby providing strong stimulus for the imagination. Moreover, the fusion of imageries and the mishmash anachronisms of mutually incoherent objects are recruited to tell a nonsensical tale about lethal competition and vengeance, and can be viewed as a straightforward commentary about the disorientating forces of capitalism and intensive and multidirectional globalization processes.

Black characters or references to black culture in anime have always been a means to speak of Japanese society and culture, or, quite conversely, to create distance from Japan. In the United States, however, the anime-inspired cartoon *The Boondocks* is very critical of the sociocultural politics of African Americans and their relations with white America. Its anime-style dialogue enhances the show's cool look and aesthetics. For those in the know, that is, those who are familiar with contemporary anime works, particularly those of Watanabe, *The Boondocks* reintroduced into the visual imagery of anime a sociocultural critique of African Americans that nonetheless affirms the individualistic eccentricity and resistant spirit that has come to be part of the construction of "black American culture" in Japan.

Amy Fitzgerald has written about the merging of samurai and hip-hop culture in *Samurai Champloo,* arguing that one of the embedded messages explores cultural identity in an age of globalization and shows that globalization does not necessarily entail the belittling of one's culture. It is possible to remain true to local culture while enacting it within the framework of a global, modern society. In other words, you can remain, and even be truer to being, "Japanese" by enacting your Japaneseness through hip-hop. Likewise, in his work, McGruder communicates, enacts, and develops the causes that define his own identity as a black American with an imported means of communication, namely, anime.

With the growing number of multinational and multicultural productions of animation, the meanings of symbolic representations in these creations, be they visual or thematic, become further destabilized. This is not specific to animation alone; we see similar cross-cultural interactions leading to the destabilization of symbolic meanings in all of today's media.

Conclusion: The Limits of Anime as Transcultural Style

The substantial normative impact of anime on American popular culture, and particularly on youth culture, is one of the most significant aspects of anime expansion into the U.S. market. Anime visual styles, imageries, and storytelling techniques have come to be the heritage of animators around the world. The influence of anime in general and specific anime creators in particular on non-Japanese animators is exhibited in a variety of ways and in many mediums beyond television animation in animation produced outside of Japan. The anime-inspired cartoons discussed in this chapter reflect this influence most explicitly.

But anime-inspired cartoons may have represented an interim stage in a larger process of cross-cultural pollination, as this category is practically obsolete in the United States. This is, first of all, a reflection of the fact that the anime boom years are commercially over and that the term "anime-inspired cartoon" can no longer benefit producers and marketing professionals as a marketing strategy. Moreover, it reflects the fact that the visual styles, imageries, and storytelling techniques of anime have by now become an established part of a sophisticated and diverse tool kit comprising various sources of inspiration that is available to the contemporary animator and producer. In that sense, anime has become a transcultural animation style. Nothing illustrates this better than an article published in the web magazine *Creative Bloq* in December 2014 delineating the five new transformative global trends in animation.[18] The article discusses what it terms "mixed styles" according to which, "with an entire generation of Western animators influenced by the likes of Miyazaki Hayao now coming to the fore, we can expect a cross-continental mix to grow more and more important on both sides of the Pacific."

Nevertheless, for those in the business of anime, there is still a huge gap between Japanese anime and animation around the world, including the United States. We have argued more than once in this book that one of the cultural impacts of anime is that it helped to push the boundaries of animation in the United States from being a child-oriented medium to one that is also appropriate for adults. However, if we compare the Japanese and American anime industries as the two largest and most influential producers of animation in the world, unlike in Japan where animation rivals the film industry for its diversification, animation for young adults and adults in the United States is almost entirely restricted to satire. With the exception of a few projects, there are no dramatic television cartoon series that debate complex psychological or philosophical issues. There are hardly any commercial television cartoons for mature audiences. And finally, there are no theatrical animated features in the United States that target a young adult or an adult-only audience. Anime developed as a medium in Japan under specific economic, industrial, and cultural conditions that allowed it to become the animated rival of the film industry. Whether the medium of animation around the world will ever follow suit remains to be seen.

CHAPTER 5

Japan's Anime Policy

Supporting the Industry or "Killing the Cool"?

In January 2015, the Japanese Ministry of Foreign Affairs (MOFA) announced that in the next two years it would be setting up new cultural centers in London, Los Angeles, Sao Paulo, Hong Kong, Jakarta, and Istanbul to actively promote Japanese culture and technology through displays of anime, manga, and culinary culture. The ministry is, accordingly, hoping that the facilities, to be located in busy urban areas and headed by local staff, will sway global opinion in Japan's favor regarding its various disputes with China and South Korea. The previous year, Foreign Minister Inada Tomomi, responsible for the coordinated strategy to promote Japan's culture and products abroad, took things a step further and appeared in a purple gothic Lolita dress at a cosplay event in Paris. According to Minister Inada, "Cool Japan," as this strategy is called, will serve as a "control tower" for the various ministries and agencies involved in Japan's cultural exports and coordinate the country's various "cool" initiatives.[1]

These steps are indicative of the way that anime, and more broadly Japanese popular culture, has not only globalized but also compelled the Japanese government to respond. In recent years, the Japanese government has become increasingly aware of Japan's contemporary cultural appeal, especially in the fields of anime and fashion, and has been attempting to utilize them abroad as part of its charm offensive. In the past, the Japanese government was reluctant to actively support Japan's anime exports, considering it economically marginal and diplomatically unimportant. Following the success of the private sector in the export of contemporary culture and fashion, however, the government has become progressively proactive in its attempts to utilize anime as part of its exertion of "soft power" meant to raise the country's profile in the world of nations (Otmazgin 2012: 50–54). As early as the 1990s, the mass media was already heralding the anime boom as something the Japanese should be proud of and calling on the state to make better use of its cultural resources. In recent years, television shows, popular books, and magazine covers have dealt extensively with Japan's "cool exports," thereby providing a strong tailwind for the government to hold on to.[2] Commenting sarcastically on the global anime boom, Suga Chizuru, a METI official, expressed that the Japanese government has decided "to back the winning horse."[3] For this reason, as Ōtsuka and Ōsawa (2005: 258–59) argued, the global outreach of anime should not be seen as a state endeavor or the result of state policy but as the consequence of commercial anime productions going abroad as part of transnational market liberalization. In other words, it is a case of the tail wagging the dog: the Japanese government is not the reason for the success of anime abroad, and its support of the globalization of the anime sector in the past was rather insignificant, if not harmful. But the success of the private sector and the enthusiastic acceptance of anime by consumers overseas have sparked the government's interest, and for over a decade now, it has been searching for a role in this highly promising sector.

Amid the increasing involvement of the Japanese government in the cultural sector, the intriguing question is how the state should intervene in Japan's anime industry or whether it should even intervene at all. One option is for the state to stay far away from the anime sector and let the private sector deal independently with the rising costs of production, increasing global competition, and the various market failures—as has been the case throughout most of the postwar period. Another option is to strategically allocate resources and attention to promote anime as an export-led industry, as has been done in Japan's more internationally renowned industries such as automobiles and electronics. This, however, runs the risk of "killing the cool," meaning that the government may choose to promote cultural products and fields that are not necessarily favored by consumers, or even worse, consumers may be intimidated by state-sponsored cultural campaigns (Daliot-Bul 2009). In China and

South Korea, for example, where negative recollections of Japan as oc-
cupier and colonizer continue to simmer, consumers may opt to stay away
from Japanese-made anime once the Japanese government is involved.
There are, of course, various other options in between these two extremes.

In this chapter, we analyze the response of the Japanese state to the
growth of the overseas anime market that has gradually come to be viewed
as economically profitable as well as embodying diplomatic advantages,
which could boost Japan's image abroad. Based on interviews with both
government officials and industry personnel, the chapter examines the
different initiatives taken by the Japanese government to enhance the
position of Japan's anime industry within the global animation industry
and the response of the anime industry to these initiatives. We also feature the voices of key figures in Japan's anime industry, who have shared
with us their reservations and concerns about Japan's anime policy. The
central argument we present in this chapter is that while initially the
Japanese government was neither interested in anime export nor responsible for its success during the boom years, it has, over the past fifteen
years, become increasingly involved in the field, encouraged by its economic potential as well as by the chance to accumulate soft power from
a global affinity for anime and its related products. The government is
struggling to find the right way to support the anime industry, however,
and its various initiatives are largely uncoordinated and uninspiring, and
thus overwhelmingly ineffective.

We should point out that this problem of how the state should
intervene in the promotion of its cultural industries is not unique to
Japan. There is an inherent tension between a highly formalized and bureaucratized organization, such as the government, whose mission is
to standardize and organize, and the creative industries—the basis of
anime production—which, by their very nature, aim to produce and
valorize new ideas and emphasize differences. A look into government
involvement in the anime sector in Japan will, in our opinion, provide
constructive insights as to what the right policy is in this context. It may
also help us to address wider questions related to patterns of involvement
in the anime sector and, more broadly, preferred relations between cultural production and the state in market-led economies. These are critical questions that have not been sufficiently addressed in the available
literature.

Soft-Powering Anime: The Official Soft Power Push

Unlike during most of the postwar period, the production and export of anime in Japan is currently seen as economically profitable and diplomatically useful, and is therefore deemed a legitimate object of state intervention. As indicated in previous chapters, the revenues from the export of anime, and more generally, popular culture, were most significant in the 1990s and the early 2000s, and this caught the attention of the Japanese government. Moreover, it is widely acknowledged that the anime sector is key for the development of all content industries today. Anime and anime-inspired images appear in video games, commercials, magazines, music clips, accessories, clothes, and other related goods—and not only in anime series or movies. Anime is consumed via television sets, cellular phones, DVDs and other electronic appliances, and together with other cultural visuals and sounds, is necessary for the existence of industries such as featured movies, television dramas, and music clips. In other words, anime has a broader media ecology and maintains a close synergy with other industries and a variety of media formats, a pattern referred to as "mixed media" or "media mix" (Ito 2006; MacWilliams 2008: 6; Steinberg 2012).

In recent years, academics, journalists, politicians, and bureaucrats in Japan have started emphasizing the growing importance of commodified culture for the country's future, encouraging the government to intervene, and at times even referring to the export of Japan's contemporary culture as a resource of soft power and as a manifestation of Cool Japan. This indicates a process of bureaucratization in which the anime sector is given higher priority and is firmly placed within the national agenda. The influx of government reports are further proof of this point. According to Kukhee Choo's study (2012: 86–89), government reports dealing with the content industries increased from 97 in the 1990s to 516 in the 2000s, with anime and manga increasing almost 15-fold and 37-fold, respectively, and video games tripling. These reports typically express optimistic prospects for the industry and encourage state intervention. A more concrete initiative was the establishment in July 2011 of the

Ministry of Economy, Trade, and Industry's (METI) Creative Industries Division, better known as the Cool Japan Division. The purpose of this division is to supervise the international promotion of Cool Japan and to assist Japanese small- and medium-size culture-related firms to pursue a global strategy.

Anime is one of the major objectives of METI's Cool Japan Division (see fig. 4), along with food, fashion, and other related cultural goods. More recently, the government announced that in 2016 it would allocate a record high of JPY 70 billion (approximately US$500 million) for a global public relations campaign, more than triple the previous year's budget of JPY 20 billion. Essentially, the campaign aims to reach global audiences and project a more positive image abroad through the support of local Japan-related associations and consultations with local opinion leaders. A portion of this sum will be allocated to improving the government's ability to analyze and respond to developments in global opinion and to ensure that Japan's messages get across.[4]

From a diplomatic point of view, anime is viewed as a useful tool for influencing mass opinion and boosting Japan's image abroad as part of "Japan's brand strategy" (Daliot-Bul 2009). Anime leads the worldwide transformation of images of "old Japan," represented by traditional customs and practices such as tea ceremony, *noh* theater, and pottery, with images of a new and "avant-garde Japan," represented by contemporary media and media-related products and practices. As journalist Douglas McGray (2002) observed at the turn of the millennium, Japan's booming contemporary cultural innovations and lifestyles, which he referred to as "Japan's Gross National Cool," make Japan look more like a cultural superpower today than it did in the 1980s, when it was widely acknowledged as an economic superpower.

Endo Nao, the director of the Japan Foundation in Sydney, explained Japan's ambiguous image abroad and its dual representation as both traditional and contemporary.[5] In his opinion, although traditional culture embodies "true" Japanese ideas more genuinely, the audience demands anime, and he recognizes that for the Japan Foundation to remain relevant and interest people abroad in Japan, they must exhibit contemporary forms of Japanese culture. This ambiguous attitude toward anime, namely, acknowledging its popularity on the one hand but at the same time wanting to promote traditional culture, poses a major question for Japanese

FIGURE 4. Cool Japan Events are organized by METI (Japanese Ministry of Economy, Trade, and Industry) as a way to explore the commercial value of Japanese contemporary culture. Singapore, October 2011. Courtesy of Dentsu Singapore.

officials: what artifacts and fields best represent Japan and should therefore be given priority for foreign exposure? Ogura Kazuo (2004), then president of the Japan Foundation, called for a policy shift by propagating more contemporary art forms abroad, such as anime, music, and manga, alongside Japanese high culture, such as *noh* theater, *bunraku* (puppet theater), *ikebana* (the art of flower arrangement), and *chanoyu* (tea ceremony), which still, in his personal view, "transmitted the Japanese spirit" and offered the world "international assets."

Excited about the idea of linking the marketing of cultural products together with consumer products, the Japanese government has launched a series of campaigns and initiatives aimed at improving the international image of Japan and increasing the visibility of Japanese products in foreign markets. One such initiative that indicates the movement of anime into the mainstream is the appointment of famous anime characters as special ambassadors. Doraemon, a blue robotic cat character from one of Japan's most famous manga and anime series, was appointed by the then–Japanese foreign minister Kōmura Masahiko as a special cultural ambassador to the world at an official inauguration ceremony in Tokyo in 2008 (see fig. 5). Later that year, Hello Kitty, Japan's ubiquitous ambassador of cuteness, was appointed as the country's tourism ambassador to Hong Kong and China. In a similar vein, in 2009 MOFA announced the appointment of three "Kawaii Ambassadors"[6] to spread the message of Japanese contemporary style and fashion around the world. By participating in publicized PR campaigns, these Kawaii Ambassadors were to meet fans, take part in events, and generally bring Japanese contemporary culture closer to young people from other countries. Three young women were chosen as ambassadors: Aoki Misako, who represents the Gothic Lolita fashion; Kimura Yu, symbolizing Tokyo's Harajuku-style fashion[7]; and Fujioka Shizuka, who previously ran a fashionable school uniform shop in Tokyo and is an expert in matching the right uniform for young women. According to the MOFA announcement, "Pop culture is expected to help the people of the world have more chances to know about contemporary Japan, hand-in-hand with other traditional and contemporary cultures." The three Kawaii Ambassadors have since appeared in various symposiums and events throughout Asia and Europe.[8]

To understand the transformation Japanese policymakers had to go through—moving from a long-embraced image of Japan as home to

FIGURE 5. Doraemon (center) at his inauguration ceremony as cultural ambassador, with Kōmura Masahiko (left), minister for foreign affairs, March 2008. Courtesy of the Japanese Ministry of Foreign Affairs. © Fujiko-Pro, Shogakukan, TV Asahi, Shin-Ei, ADK.

long-standing traditional cultures, *wabi-sabi* aesthetical sensibilities, and ancient virtues passed on for generations to manifesting a rather demasculinizing image of Japan, represented by Lolita mascots, sexualized cuteness, and childish anime characters—one might imagine the United States appointing Mickey Mouse or Snoopy as its official cultural ambassadors to the world. This requires not only a change in tactics but also new thinking and a cognitive transformation of what constitutes Japanese cultural identity and how it should be displayed to the world.

METI, for its part, launched the Cool Japan campaign in October 2011 to increase the visibility of Japanese products in foreign markets. The overseas campaign, which was engineered by Dentsu Inc., Japan's largest advertisement company, kicked off in Singapore and was scheduled to last several months. It introduced Japanese fashion, food, and anime, and encouraged tourism to Japan. Cool Japan events were also scheduled for India, China, South Korea, France, Italy, the United States, and Brazil. According to Matsushita Tadahiro, the senior vice minister of METI at the time, the purpose of the campaign was to introduce new Japanese brands to the growing Asian consumer market and to attract new customers by appealing to non-Japanese who already have a generally positive impression of Japanese contemporary culture.[9] The ministry's new attitude toward Japanese anime producers who wish to expand to global markets was summarized succinctly by METI official Suga Chizuru: "We are always here for you, offering advice and providing links to global distributors."[10] She did, however, admit that METI cannot offer much financial support and lacks people with sufficient knowledge about the domestic and global anime business.

Mihara Ryōtarō (2014: 6–7), a METI official, is more critical. He claimed that while the need to promote Japan's "cool" export has been internalized in official discourse within Japan's bureaucracy, there is no concrete policy for promoting Japanese culture globally, no real discussion or feedback about the actions the ministry should take, and not much understanding about how to make use of Japan's "cool" resources. METI simply gives financial assistance to Japanese companies considered creative, but this assistance does not, in fact, reach the right places (2014: 189). In Mihara's pessimistic opinion, the Cool Japan strategy is becoming counterproductive, making people dislike Japan rather than increasing positive appreciation of the country.

The Bureaucratization of Anime

The Japanese government defines the anime industry as one of the country's "content industries," namely, industries that produce cultural, art, or media artifacts of commercial value. There is no comprehensive data about the size of Japan's content industries or even their exact definition; relevant data is only partially available in various overlapping publications on multimedia, popular culture, and art. According to Sugiura Tsutomu's calculations (2008), the global export of popular culture merchandise and related royalties, income, and services deriving from products such as recorded sound and image (music, anime, movies, video games), books, magazines, paintings, art, and handicrafts more than tripled from US$8.37 billion in 1996 to approximately US$25.4 billion in 2006. The rate of this export growth is astounding, especially given that during the same period the export of Japan's total merchandise trade (of both culturally and nonculturally related items) grew by only 68 percent, from US$447 billion in 1996 to US$752 billion in 2006. Specifically regarding anime, according to the Digital Content Association of Japan (2009), 60 to 65 percent of the world's animated cartoon series in the 2000s were made in Japan, bringing in estimated worldwide annual sales of licensed goods worth US$17 billion.

From a bureaucratic point of view, the state's support for media and cultural industries includes a wide range of initiatives that involves no fewer than thirteen government ministries and agencies, all attempting to take part in this emerging sector (Otmazgin 2011; Zykas 2011). The most prominent of these are MOFA, METI, the Japan Foundation, the Agency for Cultural Affairs (ACA, under the Ministry of Education, Culture, Sports, Science, and Technology), and the prime minister's cabinet. In practice, government involvement focuses on supporting the infrastructures needed for developing the cultural industries or for organizing international platforms. This includes programs to support the technology needed for delivering and consuming cultural content (especially the infrastructure for accessing the Internet, cable television, and satellite broadcasts); to encourage universities and training centers to cultivate human resources with relevant knowledge and skills; and to ensure the availability of venture capital for producing anime, movies, television programs, video games, and so forth. At the same time, however, government involvement is characterized by overlapping responsibilities, a lack of coordination between the various ministries, struggles over the allocation of resources, and, as we shall see later, inadequate communication with the private sector.

One of the first comprehensive initiatives to think strategically about Japan's content industry sector was the 2002 establishment of the Strategic Council on Intellectual Property within the prime minister's office. A year later, the Intellectual Property Headquarters was set up within the cabinet as an intermediary between the various government ministries. The council, headed by the prime minister, was set up to promote the growth of Japan's intellectual property—including patented technologies, designs, movies, and computer game software—as a means of revitalizing the economy. In its meetings and reports, the council outlines the technical aspects of intellectual property and the need to promote creative research in universities and collaboration between companies and research institutions (Japan's Prime Minister's Office 2008). Participants in these meetings include representatives from Japan's Strategic Council on Intellectual Property, the police, the Interior Ministry, MOFA, the Finance Ministry, the Agency for Cultural Affairs, METI, Japan Patent Office, and Keidanren (Japan Business Federation), as well as Diet members, media personnel, academics, and journalists.

As soon as Japan's content industries became part of the national economic strategy, the Japanese government was keen to tackle the issue of copyright violation. This has been considered one of the major factors discouraging Japanese anime studios from further international expansion. The Chinese market, where a growing number of websites offer free online anime in clear violation of the Japanese owners' copyright, is a major source of concern. The Agency for Cultural Affairs estimates that copyright infringement of anime and manga by Chinese pirate sites amounted to over JPY 560 billion in 2014. In July 2014, in an attempt to curb online piracy, the government joined anime production studios and manga publishers such as Shūeisha, Shōgakukan, Tezuka Productions, and Studio Ghibli in forming the "Manga-Anime Guardians Project." This campaign has sent requests to hundreds of major violators asking them to delete their illegal anime and manga postings, and has launched its own website where users can purchase anime series legally at a reduced cost of only several hundred yen. In a similar vein, in 2013, the government-sponsored Cool Japan Fund teamed up with production and advertisement giants Tōei, Sunrise, TMS, Aniplex, Asatsu-DK, Nihon Ad Systems, and Dentsu to develop Daisuki, the first Japan-centered streaming entertainment platform.[11]

In recent years, METI has emerged as a major player in directing policies that promote the anime sector. It placed itself in charge of the cultural industries' economic portfolios and has, ever since, emphasized the contribution of anime to the national economy and the need to develop related infrastructures. METI's research institute (Research Institute of Economy, Trade and Industry [RIETI]) and think tanks have been examining ways to encourage the development and export of cultural industries, mainly through studying the literature and data on this subject. They routinely produce optimistic reports predicting that the multimedia and culture-related industries will continue to occupy an ever-increasing segment of the economy. In 1992, METI estimated that of the JPY 55.3 trillion that the multimedia industries were expected to generate in 2015, approximately 62 percent would come from sales of software, motion pictures, artistic images and sound, computer games, and broadcasting. Another typical METI think tank report from 2003, which analyzed prospects for the Japanese content industry, indicated that in less than five years the share of content in the world GDP is expected to rise to 6.5 percent (from 3.6 percent in 2002), worth US$1.4 trillion. These reports, however, usually present surveys of developments and prospects for Japan's anime, manga, video games, music, and television industries, but they rarely provide inspirational insights into the industry or call for a substantial policy shift.

As mentioned at the beginning of this chapter, in July 2011 METI established the Creative Industries Division (i.e., the "Cool Japan Division"), to encourage Japanese creative industries to pursue foreign market expansion opportunities. METI allocated approximately JPY 650 billion in 2013 (approximately US$650 million at the time) to this endeavor.[12] With this budget, the division finances promotional programs and publicity campaigns abroad, and facilitates the sharing of information among the different industries and companies involved. In 2013, to support the financial infrastructure of the industry, the Japanese government approved the Cool Japan Fund, a twenty-year public–private fund earmarked for overseas promotions via the Internet and other media platforms (e.g., the marketing of Japanese-style fashions such as Gothic Lolita through social media and other socially based mediums). As of October 2013, the fund is capitalized at JPY 39 billion.[13] According to Ibuki Hideki, director of the Creative Industries Division, this is to promote the export of Japan's creative industries such as anime, fashion, and food—entirely new fields for a ministry that only started supporting Japanese movie festivals in the 1980s. Ibuki, a career bureaucrat who confesses no special knowledge or interest in anime, noted that the Cool Japan promotion budget is rather limited and not sufficient to have a strong impact on Japan's anime sector.[14]

As in other industrial sectors, METI attempts to facilitate close communication with private companies and promoters as a way of invigorating the anime sector. According to Ibuki, the evolution of a cooperative and supportive business community in the content industries is key for global outreach. He would like to see more collaboration between various companies and more people becoming involved in the anime industry. But, in his opinion, the ministry does not yet take a proactive approach toward small companies because they believe that the initiatives should come from below: "We don't try to persuade or push them to do so. If they want and need help they can come to us."[15] The initiatives that the ministry does advance more enthusiastically are PR campaigns for international events. In July 2012, for example, METI announced that it would work together with private firms to establish miniature versions of the trendy Tokyo districts Shibuya and Harajuku in a few foreign cities to boost the export of Japanese fashion and other cultural trends.[16] Since 2013, METI has also supported anime festivals in Singapore and Jakarta with the collaboration of Dentsu and other media-related firms.

Cultural policy is the responsibility of MOFA, which, together with the Japan Foundation, is charged with the international dimensions of cultural policy. In its publications and reports, the Japan Foundation routinely highlights Japan's cultural capabilities and discusses the popularity of Japanese contemporary culture overseas. In April 2003, for example, the annual report of the Japan Foundation's International Exchange Research Committee underscored the potential of Japanese culture to draw a sympathetic "national image" of Japan and to assist its overseas diplomatic aims, emphasizing the rising importance of new powers in today's diplomacy and characterizing them as "soft power" (Japan Foundation 2003). In November 2012, the MOFA-supported journal *Gaikō* (Diplomacy) featured a special issue dedicated to Japan's cultural diplomacy and soft power, with many of the articles referring to the worldwide popularity of anime and calling on the government to utilize it in Japan's growing international role.

Encouraged by its own assessments, in 2005 MOFA allocated JPY 1.16 billion (approximately US$94 million) to the promotion of Japanese animation and pop music in China. In 2006, the amount was almost tripled to JPY 3.11 billion, a move meant to preclude any further deterioration in China's image of Japan following an upsurge in anti-Japanese sentiment sparked by Prime Minister Koizumi Junichirō's visit to the disputed Yasukuni Shrine.[17] In the same year, MOFA decided to allocate additional funds to finance the export of Japanese animation to developing countries as a part of the Official Development Assistance (ODA) program (an annual budget of JPY 10 million had already been designated in previous years). The justification for these additional funds was that the animation programs would improve the perception of Japan in developing countries.[18] Arai Yūsuke, a MOFA top official in charge of public diplomacy, noted that popular culture, especially anime, is now considered an effective vehicle for winning the hearts and minds of young people in different parts of the world who otherwise could not have been approached. In this context, the effectiveness of anime lies precisely in its ability to reach people without the mediation of the state or any other agenda-setting mechanism such as the mass news media. The problem, however, is how to connect anime's cultural appeal with the government's policy goals without being seen as too interventionist. Arai himself expressed doubts regarding the efficacy of this sort of cultural diplomacy.[19]

Another indication of the Japanese government's interest in the diplomatic advantages of popular culture, especially anime and manga, is the support of recent Japanese prime ministers. In December 2004, then–prime minister Koizumi Junichirō established a think tank to examine how the government should promote cultural diplomacy. During his election campaign in September 2005, his successor, Abe Shinzō, declared pop culture to be one of Japan's strengths. Later that the same year, the Prime Minister's Advisory Institute on Foreign Relations recommended manga and animation diplomacy. This comprised international events to promote Japanese culture, an International Manga Award for outstanding foreign manga artists, and a joint study group of bureaucrats and industry personnel. Prime Minister Asō Taro, an alleged fan of manga, continued this position and supported the designation of Japanese anime characters as cultural ambassadors, as described earlier in this chapter.

In short, it is evident that support for anime within the content industries sector has been gaining bureaucratic momentum and is increasingly considered a legitimate arena for state intervention, although, as will be discussed below, very few of the initiatives have actually materialized. METI, which for most of the postwar period showed very little interest in anime, has emerged as a major player, even establishing a special division for its promotion. For MOFA officials, anime offers a new platform for reaching fresh international audiences and increasing interest in Japan, but they do not really know how to best exploit it as part of public policy. If, in the 1990s and 2000s, it was the success of anime in Western markets, particularly in the United States and France, that caught the attention of the Japanese government, in recent years it is Asian markets that are being seen as the potential for the expansion of Japan's content industries. According to Mihara Ryōtarō, in spite of copyright concerns, the Chinese market, together with smaller hubs in Southeast Asia such as Singapore and Indonesia, are viewed as the future markets for Japanese anime, and are thus being targeted by the ministry's Cool Japan policy.[20]

Anime Policy: An Industry Perspective

> Bureaucrats are smart people, right? I wish they would use their heads!
>
> —Kogake Shintarō[21]

While the government has initiated programs to support the anime sector and its attitude toward content industries has become more proactive than ever, there is much disagreement within Japan's anime industry about the effectiveness of this policy. Among the anime industry personnel we interviewed, there was general agreement that government policy is barely felt and has not, as yet, been proven to be significant or constructive to the industry. In particular, there was a wide consensus that (1) the government does not really help, and (2) there is little that the state can actually do. In the candid words of our interviewees, the government does not know where to invest its money and has no concrete policy.

Kogake Shintarō, executive producer at Dentsu, admitted that while government ministries and agencies have indeed become more involved in Japan's anime market, they do not know how to approach this sector, lack a true vision for advancing Cool Japan in the world, and are experimenting with various initiatives rather than initiating or leading new policy.[22] This, he believes, is due to lack of experience and, more fundamentally, a lack of enthusiasm for promoting anime and giving it higher priority on the state's agenda. Sonobe Yukio, senior director at Fuji Creative Corporation, argued that government support for the anime industry is "not really felt" and "not yet helpful."[23] He indicated that in recent years the government has been trying to tap into the wave of anime success of the 1990s and 2000s, but, he stressed, there is a difference between being involved and actually having a constructive input on the anime sector. Similarly, Shinoda Yoshihiko, managing director of Fujiko Pro, does not have high regard for state support of the industry, accusing the government of not understanding the business: "They have the money but not the knowledge," he lamented angrily.[24]

Ironically, this criticism is shared by Mihara Ryōtarō, who was responsible for Japan's "cool" promotion. Mihara claimed that there is not enough familiarity or intimacy between METI officials and the anime sector, and therefore government officials do not know much about this sector. METI officials do not "read" the market well (*kūki ga yomenai*) and do not understand the conditions and circumstances that private companies face.[25] According to Mihara, there has been no leadership, and anime-related policies are going in the wrong direction. In his opinion, policies should not be long-term or strategically constructed but rather should enhance the relations between anime producers and fans, thus ensuring that new anime productions are interesting.

In Shinoda Yoshihiko's opinion, the government can still play a constructive role in Japan's anime business by assisting the industry in cultivating new business trajectories and new platforms for circulation and consumption, such as the development of digital comics (*denshi manga*).[26] This, he believes, requires closer communication and consultation between the government and the private sector. Mukai Junichirō, director of licensing and media development at Sega, the Japanese multinational video games developer and publisher, suggested that besides financial support, the government could assist the industry by developing the infrastructure and streaming technology "to establish a server farm in Tokyo to make it the center of connection for the whole world."[27]

Shichijō Naohiro, a senior research fellow at the National Institute of Science and Technology Policy, a Professor at Tokyo University of Technology and one of Japan's leading experts on the anime industry, believes that it is imperative to foster better communication between state agencies and anime producers, as the process of making anime involves constant negotiation and consultation regarding both artistic and executive decisions. Developing anime takes a long time, and there is no guarantee that an anime series will be successful once it goes out to the market. Shichijō believes that during the gestation period of an anime series, consultation and assistance from the state, both financial and administrative, could help reduce uncertainty and thus encourage anime producers to proceed with their ideas, in particular regarding the marketing of anime abroad, an area in which Japanese anime producers have very little knowledge or expertise.[28]

According to content producer Sakurai Takamasa (2009: 168–80), who has researched the reception of anime in different parts of the world, the advantages of what he calls "anime culture diplomacy" are twofold: it attracts young consumers around the world and makes them interested in Japan, and, at the same time, it enhances a new and creative "Japan brand" recognizable through dynamic, contemporary culture. He sees the challenge of cultural diplomacy not in the appeal to people who already like anime but rather to the people who do not. For this reason, he argued that Japan's cultural diplomacy should move away from organizational support of the industry in the form of infrastructure or finances and toward a better understanding of the needs of anime consumers around the world by the dispatch of state officials and Japanese embassy staff to interact with fans and learn about them (2009: 202–9).

Some of our interviewees indicated that intellectual property is another field where government help could be beneficial. One of the factors discouraging Japanese anime producers from expanding into global markets is the problem of online piracy, which is particularly rampant in

China, as discussed earlier. The problem is not only the abundancy of online piracy and the lax police enforcement of copyright violations but also the fact that it is technologically easier to download and watch anime series illegally than to buy them online legally. The government could offer practical assistance by raising this issue with foreign governments and even exercising pressure to regulate the markets. According to Sonobe Yukio of Fuji Creative Corporation, the government could initiate PR campaigns in places where anime has very little commercial presence, such as South America, Africa, and the Middle East, and in this way help the anime industry establish footing in new markets.[29] Miyagawa Daisuke, corporate officer at Polygon Pictures, one of Japan's most active anime studios, thinks that the government could assist anime expansion even in relatively familiar places such as the United States. He claimed that Japanese companies do not really understand the complexity of American society and thus need to rely on mediators.[30] Another practical way that the government could help, according to a few of our interviewees, is with the provision of legal support for Japanese anime producers when signing agreements with international distributors or teaming up with foreign companies. In such cases, the state's experience and knowledge of trade and industry-related negotiations with other countries and with multinational corporations could be used to serve the anime sector and reduce some of the anxiety and the cost of expanding into foreign markets.

There is one area, however, where it is believed that the government should not interfere, and that is in the content of the anime. Mihara Ryōtarō claimed that one of the reasons for the decline of the U.S. anime boom was that too many low-quality anime series were marketed in a short period of time.[31] Suga Chizuru, also a METI official, similarly emphasized that before devising a global marketing strategy, it is essential to ensure that Japanese studios are making high-quality and interesting anime. At the same time, however, this does not mean that the state should actively intervene in the content of anime.[32] Our interviewees all emphasized that the state should refrain from influencing content by actions such as censoring anime that contain "extreme" depictions of violence or sexual acts, or prioritizing anime products and genres that portray ostensibly "authentic" or "genuine" messages of Japanese culture. Such an approach, they believed, would risk "killing the cool." According to Wada George, president and CEO of Wit Studio, animators should not try so hard to make "cool" anime from the outset, because no "cool" will come out of it. He claimed that anime producers must be encouraged to think creatively and make interesting anime stories and visuals, and that these may subsequently turn out to be "cool." But asking them to make something "cool" from the start makes no sense to him.[33] In other words, the vitality and uniqueness of anime is the product of its uncontrollable and informal nature and not of intentional policy.

As reflected in our interviews, in spite of the Japanese government's engagement in the promotion of the anime sector, there is wide distrust and very little appreciation of its actions. Even in the eyes of state bureaucrats, the encouraging attitude of the Japanese government toward the anime sector, meant to spur development and its globalization, is simply not enough. There is also a sense that the government has entered the game too late. According to Amagi Yukihiko, a top executive at NHK Enterprise, METI has undeniably been flying the Cool Japan flag—but only now, years after the anime boom reached its peak. It is thus time for new thinking.[34] As summarized by JETRO official Toyonaga Mami, anime productions, as well as other forms of contemporary culture and fandom, should be seen as economically important and thus afforded professional help rather than merely being officially applauded. For Toyonaga, who lived in France and has an understanding of French bureaucracy, "pressing 'like' on Facebook is not enough . . . [state officials] need to do their work passionately like the French government."[35]

Conclusion: State Involvement in Japan's Anime Industry

As we have seen, the market-led globalization of Japanese anime has ignited government interest in anime. Anime has become a global commodity on which the government tried to capitalize for its Cool Japan policy. Government initiatives to assist Japan's anime industry establish a better footing on the world stage have so far been limited to launching public relations campaigns and raising concerns about the damages inflicted by illegal downloading of anime in many parts of the world. METI and MOFA have emerged as the two central government players, each emphasizing different aspects of anime promotion: anime as an economic commodity and as a diplomatic harbinger, respectively. As both anime personnel and government officials have emphasized, however, the government is not the force driving the globalization of anime, nor does it have a significant role in the production and marketing of anime. The government's attitude has instead been responsive and accommodating, attempting to tap into anime's success as a mainstream genre for economic and diplomatic purposes. In other words, the Japanese state views anime and other forms of popular culture as a means to revitalize the economy and boost the country's image abroad. Thus, anime should be seen as one of the mediums being employed by the state to further its interests both domestically and abroad.

According to Ibuki Hideki, it is still too early to evaluate the results of the Cool Japan campaign abroad. Events are scheduled to continue through the next few years and are still in their experimental stage, and thus they can, he believes, be seen as only markers of future government strategy. In the interview, he hinted that a few connections have been established between Japanese companies and local promoters in various international locations, but he did not elaborate.[36] Some anime companies may have benefited from this new policy. Miyagawa Daisuke of Polygon Pictures, for example, indicated that they are simply happy with the money given to them by the government as another source of funding.[37] While it is possible that some companies have started doing business thanks to the Cool Japan campaign, the one company that has definitely profited from the campaign is Dentsu, Japan's biggest advertising company and the fourth largest in the world, which was assigned to manage and promote the campaign. Dentsu has received much of the government budget to run the campaign and has, furthermore, enhanced its position as a bridge for Japanese companies wanting to do business abroad. Dentsu is certainly more experienced than any of the government ministries in designing commercial-driven campaigns for foreign markets, but it is perhaps a little risky to depend on Dentsu alone for promoting Japan's anime abroad.

It was interesting to note that in many of the interviews we conducted with both Japanese government officials and industry personnel, the Korean government's support of Korean popular culture was cited as both an example and a challenge. While the wave of Korean contemporary culture, known as *Hallyu,* swept the world a full decade after Japanese contemporary culture did, the Korean government got on board straightaway and is more strategic and proactive in advancing the expansion of Korean cultural industries abroad (Otmazgin 2011). Our interviewees saw the Korean government as an example of how the Japanese government should support the country's creative industries. Ibuki Hideki even admitted that sometimes they just "basically copy what the Koreans are doing."[38] In another interview, we were told that the Cool Japan division was established in order not to lose out to the Koreans (*makenaiyōni*). In this interview, he also acknowledged that Korea is doing a better job at cultivating and distilling creativity from individuals and conceded that this is something that METI needs to improve on.

Amagi Yukihiko of NHK sees the role of the Korean government as key to understanding the phenomenal success of Korean television dramas. He claimed that the Korean government, unlike the Japanese government, offers direct assistance to the industry by removing logistical and legal impediments to the broadcasting of television content both domestically and abroad.[39] Ishikawa Shinichirō—founder and representative director of Studio Gonzo—was even more blatant when he explained how the Korean government has managed through subsidies and tax rebates to position Korean television drama as industry leaders throughout Asia and even encouraged Japanese investment in Korean productions.[40] The Korean example was indeed highlighted in many of the interviews as a country whose government acts more strategically and involves the private sector in its work; in Japan, it is the market that is strong, whereas in Korea it is the government.

In spite of the appreciation given to the Korean government in its promotion of Korean popular culture abroad, some of our interviewees nonetheless emphasized that a too-interventionist policy, especially in the content of anime, is problematic and can be counterproductive. Highly institutionalized arrangements, especially those designed by the state, will never be able to catch up with or accommodate the dynamism of cultural industries and the volatilities of cultural markets. The government, it was felt, should keep a free sphere where culture can cultivate and cultural innovations can evolve and interact naturally with the established industry while at the same time supporting the organizational infrastructure that translates cultural creativity into a commodified set of marketable products. This can be done by helping anime studios connect with international distributors, offering legal support, providing the seed money for new anime production and tax incentives for investment in anime, and encouraging foreign investment in Japan's anime industry. Much of Japan's anime creativity is cultivated and commodified in small studios by creative individuals, and sometimes even amateurs, and it is they who need more substantial support. The emphasis should thus be on stimulating the growth of small firms that are engaged in various anime productions and anime-related cultural commodification, and are embedded in the local economy but aspire to export their products and services abroad.

CONCLUSION

Anime Artistry, Creative Industries, and Global Business

We need to try and keep Japanese properties within the hands of Japanese companies, and tie with American companies such as Disney and Saban. We need to help create a movement and not only enjoy the occasional hit. I strongly believe that the current movement is really good, and I support and encourage American guys who are trying to imitate Japanese anime. It could lead to real success. Shūeisha, Shōgakukan, and Kōdansha could even become bigger than Disney. I would love to be part of this. My friends work there, so I can work with them.

—Ishikawa Shinichirō, founder and representative director of Studio Gonzo[1]

The End of the Anime Boom?

Twelve years ago, in their in-depth study of anime in the United States, Ōtsuka and Ōsawa (2005) drew a pessimistic view of the future of Japan's anime production and its export to the United States, which, according to them, was subject to a lack of visionary productions, bad marketing decisions, and ineffective state policy. They argued that South Korean and Chinese animation productions were likely to take over Japanese productions in the near future thanks to the Korean market's growing creativity and dynamism and the Chinese market's size and capacity (2005: 278). Fast-forwarding to the present, their prediction has not yet materialized. Some might argue that given more time it will, but we believe that there is more resilience in the anime industry than Ōtsuka and Ōsawa attribute to it.

For one, Ōtsuka and Ōsawa's prediction ignores the huge pool of creative professionals making manga and anime in Japan and the ability of the Japanese market to constantly generate new genres and images to feed a consumer-driven domestic demand—a process cultural anthropologist Ian Condry (2013) has called "collaborative creativity." Indeed, from our interviews with industry professionals, a more complicated picture emerged. In 2011, Sam Register revealed that his experience with outsourcing work to Korean studios has so far been only partially successful and that they still do not reach the same level as Japanese studios. The Japanese studios "are not cheap but there is plenty of available talent."[2] Daryl Surat, an American anime expert, used stronger words. According to him, commercial Korean and Chinese anime productions are still, as they have been for many years, at the stage of "copying" Japan rather than inventing new ideas themselves. He gave the example of the Korean animated film *Taekwon V* (1976), which is basically a Korean version of the Japanese animated series *Mazinger Z* (1972–73). Dedicated Internet fan sites list many more plagiarisms, particularly from the 1970s and 1980s. But another more recent and less direct example of an emulation of Japanese animation is the Korean animated movie *Sky Blue* from 2003, which is based on themes and storytelling that have long existed in Japanese anime. The technical and visual parts of the movie are advanced, but it lacks creativity. A large number of Chinese animated series and movies also suspiciously resemble Japanese anime. A few recent examples include the plot and character design of the 2006 Chinese animation *Chess King*, which seems to be based on the Japanese anime *Yugioh!*; the 2007 series *Big Mouth DoDo*, which borrows the voice acting and style of *Crayon Shin-Chan*; and the 2008 series *Golden Hero*, which bears a striking resemblance to *Ultraman*. According to Surat, Korean and Chinese producers still need to develop their own original features.[3]

It is only fair to point out here that while the Korean commercial animation industry has yet to make its mark on the global commercial animation industry, in recent years Korean artistic animation shorts have won prestigious prizes in various international animation festivals. In 2014, for example, Joung Yumi's *Love Games* and Jeong Dahee's *Man on the Chair* won the top prizes for short films at the Animafest Zagreb 2014 and the Annecy International Animated Film Festival, respectively. It is possible that the Korean animation industry is going through a process previously witnessed in other popular culture fields, such as television dramas and pop music, which initially derived huge influence from Japan, only later developing their own recognizable characteristics, becoming major export industries to other countries. As explained by Eugene Kang,[4] founder and president of Synergy Media, one of Korea's successful media companies, compared with Japanese and American studios, Korean animation studios are very small and from the very beginning must reach out to global markets, establish global links, and cultivate synergy between different media fields. According to him, this is the only way for Korean animation to survive between the other two giants and develop its own identity.

It is important to remember that anime had a strong normative impact on the animation industries of other countries in Asia, the United States, and beyond, and thus when considering the future of anime in the global market, it should not be evaluated in terms of its commercial success alone. Anime represents a recognizable model for other productions, and its global appeal has extended beyond its sales record. In a few Asian countries (China, Korea, Singapore, Thailand, and Indonesia), Japanese studios, and not Walt Disney, are the model to learn from, and a vast range of adaptation and imitation is indeed taking place. In Asia, many animators gained their first experience in animation while working for companies that collaborated with Japanese firms as subcontractors. Local animators hired for this purpose subsequently came to view the Japanese productions as the model and the standard. This is the case in Thailand, where the media industry in the 1990s and early 2000s consciously started to build its own anime productions according to the Japanese model, and even sent representatives to Japan to learn about the industry. The growth of Thailand's television market during that period created a demand for both imported television content and television production know-how. Kantana, Thailand's biggest television production company, initially imitated Japanese anime series and later sent their producers on study tours in Japan. This has given rise to various new local productions based on Japanese formats (Otmazgin 2013: 140–41). Similarly, in Korea and Hong Kong, the consumption of Japanese anime series in the 1970s and 1980s among young people made it a mainstream phenomenon. Local animators were heavily influenced by the aesthetic perceptions, production techniques, and visual framing of Japanese anime, and subsequently incorporated them in their work (Chow 2013; Koh 2013).

At the same time, however, we should not ignore the fact that Japan's anime industry is far from its heyday of the 1990s and 2000s when anime series massively expanded to global markets and generated substantial revenues for the Japanese economy. The U.S. market, as we have shown in this book, soon became oversaturated with low-quality anime, and the boom rebounded, forcing the Japanese anime studios to refocus on the domestic market and American anime promoters to search for other opportunities. Nowadays, the Japanese anime industry is finding it difficult to reconfigure itself in the face of global challenges and to maintain a sustainable position in the United States. Many Japanese studios are reluctant to invest in an expansion strategy, the marketing pathways into the American market have narrowed, and the government's attempts to encourage the growth of the anime industry have so far been uncoordinated and mostly ineffective (chapter 5).

The Japanese case raises a series of theoretical and analytical questions that go beyond the case of Japan's anime industry and touch on the way that global creative industries operate across time. Specifically, it highlights the social and organizational mechanisms that produce and disseminate commodified culture, the creative forces that make the industry, the new genres that are being developed as part of the creative and organizational input, the role of transnational agencies in delivering content, and the state attempts at intervention. In short, findings from the specific context of Japanese anime can help us understand similar developments in other parts of the world and the actual workings of globalization in the creative industries.

In what follows, we reevaluate the anime industry's position in the global market, discuss its achievements, and outline the opportunities it lost. Our conclusion suggests that the rise and fall of the anime boom in the United States should be viewed as a reflection of the upheaval of the media convergence revolution, and that the future of the anime industry in the global arena, and possibly also in the domestic market, lies in the industry's ability to restructure itself as a global player.

The Collision of Old and New Media

According to a JETRO industrial report from 2005 (itself based on a METI report from 2003), around 60 percent of the anime shown worldwide at the time was made in Japan. During our interviews we heard much criticism of this inflated data, but even if the actual data is smaller, there is no doubt that products of the anime industry have had a significant presence in the global market of television animation for several decades. These products went somewhat incognito (at least in most countries where they aired) until the late 1990s, but since then, their Japanese identity has been celebrated with much fanfare. It remains intriguing that much of this was accomplished despite the fairly passive attitude of most players in the anime industry. Rather, it was accomplished thanks to a few non-Japanese entrepreneurs who recognized the potential of anime and were able to successfully localize it. A new generation of entrepreneurs, such as Ishikawa of Studio Gonzo, joined the anime industry in the 1990s, because they understood that the digitalization of media was revolutionizing the production and distribution of anime and that what they were seeing was only the tip of the iceberg. But even though they could detect an upcoming revolution, it was very hard to predict its outcome. Others, such as Sam Register (from a producer's standpoint) and Glen Murakami (from, mostly, an animator's standpoint), had an intimate knowledge of the American market and knew how to localize anime to accommodate American tastes and target the right audience.

Since at least the mid-1990s, media and public communication have indeed been undergoing a significant evolution. This evolution is centered on the advent of social media, where cultural content is delivered and consumed almost instantly, coupled with the dissemination of accessible devices for consuming culture such as laptops and smartphones. These processes limit the state's ability to regulate the multidirectional movement of cultural content and have encouraged the cultural industries—as well as media entrepreneurs and promoters—to seek new marketing routes and develop new models for profiting. As media scholar Jim Mc-Namara described it:

Convergence, digitization, hybridization, disintermediation, disaggrega-tion, while important, are predominantly processes of reforming and rear-ranging content and practices. Meanwhile, out of the stew of convergent media ecosystems and colliding commercial, social, and cultural practices, new forms of media and communication practice are emerging with char-acteristics, properties and potentialities unlike their predecessors. (2010: 7)

And yet, refocusing on the globalization of anime, this book is not only about the new forms of anime that have emerged in the past two decades in the context of Japanese–American cultural relations but about what is happening to old or traditional media and communication practices that are still struggling to adapt to this convergence, digitization, hybridiza-tion, disintermediation, and disaggregation. More specifically, the pro-cesses described in this book should be understood as reflecting what me-dia scholar Henry Jenkins (2006: 2) has referred to as the collision of old and new media within the phenomenon of media convergence, where grassroots and corporate media intersect and the power of the media pro-ducer and media consumer interact in unpredictable ways. It is thus that the perspective we have adopted in this book by looking at the global ani-mation industry, and within it at the Japanese anime industry, may pro-vide insights into the struggles of the television industry in general but also the music, radio, film, and publishing industries. Traditional media have lost their long-held monopoly over production and broadcasting. The old ways of doing business are not as profitable as they used to be, induc-ing feelings of malaise or crisis among leading figures in the different tra-ditional media industries. Summing it up somewhat dramatically in his much-quoted lecture, Steven Spielberg argued in December 2013 that an "implosion" in the film industry is inevitable.[5]

We showed in chapter 2 that the American television animation in-dustry with its mega animation studios has greater durability than its Japanese counterpart. This is because of its well-established local and global traditional television distribution infrastructures, which are still very productive, and also because most of its titles (for television) are for children whose viewing is under adult supervision and is television- rather than Internet-based. The Japanese anime industry, however, sticking mostly to its traditional domestic business models that rely on local television broadcasting and local merchandizing rather than the global market, is not doing so well these days in terms of generating profit and expanding abroad. It is fortunate for the anime industry that although the local market in Japan is shrinking due to the rapid aging of Japanese society, it can still rely on this traditional business model thanks to a very strict copyright system and ever-compliant consumers.

A stroll through the prime location at Shibuya's Tsutaya books, music, and movie store in 2016—with its seven floors above ground and two floors underground, most of them devoted to the sale and rental of new and old CDs and DVDs—showcases Japan's ongoing conservative business model. Japan is probably the last place on earth where the CD and DVD market is still lucrative. This may inspire in the foreign visitor renewed appreciation for the determined support of Japan's creative industries by Japanese consumers. However, in the "brave new world" where information and creative media are at consumers' fingertips around the world, Japanese consumers, who have been taught since the 1980s to view themselves as living in an advanced "information society" (*jōhōshakai*) (Castells 2000; Skov and Moeran 1995: 11), are at a great disadvantage— to say the least. One wonders how much longer these circumstances can endure.

The digitalization of media was an opportunity to replace the old monopoly on production, (global) broadcasting, and (global) distribution traditionally held by American media megacompanies with different paradigms and business models in which new, possibly smaller media companies and independent creators impact market trends and enable a more competitive environment. This could have been a particularly interesting opportunity for the Japanese anime industry. Unfortunately, Japanese players did not play an active role in shaping the ecosystem of the newly emerging global animation industry and therefore did not secure for themselves a leading position within it. As we have shown in this book, this was partly the result of an ambiguous attitude of the Japanese anime industry toward global markets, which were seen as both an opportunity but also a major risk.

Concurrently, over the past fifteen years, we have seen the emergence of new national animation industries (e.g., Philippines, Malaysia, Singapore, Vietnam, Thailand, India, Indonesia), the strengthening of national industries that had a history but that were not prominent in the global market (such as the Chinese animation industry), the intensification of international collaborations enabled by a greater mobility of talents, and, most important, a growing shift toward using the Internet, and more broadly social media, for distributing and consuming animation. In addition, we have more recently been witnessing how online streaming has become a prominent model for fighting Internet piracy and generating revenues. In all of these transformations, the Japanese players, with the exception of a handful of media companies/anime production companies, are falling behind. At most, they are—as we were told by some of our more critical Japanese interviewees—following market trends.

To delineate the urgency in transforming media business paradigms, we have shown that even the more resilient American animation industry is actively looking for new business models that would better fit the transformations of media consumption engendered by new technologies (chapters 2 and 4). We described how in 2013, DreamWorks, which unlike other major U.S. animation studios does not own its own distribution arm, signed a multiyear agreement with Netflix. This was a bold initiative designed to expand DreamWorks production and distribution worldwide. In 2014, *Bloomberg Businessweek* reported that while the world of online video, particularly content favored by younger users, has been built by tiny operations drawing huge audiences to low-budget works, more recently a steady stream of acquisitions has marked the arrival of big money to the YouTube market.[6] The names of the media companies that have put up the money is revealing: Disney bought Maker Studios, a supplier of online video content to YouTube, for US$500 million; DreamWorks Animation bought Awesomeness TV, a smaller competitor of Maker Studios, for US$117 million. It should come as no surprise by now that there are no Japanese names in this game.

Where, one might wonder, is the entrepreneurial spirit that drove many Japanese industries to go global prior to the early 1990s? It is too easy and impossibly apologetic to point out that competing in the global market of automobiles and electronics (two sectors that were dominated by Japanese firms in the 1980s and early 1990s) is in many ways simpler, more manageable, and more controllable than competing in the global market of IPs and content. As demonstrated by the example of Japan's Sony Corporation in the late 1980s, moving to the global market is a question of leadership (see chapter 3). Sony Corporation made the strategic decision to go beyond electronic appliances and expand its business to music, video games, motion pictures, and television in 1989 when it bought all of Coca Cola's entertainment holdings, becoming the owner of labels such as Columbia Pictures Entertainment and Tri-Star Pictures. Having made daring and risky acquisitions as well as outstanding managerial decisions, Sony thus established its U.S. subsidiary, Sony Picture Entertainment Inc., in 1991, which today is extremely influential in the global content market. It is no wonder that Sony Picture Entertainment Japan Inc. is the majority shareholder of Animax, the anime satellite television network, and a shareholder of Daisuki, an online anime streaming service—two daring business initiatives that we discussed earlier.

There are, however, two informed hypotheses that provide, in our opinion, some explanation for why the Japanese television anime industry was not able to profit enough from the opportunity presented by the digitalization of media. The first is that apart from a handful of outstanding examples, Japanese companies in the export sector did better in the global business environment prior to the 1990s because it was managed through trade, acquisitions of foreign assets, and investments. These strategies allowed Japanese companies total control of their overseas business and assets. Approaching the new millennium, the global business environment became more dependent on strategic alliances and collaborations, which require a more flexible, agile, and risk-taking approach that is foreign to Japanese corporate and business culture.

The second hypothesis suggests that to lead innovative business models, the Japanese anime industry should not only have ventured into the uncharted and risky territories of global content distribution but also should have reinvented itself from the core by revamping its organizational structure, organizational culture, and strategic priorities. For anime producers and members of anime production committees in Japan, a shift in focus to proactive expansion in the global market that goes beyond producing more anime series to increase supply would have necessitated a dramatic structural and cognitive change. It is not only a matter of deciding on a new business expansion strategy but accepting the notion that Japan's anime industry is undeniably part of the global market and should be oriented outward from the very beginning.

Animation May Be a Global Industry, Anime Is Not

In chapter 1, we described the tension between the business and creative aspects of the anime industry, echoing, or rather repeating Adorno's argument about the "perennial conflict between artists active in the culture industry and those who control it" (1991: 100–101). Indeed, this sort of tension exists not only in anime but also in many of the cultural industries where creativity is commodified and sold as part of corporate success and in the process unavoidably loses part of its dynamism and free spirit (Baker and Hesmondhalgh 2010; Bilton and Cummings 2010; Caves 2002). As for addressing anime within the context of a global animation industry, however, there seems to be not much conflict. Not only are most media entrepreneurs in Japan reluctant to review their global business strategies, likewise, creative talents in the industry do not see themselves as part of a global industry. As bluntly explained by Makihara Ryōtarō, a senior animator at Wit Studio (*Haru* [*Hal*] 2013, *Shingeki no kyojin* [*Attack on Titan*] 2013): "I don't care about which anime can sell better and about other commercial considerations, I just do what I personally think is interesting."[7] This reflects a general ambience. Almost none of our Japanese interviewees—animators, producers, scholars, or policymakers— had ever heard of the term "anime-inspired cartoon" (see chapter 4). Generally speaking, they expressed little interest or familiarity in television cartoons made outside of Japan. This echoes what we mentioned in chapters 1 and 3, namely, that unlike the interviewed artists and producers from Europe, North America, Israel, and even South Korea, Japanese animation artists and producers do not as a whole feel part of a global industry that can offer them opportunities for employment or sources of inspiration.

A comparison of the anime industry with the video game industry is illuminating in this context, proving that this situation is not an unavoidable predicament. Unlike the anime industry, which has always tended to consider the global market as nothing more than "plus alpha" (see chapter 2), the Japanese video game industry was seen after the 1980s as the epicenter of the global video game industry and culture, with Japanese designers gaining legendary status, Japanese game consoles setting the standards, and Japanese games ruling the lists of "Top 100 Games of All Times" (Kohler 2004). Since the early 2000s, however, Japan has been losing the grip it once held on the gaming world.[8] In contrast to anime, veterans of the video game industry, such as game creator Inafune Keiji (creator of *Mega Man* and *Dead Rising*), are highly critical of their home industry and are vigorously fighting to explore new models in an attempt to recover its former cutting-edge innovative spirit and global leadership.

The present discussion is not the place to delve into the technological and cultural challenges facing the Japanese video game industry in the global market, or its responses to these challenges. Suffice it to say that as in so many other Japanese industrial sectors (including the anime sector), amid the global decline of the Japanese video game industry there is a tendency among many Japanese video game producers to focus only or mostly on the local market. Meanwhile, however, newly devised strategies designed to reclaim the global dominance of the Japanese industry are also coming to the fore, as is a collective narrative on the struggle of the industry as a whole to snap out of its temporary stagnation and regain its rightful position as the spiritual home of video games. The sudden worldwide success of *Pokémon Go* in the summer of 2016, which generated substantial economic gains for Nintendo, is a recent indication that Japan's video game industry is still a major global player. It seems to us that the desire of the Japanese video game industry for global reach is enabled by its organizational structure and culture, and most important, by the strategic priorities of the people making up the industry who grew up seeing themselves as global players.

Seclusion and Creativity?

Anime visual styles, imageries, and storytelling techniques have now become part of the tool kit of animators the world over. This should suggest that anime products, visual styles, and storytelling techniques would no longer be marked as Japanese. And yet, this is not the case. From the industry point of view,[9] anime products and related techniques and styles still keep their distinct identity as made in, or at least originating from,

Japan. During our interview with Sam Register, he explained that as a producer he is developing 2D animation products and 3D animation products as well as anime products.[10] For him, anime products are a category on their own. Indeed, according to many in the global animation industry, anime is a medium, a genre, or a technique unto itself, distinguished from all other animations.

Beyond the business or the industry, from a cultural production point of view, although anime has become a transcultural style that is emulated in many ways (see chapter 4), it has not lost its Japanese identity—or at least not entirely. In many cases, anime influences are still adopted and interpreted as influences from Japan rather than as deterritorialized influences. Could it be that this distinctive mark of Japanese animation is the lingering result of the relative seclusion of the anime industry, which has created and is still creating unique products? In other words, could it be that the so-called Galapagosization of the anime industry has the wonderful result of nurturing uniquely creative Japanese animation products with a unique visual language? In line with these thoughts, in response to these critical times and to recover and find its vigor again, perhaps, as has been suggested to us by several of our Japanese interviewees, the anime industry should refocus its energy solely on the local market, repeating Japan's long history of cyclical cultural isolation that has resulted in some unique cultural heritages.

As described in this book, one obvious result of the contemporary seclusion of the anime industry is that these days many anime series are formulaic products designed for specific niche audiences (*otaku*), causing anime to further lose its global appeal and its connection to wider social and humanistic pulses. According to animator Makihara Ryōtarō, anime studios today are making fewer stories that depict universal values. However, he sees his mission as an animator to tell universal stories that can reach the hearts and touch the sensibilities of many people, both in and out of Japan, regardless of their cultural or social backgrounds. He wishes to make new anime without thinking too much about audience targeting, financial risks, the needs of the market, and other commercial considerations that put heavy constraints on the anime industry.[11]

Media scholar Marco Pellitteri observed that anime ceased to be universally popular when it abdicated its initial role, mission, and talent for telling intense stories about suffering, trauma, achievement, and heroism.

When anime series stopped addressing just the average, regular kids and teenagers and started giving all their attention to the *otaku* fringe (previously the minority), the basis of the new stories became narrow: *moe, kawaii,* sex-related puns, pseudo-philosophical discussions, millenarianism, and so on. According to Pellitteri, the appeal of anime always lay in the stories that were intense, dramatic, and rich in values but without any pedantry. The superb graphical aspects were of course important, as were the developed cinematic codes and dynamic visions, but these only complemented the story. In his harsh words: "Anime got far away from their original, huge audience in Japan and around the world and became (again) a show for niches. It is paradoxical, because anime were mainstream twenty years ago, and now anime companies *think* they are mainstream but they have stepped back to geek culture and fan culture. Exactly the opposite of what they wanted."[12] Cultural history provides us with an abundance of proof that cultural isolation means stagnation and decay (Diamond 1993). This process may be reflected as well in the increasing focus on the *otaku*-oriented market of anime in Japan. The rich history of Japanese anime is a history of cross-cultural interchanges that we have referred to as a "cultural ping-pong." The tendency toward seclusion in the anime industry today will have no positive creative effect, not even on the maintenance of the distinctive identity of anime as a separate medium. As has been argued before, it is when cultures interact that, even though they become more and more similar, diversity increases as well (Cowen 2004).

What Is Next?

Since the 1990s, the industrialized world has been undergoing a major transformation brought on by extensive digitalization, globalized information, and transnational telecommunication (Perez 2010). As with all techno-economic paradigm shifts, this one also disrupts old business models, industry structures, organizational frameworks, public policies, and, in our particular case, media regulations, including copyright issues, causing a process that economist Tyler Cowen (2004) has called "creative destruction." Specifically in the world of media, there have been major changes in the organization of cultural commodity production and consumption due to an increase in the utilization of alternative distribution channels invigorated by information technology and social media, resulting in a need for companies to revise their marketing strategies to accommodate these changes. On the other hand, technological changes have enabled many consumers to access cultural content through various media forms, such as viewing television content online and accessing pop music via social media. The Internet, in particular, has provided a new marketing avenue for content, which in turn has weakened the control of the established industry over its marketing (Otmazgin 2015: 81–83). Many Japanese industries—adept business players before this techno-economic shift—are having a hard time adapting to this new reality. Japanese cultural and media industries, which could have profited from the digital revolution by inventing competitive new media silk roads, are, at most, dragging along.

At the time of writing these last few lines, it remains to be seen whether the spectacular Japanese anime industry will manage to rise up to the present challenges and continue to play the major role it has been playing for several decades by expanding the boundaries of animation around the world. As we hope we have made clear throughout this book, we do not disregard cultural differences and cultural tastes as important criteria for global popularity. But in evaluating the reasons for the success of media products around the world, we see the processes of mediation and distribution as critical. In other words, the Japanese anime industry does not need to "Disneyfy" its products to compete successfully in the global arena; rather, it needs to find ways to shape and create global audiences for its locally grown products. To rejuvenate, the anime industry, replete with talent and skill, will, we believe, have to come up with innovative business models and reform industry structures and organizational frameworks. It will, in addition, need the support of a completely new approach to public policies, most urgently regarding the thorny issue of copyrights.

Notes

Introduction

1. Character-related data does not include the merchandising of the highly popular *Hello Kitty, Domo-kun, Power Rangers,* and *Transformers.*

2. Roland Kelts, interview, Baltimore, July 31, 2011.

3. For a definition of globalization, we follow Tomlinson (1999) who defined globalization as *complex connectivity* that is derived from the rapidly developing and ever denser network of interconnections and interdependencies that characterize modern social life. In this book, however, more often than using globalization, we use cultural globalization or the globalization of culture/media/content/anime. In so doing, we refer to the ways in which ideas, values, knowledge, and symbolic vehicles of meanings are transmitted across the globe and between cultures.

4. Creative industries, which are also referred to as cultural industries, have been variously defined since Adorno and Horkheimer coined the term "cultural industries" for their critique of mass society in their 1944 book *Dialectic of Enlightenment* (Adorno and Horkheimer 2007). We adopt a much more pragmatic definition for creative industries, coined by the British Council for U.K. international cultural relations and educational opportunities: the socioeconomic activities that trade with creativity, knowledge, and information. British Council, Creative Cities, http://creativecities.britishcouncil.org/creative-industries/what_are_creative_industries_and_creative_economy (accessed July 19, 2016).

5. Fansubs (short for fan-subtitled) are fan-translated versions of anime programs (as opposed to officially licensed translations done by professionals) and subtitled into a language other than the original. See Anime News Network http://www.animenewsnetwork.com/encyclopedia/lexicon.php?id=63, accessed April 22, 2017.

6. The Pokémon Company, Pokémon in Figures, http://www.pokemon.co.jp/corporate/en/data (accessed July 29, 2017).

7. Quoted in "Sony: Bad Strategy or Bad Management," *The Economist,* Mar. 10, 2005, http://www.economist.com/node/3738979.

8. We thank Marco Pellitteri for bringing this point to our attention.

9. *Animation: An Interdisciplinary Journal,* home page, http://www.uk.sagepub.com /journals/Journal201763 (accessed Dec. 2, 2014).

10. The first Comiket was an intimate event that drew about six hundred people (Yonezawa 1987: 75–88). It soon developed into a huge fan convention, which today draws nearly six hundred thousand people over three days, twice a year.

11. The nickname *otaku* is said to have been invented by Nakamori Akio in a 1983 editorial piece titled "Otaku no kenkyū 1" (A Study of *Otaku,* 1) in the manga magazine *Manga Burikko.* Nakamori suggested referring to these fans of drawn worlds as *otaku* instead of *mania,* the term that is usually used for describing enthusiastic fans in Japanese (*mania* derives from the English word "mania," but is closer in meaning to "maniacs"). According to Nakamori, *mania* does not evoke the unique characteristics of these fans, who are great experts in their topics of interest but lack social skills. Clearly demonstrating this social awkwardness among themselves, the fans commonly use the term *otaku,* which is a deferential, formal second-person pronoun. However, according to Murakami Takashi (2001: 62), the eccentric use of *otaku* as a colloquial second-person pronoun did not start due to a lack of social skills but as a sociolect in the anime *Chōjikū yōsai makurosu* (Super Dimensional Fortress Macross, created by Kawamori Shōji, directed by Ishiguro Noboru, Studio Nue, 1982). Hikaru Ichijo, the protagonist in the anime series, often uses the pronoun *otaku* when addressing others. Fans of the studio's work began using the term, and it entered common use among the fans who gathered at comic markets, fanzine meetings, and the all-night parties held before major anime movie releases.

12. We conducted three wide-scale surveys for this research. The first was conducted between 2009 and 2010 with the aim of producing a database of anime series that were commercialized in the United States or broadcasted on American television between 1993 and 2010. The second was conducted between 2009–2012 with the aim of producing a database of Japanese–American and Japanese–European collaborations in television animation projects that aired in the United States and in Europe between 1982 and 2011. The third was conducted between 2009–2015 with the aim of producing a database of anime-inspired cartoons produced around the world between the late 1990s until 2015.

13. "An Exclusive Interview with Glen Keane," interview by Michael J. Lee, *Radio-Free.com,* Oct. 24, 2010, http://movies.radiofree.com/interviews/tangled_glen_keane .shtml.

Chapter 1

1. Sam Register, interview, Los Angeles, Apr. 4, 2011. At the time, Register was executive vice president at Warner Bros. Animation.

2. *Teen Titans* (coproducer, 2003); *Hi Hi Puffy Ami Yumi Show* (creator and executive producer, 2004), *Ben Ten* (executive coproducer, 2005); *ThunderCats* (executive producer, 2011). He is also a coproducer of the anime version of *The Powerpuff Girls: Demashita! Powerpuff Girls Z* (2006).

3. For an account of the Japanese television animation productions that preceded *Astro Boy,* see the introduction to this book.

4. Some of these iconic television series, such as *Buck Rogers,* were based on earlier comic strips (1928–). These comic strips arrived in Japan and influenced manga writers in the immediate postwar period. The ensuing American-inspired manga works subsequently inspired the 1970s science fiction (SF) boom in anime.

5. "George Lucas talks about the influence of Akira Kurosawa on Star Wars," http://www.youtube.com/watch?v=3eMvSjDZYb4 (accessed Aug. 22, 2011).

6. Iwabuchi has been widely quoted since introducing the keyword *mukokuseki* to refer to non-Japaneseness as a strategic approach to promote the marketability of anime over the years. Although some have challenged his approach (Pellitteri 2011: 62), in a recent interview from May 2014, Wada George, producer at Production I.G and president of I.G port subsidiary Wit Studio, confirmed that *mukokuseki* is indeed a market strategy for assuring exportability in the anime industry.

7. Matthew Chozick and Akane Suzuki, "Hiroki Azuma: The Philosopher of 'Otaku' Speaks," *Japan Today,* Oct. 3, 2011, http://www.japantoday.com/category/arts -culture/view/hiroki-azuma-the-philosopher-of-otaku-speaks.

8. The anthology included *Demon Dragon of the Heavens Gaiking* (*Daikū maryū gaikingu,* created by Nagai Gō and directed by Katsumata Tomoharu, 1976), *Planet Robo Danguard Ace* (*Wakusei robo dangādo ēsu,* created by Matsumoto Reiji and Kobayashi Dan, directed by Katsumata Tomoharu, 1977), *Getter Robo G* (*Gettā robo jī,* created by Nagai Gō and Ishikawa Ken, directed by Katsumata Tomoharu, 1975), *UFO Robot Grendizer* (*UFO robo gurendaizā* or *Gurendaizā,* created by Nagai Gō, directed by Katsumata Tomoharu, 1975–77), *Science Fiction Saiyuki Starzinger* (*Esu efu saiyūki sutājingā,* created by Matsumoto Reiji, directed by Serikawa Yugo, 1978).

9. The two series were *Beast King GoLion* (*Hyakujūō goraion,* created by Tōei staff and directed by Taguchi Katsuhiko, 1981) and *Armored Fleet Dairugger XV* (*Kikō Kantai Dairagā Fifutīn,* created by Tōei staff and directed by Morishita Kozo, 1982).

10. *Robotech* is a space opera-*mecha* American cartoon. It was created by the television production and distribution company Harmony Gold together with the Japanese animation company Tatsunoko Production by combining three different anime series that were originally produced collaboratively with, or entirely by Tatsunoko: *The Super Dimension Fortress Macross* (*Chōjikū yōsai makurosu,* created by Kawamori Shōji, directed by Ishiguro Noboru, 1982), *Super Dimension Cavalry Southern Cross* (*Chōjikū kidan sazan kurosu,* created by Tatsunoko staff and directed by Hasegawa Yasuo, 1984), and *Genesis Climber Mospeada* (*Kikō sōseiki mosupīda,* created by Aramaki Shinji and Kakinuma Hideki and directed by Yamada Katsuhisa, 1983). *Captain Harlock and the Queen of a Thousand Years* was a space opera American cartoon also created by Harmony Gold, partnered this time with Tōei Animation. The series was created by combining two series produced by Tōei Animation, both created by Matsumoto Reiji: *The New Bamboo Cutter Tale: Queen Millenia* (*Shin taketori monogatari: Sennen Joō,* directed by Nishizawa Nobutaka, 1981) and *Space Pirate Captain Harlock* (*Uchū kaizoku kyaputen hārokku,* directed by Rintaro, 1978).

11. See Emru Townsend (1995: 2). Also available in *The Critical Eye,* http://purpleplanetmedia.com/eye/film/akira.php (accessed July 15, 2015).

12. The interview with Alex Orrelle was conducted by skype while he was in Australia on Aug. 23, 2011.

13. http://www.storyboardpro.com/exosquad/exosquad_landing_01.html   (accessed Sept. 15, 2011). (The page was later removed and is only partly available as a cached page.)

14. http://groups.google.com/group/rec.arts.anime/browse_thread/thread /a54afcb1b5844395/34beb481026001eb?#34beb481026001eb (accessed Sept. 15, 2011).

15. "An Exclusive Interview with Glen Keane," interview by Michael J. Lee, *RadioFree .com,* Oct. 24, 2010, http://movies.radiofree.com/interviews/tangled_glen_keane.shtml.

16. Shinoda Yoshihiko, interview, Tokyo, Aug. 21, 2013.

17. *Box Office Mojo,* http://www.boxofficemojo.com/movies/?id=pokemon1.htm. (accessed Aug. 22, 2015).

18. From the mid-1980s, a number of U.S.-based Japanese and American companies were established for the specific purpose of opening licensing and distribution channels for Japanese animation in the American market, on television and through direct sale of VHS tapes and DVDs. Some examples include Streamline Pictures (1988–2002), VIZ Media (1986–), U.S. Renditions (1987–mid-1990s), AnimEigo (1988–), Central Park Media (1990–2009), ADV Films (1992–2009), Funimation Production (originally Funimation Entertainment, 1994–), Urban Vision Entertainment Inc. (1996–), Bandai Entertainment (1998–2012), Synch-Point (2001–8), and Geneon Entertainment USA (originally Pioneer Entertainment, 2003–7). At the time this book was written many of these companies were defunct.

19. Sam Register, interview, Los Angeles, Apr. 4, 2011.

20. Berthe Lotsova, interview, Tel Aviv, Aug. 4, 2013.

Chapter 2

1. "The Anime Biz," *Bloomberg Businessweek,* June 26, 2005, http://www.business week.com/stories/2005-06-26/the-anime-biz.

2. Alex Martin, "Future of 'Anime' Industry in Doubt: Money, Success Elude; Outsourcing, Piracy Abound," *Japan Times: News,* Mar. 9, 2009, http://www.japantimes.co .jp/news/2009/03/04/national/future-of-anime-industry-in-doubt/#.VSDslO6UfIU.

3. See chapter 1, note 29.

4. One interesting anecdotal story we heard during our interviews was that Disney executives were not happy with Pixar Studio's hugely successful creation *Up* (2009), which was a box office success and won an Academy Award, because it didn't have enough merchandisable characters.

5. Todd Spangler, "Toy and Game Company to Pay Mouse House up to $225M in Additional Star Wars Royalties, $80M Additional for Marvel," *Variety,* July 22, 2013, http://variety.com/2013/biz/news/hasbro-extends-disney-pact-for-marvel-star-wars-toys -and-games-1200566115/.

6. Michelle Orrelle, interview, Tel Aviv, July 22, 2013.

7. The best-known television content festivals are MIPTV (Marché International des Programmes de Télévision), held every year in Cannes, France, and its North American counterpart, NATPE (National Association of Television Program Executives). According to Ishikawa Shinichirō, it was at these content festivals in the early 2000s that new companies such as Funimation, Studio Gonzo, and A.D. vision set up booths as content

start-ups and began flaring the anime boom in the United States (interview, Tokyo, Feb. 15, 2012).

8. Michelle Orrelle, interview, Tel Aviv, July 22, 2013.

9. Leonard Devin, "'South Park' Creators Haven't Lost Their Edge," *CNN Money,* Oct. 27, 2006.

10. "Matt Stone, Trey Parker, Larry Divney 'Speaking Freely' Transcript," First Amendment Center, Mar. 1, 2012, http://www.webcitation.org/5mq7vTf06.

11. David M. Halbfinger, "'South Park' Creators Win Ad Sharing in Deal," *New York Times,* Aug. 27, 2007.

12. Bill Carter, "Comedy Central Makes the Most of an Irreverent, and Profitable, New Cartoon Hit," *New York Times,* Nov. 10, 1997.

13. Shichijō Naohiro, interview, Tokyo, Oct. 11, 2012.

14. Toyonaga Mami, interview, Tokyo, Feb. 10, 2012.

15. Tanaka Eiko, interview, Tokyo, Feb. 17, 2012.

16. Kogake Shintarō, interview, Tokyo, Feb. 16, 2012.

17. Wada George, interview, Haifa, May 26, 2014.

18. Wada George, interview, Haifa, May 26, 2014.

19. Amid Amidi, "DreamWorks Moves Forward with Big TV Animation Plans," *Cartoon Brew,* Aug. 1, 2013, http://www.cartoonbrew.com/tv/dreamworks-moves-forward -with-big-tv-animation-plans-86881.html.

20. Roxborough Scott, "MIPCOM: With 'Scandal' and 'Scooby-Doo' Germany Super RTL Takes on Disney Channel," *The Hollywood Reporter,* Aug. 10, 2013.

21. Berthe Lotsova, interview, Tel Aviv, Aug. 4, 2013. In 2016 Marathon Media merged with Banijay Group, a global production and distribution company.

22. Kogake Shintarō, interview, Tokyo, Feb. 16, 2012.

23. "Plus alpha" in this case means that the main revenues precalculated for an anime production business model are generated within Japan's domestic market, and anything beyond them (revenues from the international market) are considered alpha.

24. Mihara Ryōtarō, interview, Tokyo, Feb. 15, 2012, Tokyo. A few months after the interview, Mihara resigned from METI.

25. Sonobe Yukio, interview, Tokyo, Aug. 20, 2013.

26. Shinoda Yoshihiko, interview, Tokyo, Aug. 21, 2013.

27. Toyonaga Mami, interview, Tokyo, Feb. 10, 2012.

28. Ishikawa Shinichirō, interview, Tokyo, Feb. 15, 2012.

29. Sam Register, interview, Los Angeles, Apr. 4, 2011.

30. Matt Kamen, "How the Streaming Revolution Is Changing the Japanese Animation Industry," *WIRED.CO.UK,* May 9, 2012, http://www.wired.co.uk/news/archive /2012-05/09/anime-streaming.

31. Mihara Ryōtarō, interview, Tokyo, Oct. 15, 2012.

32. "Ask John: Will Anime Distribution Ever Go All Digital?," *AnimeNation,* Feb. 20, 2012, http://www.animenation.net/blog/2012/02/20/ask-john-will-anime-distribution -ever-go-all-digital/.

33. Nadav, "The Future of Anime in the US," *Anime Review,* Jan. 8, 2012, http:// animereviews.co/articles/the-future-of-the-u-s-anime-market/.

34. "Anime Distributor Launches Piracy Assault, Sues 1337 BitTorrent Users," *TorrentFreak,* Jan. 26, 2011, http://torrentfreak.com/anime-distributor-launches-piracy-assault-sues-1337-bittorrent-users-110126/.

35. David Lieberman, "Peter Chernin Takes Control of Anime Provider Crunchyroll," *Deadline Hollywood,* Dec. 2, 2013, http://deadline.com/2013/12/peter-chernin-takes-control-of-anime-provider-crunchyroll-646003/.

36. "Netflix to Run Original Animation Series from Dreamworks," *Entertainment Weekly,* June 17, 2013, http://www.ew.com/article/2013/06/17/netflix-dreamworks.

37. James Rainey, "DreamWorks Animation Expands Netflix Pact, Sets Guillermo del Toro 'Trollhunters' Series," *Variety,* Jan. 3, 2016, http://variety.com/2016/biz/news/dreamworks-animation-guillermo-del-toro-trollhunters-voltron-netflix-1201672250/.

38. Kamen Matt, "Netflix Announces First Original Anime Series: 'Perfect Bones'," *Wired,* Feb. 25, 2016.

39. Ishikawa Shinichirō, interview, Tokyo, Oct. 10, 2012.

Chapter 3

1. Sam Register, interview, Los Angeles, Apr. 4, 2011.

2. Tanaka Eiko, interview, Tokyo, Feb. 17, 2012.

3. Kogake Shintarō, executive producer at Dentsu, interview, Tokyo, Feb. 16, 2012.

4. "Tie-up" is a marketing strategy commonly used by Japanese companies to conjointly promote sound and image with the aim of commercializing devices through the use of various media forms, such as using anime images or catchy pop songs in automobile commercials.

5. Hasegawa Yoshihiko, chief strategic solution director at Dentsu Asia Pacific, interview, Singapore, Nov. 13, 2011.

6. Ishikawa Shinichirō, interview, Tokyo, Feb. 16, 2012.

7. Christine Yoo, interview, Seoul, Jan. 29, 2013.

8. Sasaki Hiroshi, interview, Singapore, Nov. 10, 2011. Since its establishment in 1995, Aniplex has been involved in more than 120 anime productions including *Fullmetal Alchemist, Blood: The Last Vampire, Persona 4: The Animation, Birdy the Mighty, Angel Beats!* and *Rurouni Kenshin.*

9. Fujisaku Junichi, interview, Tokyo, July 19, 2014.

10. Karasawa Ted, interview, Tokyo, Feb. 16, 2012.

11. Ishikawa Shinichirō, interview, Tokyo, Feb. 16, 2012.

12. Kogake Shintarō, interview, Tokyo, Feb. 16, 2012.

13. Amagi Yukihiko, interview, Tokyo, Feb. 16, 2012.

14. Anthony Kang, interview, Singapore, Nov. 13, 2011.

15. Sasaki Hiroshi, interview, Singapore, Nov. 10, 2011.

16. Daryl Surat, interview, Baltimore, July 31, 2011.

17. Toyonaga Mami, interview, Tokyo, Feb. 10, 2012.

18. Mihara Ryōtarō, interview, Tokyo, Oct. 15, 2012.

19. Marco Pellitteri, interview, Kyoto, Aug. 31, 2015.

20. Sam Register, interview, Los Angeles, Apr. 4, 2011.

21. Shichijō Naohiro, interview, Tokyo, Oct. 11, 2012.

22. Wada George and Makihara Ryōtarō, interview, Haifa, May 25, 2014.

23. Shimizu Yoshihiro, general manager of Tezuka Productions, interview, Tokyo, Oct. 15, 2012.

24. "Cross Media International to Bring Tezuka Productions' Animated Properties and Characters to North America," *Bloomberg News,* Jan. 16, 2014, http://www.bloomberg.com/article/2014-01-16/a7HkPx7A97XU.html.

25. According to Internet sources, in contrast to the four live-action theatrical films based on Marvel Comic characters produced prior to 1998, as many as around forty films have been produced from 1998 until today. See *Wikipedia,* s.v. "List of Films Based on Marvel Comic," last modified Mar. 30, 2017, http://en.wikipedia.org/wiki/List_of_films_based_on_Marvel_Comics (accessed Sept. 22, 2014).

26. For a fuller and more complex discussion of Marvel's economic rehabilitation, see Johnson 2013.

27. Ishikawa Shinichirō, interview, Tokyo, Feb. 15, 2012.

28. Tanaka Eiko, interview, Tokyo, Feb. 17, 2012.

29. Kogake Shintarō, interview, Tokyo, Feb. 16, 2012.

30. "TV TOKYO Enter into Gaming Partnership with iDreamSky," *Yahoo Finance,* Sept. 17, 2014, http://finance.yahoo.com/news/tv-tokyo-enter-gaming-partnership-140000454.html.

31. Sam Register, interview, Los Angeles, Apr. 4, 2011.

32. Kogake Shintarō, interview, Tokyo, Feb. 16, 2012.

33. Berthe Lotsova, interview, Tel Aviv, Aug. 4, 2013.

34. Kogake Shintarō, interview, Tokyo, Feb. 16, 2012.

Chapter 4

1. As with monsters in monster movies, which are most scary when not exposed to the camera, there are no actual Japanese in the movie.

2. Tim Long, commentary on "Fat Man and Little Boy," in *The Simpsons: The Sixteenth Season* (20th Century Fox, 2013), DVD.

3. Craig McCracken acknowledged the influence of anime on *The Powerpuff Girls,* although he also said that it was not a definite homage to anime. Interview by Keith Phipps, A.V. Club, June 21, 2000, http://www.avclub.com/article/the-powerpuff-girls-13665. In 2006, *The Powerpuff Girls* was reproduced in Japan as *Demashita! Pawapafu gāruzu zetto* (Powerpuff Girls Z). The anime was animated by Tōei Animation and co-produced by Cartoon Network Japan, Aniplex, and Tōei Animation.

4. "Episode 133: Inspired by Anime," http://player.fm/series/animation-aficionados-podcast-feed/episode-133-inspired-by-anime (accessed Apr. 2, 2014).

5. "Interview: *Avatar*'s Bryan Konietzko and Michael Dante DiMartino," by Eduardo Vasconcellos, IGN TV, Feb. 21, 2005, http://tv.ign.com/articles/818/818284p1.html.

6. This is a widescale survey conducted between 2009 and 2015 on anime-inspired cartoon series that were produced around the world from the late 1990s until 2015.

7. Berthe Lotsova, interview, Tel Aviv, Aug. 4, 2013.

8. Sam Register, interview, Los Angeles, Apr. 4, 2011.

9. "Aaron McGruder Sounds Off on the Boondocks–Season 2," *MovieWeb*, Oct. 9, 2007, http://www.movieweb.com/news/aaron-mcgruder-sounds-off-on-the-boondocks-season-2/lists.

10. "Interview with Aaron McGruder," A.V. Club, Oct. 6, 1999, http://www.avclub.com/articles/aaron-mcgruder,13622/.

11. The original movie directly addressed the recent memory of the Pacific War in Japan, and while the plot makes the rather problematic point of transferring the responsibility for provoking and enticing that very real war (i.e., the Pacific War) to the fictitious Black Ghost Organization, it also speaks firmly against war and its disastrous outcomes.

12. Darky iconography is the critical scholarly designation for drawing blacks with racist attributes including exaggerated lips, frizzy hair, and bulbous eyes (Martinez 2016: 199). American animated cartoons from the early 20th century to the 1960s featured countless characters that corresponded to this description (Berry and Berry 2015: 32).

13. *The Super Dimension Fortress Macross* is also important because, according to Murakami Takashi (2001: 62), this is the show that inaugurated the eccentric use of the word *otaku* as a colloquial second-person pronoun among Japanese anime geeks, a term that subsequently became part of their sociolect and eventually stuck as their subcultural nickname (see also, Daliot-Bul 2014: 150n15).

14. See chapter 1, note 10.

15. Fred Patten, "Cowboy Bebop: The Movie . . . At Last," *Animation World Network*, Mar. 31, 2003, http://www.awn.com/animationworld/cowboy-bebop-movie-last.

16. Simon Abrams, "*Cowboy Bebop:* Mushroom Samba," A.V. Club, Dec. 3, 2011, http://www.avclub.com/tvclub/cowboy-bebop-mushroom-samba-65906.

17. Charles Solomon, "American, Japanese Pop Culture Meld in *Afro Samurai:* Rap and Bushido? Anyone Who Knows RZA's Wu-Tang Clan Work Can See Why He Jumped at the Chance to Score *Afro Samurai*," *Los Angeles Times,* Feb. 2, 2009, http://articles.latimes.com/2009/feb/02/entertainment/et-afrosamurai2.

18. "5 New Animation Trends for 2015 that Will Change Everything," *Creative Bloq,* Dec. 11, 2014, http://www.creativebloq.com/3d/animation-trends-2015-111413522.

Chapter 5

1. "Foreign Ministry Details 'Japan House' Propaganda Initiative," *The Japan Times,* Jan. 5, 2015, http://www.japantimes.co.jp/tag/japan-house; Inada Tomomi, "'Cool Japan' to Provide Solutions for Global Problems," *The Japan News,* July 28, 2014, http://article.wn.com/view/2014/07/25/Message_II_Tomomi_Inada_Cool_Japan_to_provide_solutions_for_.

2. "Kūru Japan kasoku" (Speeding Cool Japan), *Sankei Shimbun,* Sept. 26, 2015, 2; *Mainichi Shimbun,* Feb. 25, 2015, http://mainichi.jp/select/news/20150226k0000m040014000c.html.

3. Suga Chizuru, interview, Tokyo, Feb. 15, 2012.

4. Jeff Kingston, "Japan's Public Diplomacy Is Expensive and Errant," *The Japan Times,* Feb. 14, 2015, http://www.japantimes.co.jp/opinion/2015/02/14/commentary/japans-public-diplomacy-expensive-errant/.

5. Endo Nao, interview, Sydney, Aug. 24, 2012.

6. *Kawaii,* usually translated into English as "cuteness" or "lovability." The Japanese culture of *kawaii* is vaguely defined as the primal innocence of childhood, epitomized by playful designs, initially driven by teenagers and young women but in recent years has spread to other segments of Japanese society. From a media industry point of view, the development of the *kawaii* culture reflects the transformation from classical aesthetics to an economic growth machine that has spread its commercial goods both domestically and globally (Yomota 2006: 134–152).

7. Located at the heart of Tokyo, Harajuku is a bustling mecca for youth culture, home to fashion designers, underground culture and creative artists, and a focal point for gathering of Japanese youth dressed in colorful styles.

8. MOFA announcement, "Introduction of the Kawaii Ambassadors," Mar. 12, 2009, http://www.mofa.go.jp/announce/press/2009/3/0312.html.

9. Matsushita Tadahiro, interview, Singapore, Oct. 6, 2011.

10. Suga Chizuru, interview, Tokyo, Feb. 15, 2012.

11. "Japan Plans Campaign to Curb Manga, Anime Copyright Violations Abroad," *The Japan Times,* July 28, 2014, http://www.japantimes.co.jp/news/2014/07/28/national /crime-legal/japan-plans-campaign-curb-manga-anime-copyright-violations-abroad; Roland Kelts, "At Last, Japan Gets It," *The Japan Times,* Apr. 20, 2014, http://www .japantimes.co.jp/culture/2015/04/18/general/last-japan-gets.

12. According to Ibuki Hideki, director of METI's Creative Industries Division, JPY 150 billion are allocated on a regular basis (JPY 30 billion come directly from METI and JPY 20 billion come from the Ministry of Internal Affairs and Communications), but an additional JPY 500 billion were given specifically for promotions in 2013. Ibuki Hideki, interview, Tokyo, Aug. 22, 2013.

13. See Roland Kelts, "Cool Japan Sets Its Sights on Southeast Asia," *The Japan Times,* Feb. 12, 2014.

14. Ibuki Hideki, interview, Tokyo, Aug. 22, 2013.

15. Ibid.

16. http://www.yomiuri.co.jp/dy/business/T120724003516.html (accessed Dec. 14, 2014).

17. Founded in 1869, the Yasukuni Shrine commemorates the Japanese soldiers who died in war since the Meiji Restoration. Controversy started in 1978 following the enshrinement of fourteen Class A war criminals, which included the prime ministers and top generals convicted in the Tokyo Trial in a conspiracy to start the war in the Pacific. Since the mid-1980s, the visits of Japanese top politicians to the shrine have provoked howls of protest from China and Korea, who blame Japan for "not coming to terms with its past."

18. *Asahi Shimbun,* Dec. 22, 2005, 26.

19. Arai Yusuke, interview, Tokyo, July 10, 2014.

20. Mihara Ryōtarō, interview, Tokyo, Oc. 15, 2012.

21. Kogake Shintarō expressed his frustration at what he sees as an ineffective government policy to support Japan's anime export. Interview, Tokyo, Feb. 16, 2012.

22. Ibid.

23. Sonobe Yukio, interview, Tokyo, Aug. 20, 2013.

24. Shinoda Yoshihiko, interview, Tokyo, Aug. 21, 2013.

25. http://www.yomiuri.co.jp/book/news/20140513-OYT8T50183.html?from=ytop_ymag (accessed Feb. 15, 2015).

26. Shinoda Yoshihiko, interview, Tokyo, Aug. 21, 2013.

27. Mukai Junichirō, interview, Tokyo, Aug. 1, 2013.

28. Shichijō Naohiro, interview, Tokyo, Aug. 20, 2013.

29. Sonobe Yukio, interview, Tokyo, Aug. 20, 2013.

30. Miyagawa Daisuke, interview, Tokyo, Aug. 14, 2015.

31. Mihara Ryōtarō, interview, Tokyo, Feb. 15, 2012.

32. Suga Chizuru, interview, Tokyo, Feb. 15, 2012.

33. Wada George, interview, Haifa, May 26, 2014.

34. Amagi Yukihiko, interview, Tokyo, Feb. 16, 2012.

35. Toyonaga Mami, interview, Tokyo, Feb. 10, 2012.

36. Ibuki Hideki, interview, Tokyo, Aug. 22, 2013.

37. Miyagawa Daisuke, interview, Tokyo, Aug. 14, 2015.

38. Ibuki Hideki, interview, Tokyo, Aug. 22, 2013.

39. Amagi Yukihiko, interview, Tokyo, Feb. 16, 2012.

40. Ishikawa Shinichirō, interview, Tokyo, Feb. 15, 2012.

Conclusion

1. Ishikawa Shinichirō, interview, Tokyo, Oct. 10, 2012.

2. Sam Register, interview, Los Angeles, Apr. 4, 2011.

3. Daryl Surat, interview, Baltimore, July 31, 2011.

4. Interview, Seoul, Sept. 23, 2015.

5. Paul Bond, "Steven Spielberg Predicts 'Implosion' of Film Industry," *Hollywood Reporter,* Dec. 6, 2013, http://www.hollywoodreporter.com/news/steven-spielberg-predicts-implosion-film-567604.

6. "Disney Agrees to Pay $500 Million for Maker Studios," *Bloomberg Businessweek Technology,* Mar. 25, 2014, http://www.bloomberg.com/news/2014-03-24/disney-pays-as-much-as-950-million-for-maker-studios.html.

7. Makihara Ryōtarō, interview, Haifa, May 26, 2014.

8. Sam Byford, "Japan Used to Rule Video Games, So What Happened?" *The Verge,* Mar. 20, 2014, http://www.theverge.com/2014/3/20/5522320/final-fight-can-japans-gaming-industry-be-saved.

9. The industry has a different perspective from that of consumers. Fans of anime not included, many television viewers around the world do not necessarily realize that they are watching a Japanese series or that anime influences are embedded in a series they are watching.

10. Sam Register, interview, Los Angeles, Apr. 4, 2011.

11. Makihara Ryōtarō, interview, Haifa, May 26, 2014.

12. Marco Pellitteri, interview, Kyoto, Aug. 31, 2015.

References

Ad Age. 2012. "World's 50 Largest Agency Companies," Apr. 30.

Adorno, Theodor W. 1991. "Culture Industry Reconsidered." In *The Culture Industry: Selected Essays on Mass Culture,* edited by Jay M. Bernstein, 98–106. London: Routledge Classics.

Adorno, Theodor W., and Max Horkheimer. 2007. *Dialectic of Enlightenment.* Stanford: Stanford University Press.

Alger, Chadwick. 1988. "Perceiving, Analyzing, and Coping with the Local-Global Nexus." *International Social Science Journal* 40:3321–39.

Allison, Anne. 2000. "A Challenge to Hollywood? Japanese Character Goods Hit the US." *Japanese Studies* 20, no. 1: 67–88.

———. 2006. *Millennial Monsters: Japanese Toys and the Global Imagination.* Berkeley: University of California Press.

Althusser, Louis. (1965) 2005. *For Marx.* London: Verso.

Anderson, Chris. 2004. "The Long Tail." *Wired* 12:10. Last modified Oct. 12, 2004. http://archive.wired.com/wired/archive/12.10/tail.html.

Anime sangyō repōto 2012 (Anime Industry Report of 2012). 2012. Association of Japanese Animation Database Working Group. Sept.

Anime sangyō repōto 2015 (Anime Industry Report of 2015). 2015. Association of Japanese Animation Database Working Group. Sept.

Asaba, Michiaki. 1989 (1990). "Kōdō shōhi shakai ni yūyūsuru tenshitachi" (Angels Playing in High Consumer Society). In *Otaku no hon* (The Otaku Book), edited by Ishii Shinji, 251–71. Bessatsu takarajima 104. Tokyo: JICC shuppan kyoku.

Asian Animation Industry: Strategies, Trends & Opportunities. 2010. Research and Markets. Accessed through http://www.researchandmarkets.com.

Azuma, Hiroki. 2009. *Otaku: Japan's Database Animals.* Translated by Jonathan E. Abel and Shion Kōno. Minneapolis: University of Minnesota Press.

Baker, Sarah, and David Hesmondhalgh. 2010. *Creative Labour: Media Work in Three Cultural Industries.* London: Routledge.

Bendazzi, Giannalberto. 1995. *Cartoons: One Hundred Years of Cinema Animation*. London: John Libbey.

Berry, Torriano S., and Venise T. Berry. 2015. *Historical Dictionary of African American Cinema*. Lanham, Maryland: Rowman and Littlefield.

Bielby, Denise D., and Harrington C. Lee. 2008. *Global TV: Exporting Television and Culture in the World Market*. New York: New York University Press.

Bilton, Chris, and Stephen Cummings. 2010. *Creative Strategy: Reconnecting Business and Innovation*. Wiltshire: Wiley-Blackwell.

Bolter, David J., and Richard Grusin. 1999. *Remediation: Understanding New Media*. Cambridge, MA: MIT Press.

Brienza, Casey. 2016. *Manga in America: Transnational Book Publishing and the Domestication of Japanese Comics*. New York: Bloomsbury.

Brophy, Philip, Carl Chatfield, Jonathan Clements, Jordi Costa, Luca Della Casa, Stéphane Delorme, Davide Di Giorgio, Daniele Dottorini, Stefano Gariglio, and Paul Gravett. 2010. *Manga Impact: The World of Japanese Animation*. London: Phaidon Press.

Brown, Steven, ed. 2008. *Cinema Anime*. New York: Palgrave Macmillan.

Castells, Manuel. 2010. *The Rise of the Network Society*. Malden: Blackwell.

Caves, Richard E. 2002. *Creative Industries: Contracts between Art and Commerce*. Cambridge, MA: Harvard University Press.

Choo, Kukhee. 2012. "Nationalizing 'Cool': Japan's Global Promotion of the Content Industry." In *Popular Culture and the State in East and Southeast Asia*, edited by Nissim Otmazgin and Eyal Ben-Ari, 85–105. London: Routledge.

Chow, Kenny K. N. 2013. "From Haiku and Handscroll to Tezuka: Refocusing Space and Camera in the Narrative of Animation." In *Japanese Animation: East Asian Perspective*, edited by Masao Yokota and Tze-yue G. Hu, 183–95. Jackson: University of Mississippi Press.

Condry, Ian. 2004. "Cultures of Music Piracy: An Ethnographic Comparison of the US and Japan." *International Journal of Cultural Studies* 7, no. 3: 343–63.

———. 2006. *Hip-Hop Japan: Rap and the Paths of Cultural Globalization*. Durham, NC: Duke University Press.

———. 2013. *The Soul of Anime: Collaborative Creativity and Japan's Media Success Story*. Durham, NC: Duke University Press.

Corbett, Michael F. 2004. *The Outsourcing Revolution: Why It Makes Sense and How to Do It Right*. Wokingham: Kaplan.

Cowen, Tyler. 2004. *Creative Destruction: How Globalization Is Changing the World's Cultures*. Princeton: Princeton University Press.

Crow, Heather. 2007. "Gesturing Toward Olympia." In *Animated 'Worlds,'* edited by Suzanne Buchan, 49–62. Boston: John Libbey.

Daliot-Bul, Michal. 2007. "Eroticism, Grotesqueness, and Non-sense: Twenty-First-Century Cultural Imagery of Japan in the Israeli Media and Popular Culture." *Journal of Intercultural Studies* 28, no. 2: 173–91.

———. 2009. "Japan Brand Strategy: The Taming of 'Cool Japan' and the Challenges of Cultural Planning in a Postmodern Age." *Social Science Japan Journal* 12, no. 3: 227–45.

———. 2014. "Reframing and Reconsidering the Cultural Innovations of the Anime Boom on US Television," *International Journal of Cultural Studies* 17, no. 1: 75–91.

———. 2014. *License to Play: The Ludic in Japanese Culture*. Honolulu: University of Hawai'i Press.

Daliot-Bul, Michal, and Ofra Goldstein-Gidoni. 2010. "On Cultural Otherness in the Era of Globalization 3.0: The New Israeli Cosmopolitans and Japan." In "East Asian Transnational Migrants and Culture in a Global World," special issue. *Encounters* 3: 169–93.

Diamond, Jared. 1993. "Ten Thousand Years of Solitude." *Discover Magazine,* March 1. http://discovermagazine.com/1993/mar/tenthousandyears189.

Digital Content Association of Japan. 2009. *Dejitaru Kontentsu Hakusho* [Digital Content White Paper]. Tokyo: Japan Ministry of Economy, Trade and Industry.

DiMaggio, Paul, and Hugh Louch. 1998. "Socially Embedded Consumer Transactions: For What Kind of Purchases Do People Most Often Use Networks?" *American Sociological Review* 63, no. 5: 619–37.

Erickson, Hal. 2001. *Syndicated Television: The First Forty Years, 1947–1987.* Jefferson, NC: McFarland.

Featherstone, Mike. 1995. *Undoing Culture.* London: Sage.

Fellow, Anthony R. 2010. *American Media History*. Boston: Wadsworth Cengage Learning.

Fitzgerald, Amy. 2008. "In the Way of the Samurai: Difference and Connections in Samurai Champloo." *Virginia Review of Asian Studies* 11:171–84.

Galbraith, Patrick. 2014. *The Moe Manifesto: An Insider's Look at the World of Manga, Anime, and Gaming*. North Clarendon, VT: Tuttle.

Garnham, Nicholas. 1990. *Capitalism and Communication: Global Culture and the Economics of Information.* London: Sage.

Goldman, William. 1984. *Adventures in the Screen Trade: A Personal View of Hollywood and Screenwriting.* New York: Warner Books.

Halas, John. 1976. *Film Animation: A Simplified Approach.* Paris: Unesco.

Hebdige, Dick. 1979. *Subculture: The Meaning of Style.* New York: Methuen.

Hoffer, Thomas W. 1981. *Animation: A Reference Guide.* Westport, CT: Greenwood.

Hu, Tze-Yue G. 2010. *Frames of Anime: Culture and Image-Building.* Hong Kong: Hong Kong University Press.

Hui Gan, Sheuo. 2009. "To Be or Not to Be Anime: The Controversy in Japan over the 'Anime' Label." *Animation Studies Online Journal* 4. Accessed December 31, 2014. http://journal.animationstudies.org/sheuo-hui-gan-to-be-or-not-to-be-anime-the-controversy-in-japan-over-the-anime-label/.

Ito, Mizuko. 2006. "Japanese Media Mixes and Amateur Cultural Exchange." In *Digital Generations,* edited by D. Buckingham and R. Willet, 49–66. Mahwah, NJ: Lawrence Erlbaum.

Iwabuchi, Koichi. 2002a. *Recentering Globalization: Popular Culture and Japanese Transnationalism*. Durham, NC: Duke University Press.

———. 2002b. "'Soft' Nationalism and Narcissism: Japanese Popular Culture Goes Global." *Asian Studies Review* 26:447–69.

Japan Foundation. 2003. Aratata na Jidai no Gaikō to Kokusai Kōryū no Aratatana Yakuwari [Diplomacy in a New Era and a New Role for International Exchange]. Tokyo: International Exchange Research Group.

Japan Spotlight. 2005. "Data for Content Business," May/June.

Jenkins, Henry. 2006. *Convergence Culture: Where Old and New Media Collide*. New York: New York University Press.

———. 2007. Afterword to *Fandom: Identities and Communities in a Mediated World*, edited by Harrington Lee, Jonathan Gray, and Cornel Sandvoss, 357–64. New York: New York University Press.

JETRO (Japan External Trade Organization). 2003. *Conditions and Prospects of US-Anime Market*. Tokyo: JETRO.

———. 2005. "Japan Animation Industry Trends." *JETRO: Japan Economic Monthly*, June. http://www.jetro.go.jp/en/reports/market/pdf/2005_35_r.pdf.

———. 2011. *Beikoku ni okeru kontentsu shijō no jittai* (Content Market Situation in America). Tokyo: JETRO Global Marketing Division.

Jin, Dal Yong. 2011. "Deconvergence and Deconsolidation in the Global Media Industries: The Rise and Fall of (Some) Media Conglomerates." In *Political Economies of the Media: The Transformation of the Global Media*, edited by Dwayne Winseck and Dal Yong Jin, 167–82. London: Bloomsbury.

Johnson, Derek. 2013. "From Ownership to Partnership: The Institutionalization of Franchise Relations." In *Media Franchising: Creative License and Collaboration in the Culture Industries*, 67–106. New York: New York University Press.

Kelts, Roland. 2007. *Japanamerica: How Japanese Pop Culture Has Invaded the U.S.* New York: Palgrave.

———. 2011. "Soft Power Hard Truths: Overseas Anime Market Online Only." *The Daily Yomiyuri*, Nov. 24.

Kim, Se-jeong. 2010. "North Korea Emerges as Animation Producer." *The Korea Times*, Jan. 11. http://www.koreatimes.co.kr/www/news/nation/2010/11/113_75584.html.

Kinsella, Sharon. 2000. *Adult Manga: Culture and Power in Contemporary Japanese Society*. Honolulu: University of Hawai'i Press.

———. 2005. "Black Faces, Witches, and Racism against Girls." In *Bad Girls of Japan*, edited by Laura Miller and Jan Bardsley, 143–57. New York: Palgrave.

Kodaira, Sachiko Imaizumi. 2005. "Children's Television: Trends around the World." *NHK Broadcasting Studies* 4:104–30. Accessed Apr. 4, 2015. http://www.nhk.or.jp/bunken/english/reports/pdf/05_no4_07.pdf.

Koh, Dong-Yeon. 2013. "Growing Up with *Astro Boy* and *Mazinger Z*: Industrialization, 'High Tech World,' and Japanese Animation in the Art and Culture of South Korea." In *Japanese Animation: East Asian Perspectives*, edited by Masao Yokota and Tze-yue G. Hu, 155–95. Jackson: University of Mississippi Press.

Kohler, Chris. 2004. *Power Up: How Japanese Video Games Gave the World an Extra Life.* Indianapolis: Brady Games.

Koide, Masashi. 2013. "Establishment and History of Japan Society for Animation Studies." In *Japanese Animation: East Asian Perspectives,* edited by Masao Yokota and Tzeyue G. Hu, 49–72. Jackson: University Press of Mississippi.

Kondo, Seiichi. 2008. "Wielding Soft Power: The Key Stages of Transmission and Reception." In *Soft Power Superpowers: Cultural and National Assets of Japan and the United States,* edited by Yasushi Watanabe and David L. McConnell, 191–206. New York: M. E. Sharpe.

Kuratko, Donald, and David Audretsch. 2009. "Strategic Entrepreneurship: Exploring Different Perspectives of an Emerging Concept." *Entrepreneurship: Theory and Practice* 33, no. 1: 1–17.

Kusanagi, Satoshi. 2003. *America de nihon no anime ha dō miraretekitaka?* (How is Japanese Animation Viewed in America?). Tokyo: Asahi Shimbun.

Ladd, Fred, and Harvey Deneroff. 2010. *Anime ga ninaru made: Tetsuwan atomu Amerika ni iku* (Astro Boy and Anime Come to America). Tokyo: NTT Shuppan.

LaMarre, Thomas. 2002. "From Animation to Anime: Drawing Movement and Moving Drawings." *Japan Forum* 14, no. 2: 329–67.

———. 2009. *The Anime Machine: A Media Theory of Animation.* Minneapolis: University of Minnesota Press.

Lambie, Ryan. 2011. "How Anime and Videogames Work in Tandem." *Den of Geek.* Last modified Nov. 28, 2011. http://www.denofgeek.com/games/21235/how-anime-and-videogames-work-in-tandem.

Lee, Hye-Kyung. 2001. "Participatory Media Fandom: A Case Study of Anime Fansubbing." *Media, Culture & Society* 33, no. 8: 1131–47.

Lee, Sunny. 2007. "US Cartoons Made in North Korea." *Asia Times Online.* Last modified Mar. 14, 2007. http://www.atimes.com/atimes/Korea/IC14Dg03.html.

Lent, John A. 2001. *Animation in Asia and the Pacific.* Bloomington: Indiana University Press.

Leonard, Sean. 2004. *Progress against the Law: Fan Distribution, Copyright, and the Explosive Growth of Japanese Animation.* Cambridge: Massachusetts Institute of Technology.

Lipitz, Nicole. 2010. "Animation (2)." *Chicago School of Media Theory,* September. Accessed Sept. 7, 2014. http://lucian.uchicago.edu/blogs/mediatheory/keywords/animation-2/.

MacNamara, Jim. 2010. *The 21st Century Media (R)evolution: Emergent Communication Practices.* New York: Peter Lang.

MacWilliams, Mark. 2008. Introduction to *Japanese Visual Culture: Explorations in the World of Manga and Anime,* edited by Mark MacWilliams, 3–25. New York: M.E. Sharpe.

Martinez, Michael J. 2016. *A Long Dark Night: Race in America: From Jim Crow to World War II.* Lanham, Maryland: Rowman and Littlefield.

Mascias, Patrick. 2006. *Otaku in USA: Aii to gokai no anime yunyūshi* (Love and Misunderstanding! The History of Adopted Anime in America!). Tokyo: Tamada shuppan.

McGray, Douglas. 2002. "Japan's Gross National Cool." *Foreign Policy* 130 (May/June): 44–54.

McKevitt, Andrew C. 2010. "'You Are Not Alone!': Anime and the Globalizing of America." *Diplomatic History* 35, no. 5: 893–921.

METI (Japanese Ministry of Economy, Trade and Industry). 2003. "Chūkan torimatome" (Midterm Report). In *International Strategy Study Group*. Tokyo: METI.

Mihara, Ryōtarō. 2014. *Kūru Japan ha naze kirawarerunoka: Nekkyo to reisho wo koete* (Why Is Cool Japan Hated? Overcoming Wild Enthusiasm and Derision). Tokyo: Chuokoron-Shinsha.

Morisawa, Tomohiro. 2013. "Producing Animation: Work, Creativity, and Aspirations in the Japanese Animation Industry." Ph.D. thesis, Oxford University.

Morley, David, and Kevin Robins. 1995. *Spaces of Identity: Global Media, Electronic Landscapes, and Cultural Borders*. New York: Routledge.

Morris, Michael, Daniel Kuratko, and Jeffrey Kovin. 2008. *Corporate Entrepreneurship and Innovation*. Cincinnati, OH: Thomson/South Western.

Munoz, Felix-Fernando, and Francisco Javier Otamendi. 2014. "Entrepreneurial Effort and Economic Growth." *Journal of Global Entrepreneurship Research* 2, no. 8: 1–17.

Murakami, Takashi. 2001. "Impotence Culture-Anime." In *My Reality: Contemporary Art and the Culture of Japanese Animation*, edited by Jeff Fleming, 58–66. New York: Independent Curator International.

———. 2005. "Earth in My Window." In *Little Boy: The Arts of Japan's Exploding Subculture*, edited by Takashi Murakami, 99–149. New York: Japan Society; New Haven: Yale University Press.

Nakamura, Ichiya. 2003. "Japanese Pop Industry." Stanford Japan Center Discussion Papers, Nov. 22. Accessed Apr. 4, 2015. http://sjc-r.stanford.edu/research/publication/DP/pdf/DP2003_002_E.pdf.

Napier, Susan J. 2001. *Anime: From Akira to Princess Mononoke*. New York: Palgrave.

Newton, Judith, and Deborah Rosenfelt. 1985. *Feminist Criticism and Social Change: Sex, Class and Race in Literature and Culture*. New York: Methuen.

Nye, Joseph. 1990. "Soft Power." *Foreign Policy* 80:153–71.

———. 2004. *Power in the Global Information Age*. London: Routledge.

Ogura, Kazuo. 2004. "'Kokusaizai' no shin ni kachikoso sekai ni hasshin shiyō" (Sharing Japan's Cultural Products as "International Assets"). *Chuo koron*, Oct., 210–17.

Ōshita, Eiji. 2014. *Kamenraida kara Garo he* (From Kamen Rider to Garo). Tokyo: Takeshobō.

Otmazgin, Nissim. 2011. "Commodifying Asian-ness: Entrepreneurship and the Making of East Asian Popular Culture." *Media, Culture & Society* 33, no. 2: 249–74.

———. 2012. "Geopolitics and Soft Power: Japan's Cultural Industry and Cultural Policy in Asia." *Asia-Pacific Review* 19, no. 1: 37–61.

———. 2013. *Regionalizing Culture: The Political Economy of Japanese Popular Culture in Asia*. Honolulu: University of Hawai'i Press.

———. 2014. "Anime in the US: The Entrepreneurial Dimensions of Globalized Culture." *Pacific Affairs* 87, no. 1: 53–69.

————. 2015. "Staying Relevant: The Impact of the New Media on Asia's Media Industries." In *The Routledge Handbook of New Media in Asia,* edited by Larissa Hjorth and Olivia Khoo, 80–90. New York: Routledge.

————. 2017. "Soft Powering Popular Culture." In *Modern Japan: Social Commentary on State and Society,* edited by Yoneyuki Sugita, chap. 8. Berlin: Springer.

Ōtsuka, Eiji. 2015. "Japan as Montage." *Innovative Research in Japanese Studies* 2, (Fall): 3–17. Accessed Sept. 10, 2016. http://media.wix.com/ugd/68505e_532aa3b62d01439d8 15d99a4d9563ba1.pdf.

Ōtsuka, Eiji, and Nobuaki Ōsawa. 2005. *Japanimēshon ha naze yabureruka?* (Why Is Japanimation Losing?). Tokyo: Kadokawa shoten.

Patten, Fred. 2001. "Anime in the United States." In *Animation in Asia and the Pacific,* edited by John A. Lent, 55–72. Bloomington: Indiana University Press.

————. 2004. *Watching Anime, Reading Manga: 25 Years of Essays and Reviews.* Berkeley, CA: Stone Bridge.

Patterson, Orlando. 1994. "Global Culture and the American Cosmos." *World Policy Journal* 11, no. 2: 103–17.

Pellitteri, Marco. 2011. *The Dragon and the Dazzle: Models, Strategies, and Identities of Japanese Imagination–A European Perspective.* Bloomington: Indiana University Press.

Perez, Carlota. 2010. "Technological Revolutions and Techno-Economic Paradigms." *Cambridge Journal of Economics* 34: 185–202.

Peterson, Robert S. 2011. *Comics, Manga, and Graphic Novels: A History of Graphic Narratives.* Santa Barbara, CA: Praeger.

Pilling, Jayne. 1997. *A Reader in Animation Studies.* Sydney: John Libbey.

Poitras, Gilles. 2008. "Contemporary Anime in Japanese Pop Culture." In *Japanese Visual Culture: Explorations in the World of Manga and Anime,* edited by Mark MacWilliams. New York: M.E. Sharp.

Price, David. 2008. *The Pixar Touch: The Making of a Company.* New York: Alfred A. Knopf.

Prime Minister of Japan. 2008. *Official Website.* http://www.kantei.go.jp. Accessed August 14, 2008.

Richie, Donald. 2003. *The Image Factory: Fads and Fashions in Japan.* London: Reaktion.

Robertson, Roland. 1992. *Globalization: Social Theory and Global Culture.* London: Sage.

Russell, John G. 1996. "Race and Reflexivity: The Black Other in Contemporary Japanese Mass Culture." In *Contemporary Japan and Popular Culture,* edited by John Whittier Treat. Honolulu: University of Hawai'i Press.

Ryan, Bill. 1992. *Making Capital from Culture: The Corporate Form of Capitalist Cultural Production.* De Gruyter Studies in Organization 35. New York: Walter de Gruyter.

Sakurai, Takamasa. 2009. *Anime bunka gaikō* (Anime's Cultural Diplomacy). Tokyo: Chikuma shinsho.

Salkowitz, Rob. 2012. *Comic-Con and the Business of Pop Culture.* New York: McGraw-Hill.

Samoha, Shahar. 2002. "Digimon hador haba" (Digimon, the Next Generation). *Haaretz,* Oct. 24.

Schodt, Frederik L. 1996. *Dreamland Japan: Writing on Modern Manga.* Berkeley, CA: Stone Bridge Press.

———. 2007. *The Astro Boy Essays.* Berkley, CA: Stone Bridge Press.

Scott, Sharon M. 2010. *Toys and American Culture: An Encyclopedia.* Santa Barbara, CA: Greenwood.

Sharma, Pramodita, and James Chrisman. 1999. "Toward a Reconciliation of the Definitional Issues in the Field of Corporate Entrepreneurship." *Entrepreneurship: Theory and Practice* 23, no. 3: 11–27.

Shiraishi, Saya. 2013. *Grōbarukashita Nihon no manga to anime* (Globalized Japanese Manga and Anime). Tokyo: Gakujutsu shuppankai.

Shita, Eiji. 2005. *Nihon hīrō ha sekai wo seisu* (Establishing Japanese Heroes around the World). Tokyo: Kadokawa shoten.

Skov, Lise, and Brian Moeran. 1995. "Hiding in the Light: From Oshin to Yoshimoto Banana." In *Women, Media, and Consumption in Japan,* edited by Lise Skov and Brian Moeran, 1–74. Honolulu: University of Hawai'i Press.

Steinberg, Mark. 2012. *Anime Media Mix: Franchising Toys and Characters in Japan.* Minneapolis: University of Minnesota Press.

Sterling, Marvin. 2010. *Babylon East: Performing Dancehall, Roots Reggae, and Rastafari in Japan.* Durham, NC: Duke University Press.

Storper, Michael. 1994. "The Transition to Flexible Specialization in the US Film Industry: External Economies, the Division of Labour and the Crossing of Industrial Divides." In *Post-Fordism: A Reader,* edited by Ash Amin, 195–226. Oxford: Blackwell.

Sugiura, Tsutomu. 2003. "Monetary Value of Japanese Arts and Cultural Products Based on Japan's Ministry of Finance Data." Tokyo: Marubeni Economic Research Institute.

———. 2008. "Japan's Creative Industries: Culture as a Source of Soft Power in the Industrial Sector." In *Soft Power Superpowers: Cultural and National Assets of Japan and the United States,* edited by Yasushi Watanabe and David L. McConnell, 128–53. New York: M. E. Sharpe.

Takada, Tsuneyasu. 2011. *Nihon ha naze neikai de ichiban ninki ga arunoka* (Why Is Japan the Most Popular in the World?). Tokyo: PHP shinsho.

Takahashi, Murakami. 2001. "Impotence-Culture Anime." In *My Reality, Contemporary Art, and the Culture of Japanese Animation,* ed. Jeff Fleming et al., 58–66. New York: Independent Curator International.

Takahashi, Ryosuke. 2011. "Anime niokeru enshutsu, mata ha kantoku to ha" (On Directing and Directors in Anime). In *Anime gaku* (Anime Studies), edited by Mitsuteru Takahashi and Nobuyuki Tsugata. Tokyo: NTT publishers.

Tomlinson, John. 1999. *Globalization and Culture.* Chicago: University of Chicago Press.

Townsend, Emru. 1995. "Akira: Anime Comes of Age." *Sci-Fi Entertainment* 2, no 2:38-40 (Aug.).

Toyonagi, Mami. 2010. "Pawārenjyāwo hitto saseta otoko: Haimu Saban to Nihon kontentsu" (The Man Who Turned Power Rangers into a Hit: Haim Saban and Japanese Contents). *Hitotsubashi Business Review* 58, no. 3: 36–51.

Trifonova, Temenuga. 2006. "Cinematic Cool: Jean-Pierre Melville's Le Samourai." *Senses of Cinema,* no. 39 (Apr.–June). Accessed Oct. 3, 2011. http://www.sensesofcinema .com/2006/cteq/samourai/.

Tsutsui, William M. 2010a. *Japanese Popular Culture and Globalization.* Ann Arbor, MI: Association for Asian Studies.

———. 2010b. "Japanese Popular Culture and Globalization: An Interview." *Education about Asia* 15, no. 2: 53.

Ueno, Toshiya. 2002. "Japanimation and Techno-Orientalism." In *The Uncanny: Experiments in Cyborg Culture,* edited by Bruce Grenville, 223–36. Vancouver: Arsenal Pulp Press.

Wood, Joe. 1997. "The Yellow Negro." *Transition* 73: 40–66.

Yamada, Kenichi. 2013. "Market Competition in the Animation Industry between Japan and China: How to Face China's Rising Interest in Promoting Domestically-Produced Animation." *NHK Broadcasting Culture Research Institute,* Feb. Accessed Dec. 31, 2014. http://www.nhk.or.jp/bunken/english/reports/pdf/report_13020101.pdf.

Yamaguchi, Yasuo. 2009. *Nihon no anime zenshi: Sekaiwo seishita Nihon anime no kiseki* (The Complete Anime History: The Miracle of Japanese Anime That Captured the World). Tokyo: Ten-Books.

Yano, Christine. 2004. "Kitty Litter: Japanese Cute at Home and Abroad." In *Toys, Games, and Media,* edited by Jeffrey Goldstein and David Buckingham, 51–71. Mahwah, NJ: Erlbaum.

———. 2012. "Categorical Confusion: President Obama as a Case Study of Racialized Practices in Contemporary Japan." In *Race and Racism in Modern East Asia,* edited by Rotem Kowner and Walter Demel, 499–522. Leiden and Boston: Brill.

———. 2013. *Pink Globalization: Hello Kitty's Trek across the Pacific.* Durham, NC: Duke University Press.

Yomota, Inuhiko. 2006. *Kawaii Ron* [Theory of Kawaii]. Tokyo: Chikuma Shinsho.

Yonezawa, Yoshihiko. 1987. "Komiketto: Sekai saidai no manga no saiten" (Comiket: The World's Largest Manga Fair). In *Otaku no hon* (The *Otaku* Book), edited by Shinji Ishii, 75–88. Tokyo: JICC shuppankyoku.

Yoon, Hyejin, and Edward J. Malecki. 2010. "Cartoon Planets: World of Production and Global Production Networks in the Animation Industry." *Industrial and Corporate Change* 19, no. 1: 239–71.

Zykas, Aurelijus. 2011. "The Discourses of Popular Culture in 21st Century Japan's Cultural Diplomacy Agenda." In *The Reception of Japanese and Korean Popular Culture in Europe,* edited by Takashi Kitamura, Kyoko Koma, and SanGum Li, 127–148. Kaunas: Vytautas Magnus University.

Index

Harvard East Asian Monographs
(most recent titles)

Harvard East Asian Monographs